STRATEGIES for TEACHING UNIVERSAL DESIGN

Edited by Polly Welch

Adaptive Environments
Boston, Massachusetts

MIG Communications
Berkeley, California

Strategies for Universal Design Education has been produced and co-published by:

Adaptive Environments Center
374 Congress Street, Suite 301
Boston, MA 02210
(617) 695-1225 (v/tdd) ext. 0

Elaine Ostroff, Director, Universal Design Education Project
    and Executive Director, Adaptive Environments
Soni Gupta, Production Coordinator

This book is also available in alternate formats: Braille, audio tape, large print, and diskette. For these formats, copies of this book, or additional information on the Universal Design Education Project, contact Adaptive Environments.

This book has been designed and co-published by:

MIG Communications
1802 Fifth Street
Berkeley, CA 94710-1915
(510) 845-0953; fax (510) 845-8750

David Driskell, Managing Editor
Paul Yee, Editor
MIG DesignWorks, Cover and Page Design
Renate Alexander, Production
Stuart Easterling, Production Assistant

Library of Congress Catalog Card Number 94-073139

ISBN 0-944661-23-8

Note: This book was written and produced by the Adaptive Environments Center under grant 93-CR-CX-003 from the U.S. Department of Justice, Disability Rights Section. Opinions about the Americans with Disabilities Act (ADA) are those of the authors and do not necessarily reflect the viewpoint of the Department of Justice. The Department's interpretations of the ADA are reflected in its ADA Regulations (28 CFR Parts 35 and 36) and its technical assistance manuals for Title II and III of the Act.

The National Endowment for the Arts holds as its guiding principle that the vast richness of America's culture should be made available to all. The universal design of buildings, spaces, products, and programs plays a major role in making this worthy goal possible. As important as its role is in making the arts accessible to people of all ages and abilities, universal design has a far broader impact on our society and its economy. That is because the practice of universal design improves the art of environmental design in all its facets, so that people may contribute more fully to the life of their communities and the prosperity of their nation.

America has struggled for years over how to serve populations with special physical needs: older adults, children, and people with disabilities. Progress has been impeded by misconceptions (both in the public mind and among design professionals) that users represent a small portion of the population and that designs for them are institutional-looking, inefficient to produce, and costly to maintain. Such attitudes have resulted in designed products, graphics, and environments that stigmatize even as they try to accommodate user needs.

The concept of *universal design* goes beyond the mere provision of special features for various segments of the population. Instead it emphasizes a creative approach that is more inclusive, one that asks at the outset of the design process how a product, graphic communication, building, or public space can be made both aesthetically pleasing and functional for the greatest number of users. Designs resulting from this approach serve a wider array of people including individuals with temporary or permanent disabilities, parents with small children, and everyone whose abilities change with age.

The Arts Endowment is pleased to have provided the initial funding for Adaptive Environments' Universal Design Education Project. We are also pleased that the exemplary nature of the project and its potential to influence succeeding generations of design professionals have won the endorsement of additional funders from both public and private sectors. Thanks to the generous support of NEC Foundation of America, the NYNEX Foundation, the J.M. Foundation, and the U.S. Department of Justice, the project is able to share the innovative work of the participating schools with a much wider audience.

The reach of this effort to stimulate innovation in the teaching and learning of designers is extraordinary. This support mirrors the interdisciplinary approach of the project itself, which is one of its strengths. *Strategies for Teaching Universal Design* documents significant advances in curriculum development, teaching, and learning in our nation's schools of design. Although the book targets design educators and students, everyone can benefit from its valuable guidance.

I strongly encourage you to read it, to embrace the concept of universal design, and to practice it.

Jane Alexander, Chairman
National Endowment for the Arts

Contents

Contents *continued*

Contents *continued*

Foreword

Design that accommodates people with disabilities is no longer optional for designers and architects, it is the law of the land. The Americans with Disabilities Act (ADA) is landmark civil rights legislation that promises to open up the mainstream of American life to people with disabilities. The ADA declares it discriminatory to design, build, or alter most buildings without providing accessibility and requires Federal agencies to establish and enforce standards for accessible design.

Improved standards for accessible design, better information, new products, and lower costs make it increasingly easy for design professionals to design buildings, interiors, and products to be usable by everyone. Universal design takes us one step beyond the mere compliance with accessibility standards that are often applied when the design is virtually complete. It is an approach to design that recognizes and accommodates the changes that people experience over the lifespan. It seeks, from the initial conceptual design stage, to accommodate the needs of people of all ages, sizes, and abilities.

Like the ADA, which seeks to integrate people with disabilities into the mainstream of American society, this important project seeks to integrate the universal design approach into the mainstream of design practice.

Ruth Hall Lusher
ADA Technical Assistance Program Manager
U.S. Department of Justice

Preface

The value of designing for people of all ages and abilities, known as universal design, is not taught in many American design schools. Nor is it practiced by many American designers. At best, many design students learn about building and product users as a homogenous group in the majority with a few exceptions—some special minority groups with unique needs like the elderly, the disabled, and the poor. Design education continues to segregate and stereotype people who do not fit "the norm" by ignoring their existence or, at best, teaching about them as separate subject matter. Well-meaning design research sometimes reinforces this separate treatment through its focus on specific groups having unique design needs. Products and building elements that meet the needs of older people and people with disabilities have tended to be ugly and expensive, and sometimes further stigmatize the very people they are intended to assist. For years there has been a no-market assumption by designers, builders, and manufacturers. This self-fulfilling prophecy has denied participation in community life to many people. Ron Mace points out that "legislated changes notwithstanding, it is *designers* who will decide whether accessibility will take the form of better design for everyone, or simply unattractive, costly, band-aid responses to annoying code requirements."[1]

Universal design is a holistic approach to creating environments and products that are usable by many people regardless of their abilities or age. In response to the Fair Housing Amendments Act and the Americans with Disabilities Act (ADA) as well as the impact of changing demographics on the marketplace, design education needs to embrace design for everyone.

The Universal Design Education Project (UDEP) was conceived as a vehicle for making the simple principles of universal design an integral component of design education. The project's goal is for students, in preparation for practice, to understand and reflect in their design work the multiplicity of ways in which a broad range of people actually use and experience places, products, and the built environment. The project supported faculty to develop new teaching strategies for infusing universal design values into the culture of their schools.

Although this project was a response to the civil rights legislation for people with disabilities, universal design is a concept that extends beyond the issues of accessibility for people with disabilities and offers compelling arguments for responding to the broad diversity of users who daily interact with the creations of designers. Universal design is one aspect of a larger movement in the design fields described by Weisman as a "politics of inclusion and wholeness" in place of the "politics of tolerance and competing interests." The pursuit of universal design values will help inform the creation of "a new ethic of design education and practice that values and celebrates human diversity and acknowledges humanity's debt to the earth."[2]

This book is both an effort to start bringing universal design teaching into the mainstream of design discourse as well as the descriptive documentation of a pilot project to enable future critical analysis of the long-term outcomes. As this book goes to press, Adaptive Environments has awarded a second round of funding to eight more design programs to build on what was learned from the initial project. It is important that the intentions of UDEP be carefully documented so that future evaluation is both fruitful and instructive. The strategies of UDEP are described here in such a way that the work of the twenty-two participating schools can be considered, adapted by other faculty, and critiqued in relation to the larger issue of pluralism in curriculum development and design values.

The book is organized around case studies written by the faculty team in each of the participating design schools. Each team was asked to fully document its intentions, the activities of teaching and learning, the outcomes, its evaluative effort, and the reflections of individual faculty about the experience. Class syllabi and assignments constituted a large part of the documentation effort by faculty. Although there was not space in this book to include those materials, faculty may request copies through the list of names and addresses provided in the appendix. The case-study format was developed to include extensive documentation of student work, but much of the material produced by the students was not reproducible at book scale.

The twenty-two schools developed a wide variety of strategies for teaching universal design, ranging from single courses to cross-department, cross-curriculum infusions. Schools also used a variety of teaching techniques in presenting the issues. A matrix on pages 26 and 27 provides an overview of the design disciplines, approaches, and techniques incorporated by each of the schools.

The four chapters preceding the case studies provide background on the concept of universal design, its relation to the history of disability-rights legislation, precedents for curriculum interventions in the design fields, and the evolution of UDEP. These chapters cover information and ideas presented to UDEP faculty at an orientation colloquium before they began teaching and may be useful to readers who plan to incorporate universal design into their curriculum. A final chapter summarizes the outcomes and discusses ongoing issues discussed by faculty at a symposium in Boston in the fall of 1994.

The appendices include a contact list so that readers can contact UDEP faculty for additional information and materials on individual projects. The biographies of key faculty, advisors, and staff illustrate the diversity of people who participated in the project and the wealth of experience that they brought to their teaching. Selections of some of the most useful books and articles available on accessibility and universal design are included, along with an annotated list of videotapes to encourage more use of non-print media. Several faculty put together course readers drawing from years of collecting materials in the popular press. We have tried to include those articles, where citations were available. Periodicals with which design faculty may not be familiar are also listed, along with a few other unique resources.

One of the thorniest problems for everyone who works on disability issues is language. The official terminology of the clinical and legislative worlds has perpetuated descriptors that emphasize people's differences and suggest that their identity is their disability. Attitudinal barriers have proven to be much harder to eliminate than architectural barriers, and language is central to eradicating the stereotypes that lead to discriminatory attitudes.[3] Very recent changes in federal legislation and in the names of governmental organizations have replaced the word *handicapped,* with its connotations of destitution and misery, with the term *disability.* Educators and practitioners need to set an example for students and clients by using language that conveys acceptance and respect for the whole person. The complexities of language were raised with the teaching faculty early in the project to sensitize them to its power in establishing respectful relationships between students and consultants.

This book tries to avoid popular euphemisms like *differently abled* and has been edited, when necessary, to use the convention most widely accepted among people with disabilities—*disability* and *people with disabilities.* In the interest of resisting political correctness when it would significantly alter the outcomes, several exceptions to this convention were made. All student work and commentary were left unedited and the terminology used by the Michigan State University faculty, *handicapper*—the legal and political label mandated in the state of Michigan—remains in their chapter. The word *other* is used in several chapters, in spite of its "we-they" distinction, because it has pedagogical significance for design disciplines that are struggling with self-referential values. In keeping with this posture on terminology, gender has been arbitrarily assigned when third-person singular pronouns were unavoidable.

Inaccurate use of language sometimes confused the basic goals of this project. The ADA Standards for Accessible Design[4] are the basis for universal design but by themselves constitute only one aspect of designing for all people. Going beyond the ADA Standards and the familiar concepts of accessible design to the broader issues of including all people proved difficult for some faculty with years of experience in teaching accessibility. This problem is complicated by the popular trend in advertising and print media to use the terms *barrier-free design, accessibility,* and *ADA* interchangeably with *universal design* without understanding or explaining the requisite shift in perspective.

The teaching and learning experiences documented in the following case studies reflect thoughtful, inventive work by faculty, students, and user consultants. Each strategy illustrates a unique response to the challenge of embracing inclusive design. Each faculty member managed a significant act of change within the complex politics of the academy. The experience of many faculty is captured by the comments of a few: "It was the hardest work I've ever done." "It was the most satisfying teaching of my life." Through this book we learn from their efforts and frame new avenues of inquiry.

Polly Welch and Elaine Ostroff

Notes

1. Mace, R., G. Hardie, and J. Plaice (1991). "Accessible Environments: Toward Universal Design." In *Design Interventions: Toward A More Humane Architecture,* edited by Preiser, Vischer, and White. New York: Van Nostrand Reinhold.

2. Weisman, Leslie Kanes (1994). "Toward an Architecture of Inclusion." *Outreach ACSA Women's Issues Newsletter,* October.

3. Kailes, June Isaacson (1984). *Language is More Than a Trivial Concern.*

4. The ADA Standards for Accessible Design are the enforceable standards issued by the U.S. Department of Justice as part of the Final Rule for ADA Title III. When DOJ adopted the *ADA Accessibility Guidelines* (ADAAG) developed by the Access Board, as the appendix in Title III, they became the enforceable standards for new construction and alterations. When altering any building or space it is important to use the DOJ Final Rule where you will find not only the ADA Standards but all of the requirements for barrier removal and alterations.

Acknowledgements

Both the Universal Design Education Project and *Strategies for Teaching Universal Design* were made possible by the generous financial support of the multiple funders of the project. The success of the pilot, and its potential for continuing impact, is very much related to the diversity and scope of these funders. The U.S. Department of Justice, Disability Rights Section, as part of its ADA Technical Assistance Grant Program, supported two years of dissemination activities that made it possible for the project to have a far greater reach than it otherwise would have had. The dissemination included the production of this book, advisor visits to the participating schools, national meetings, and the development of an Internet information network. The initial funding that launched the project came from a grant from the National Endowment for the Arts. NEC Foundation of America provided additional crucial funding, matching the NEA support. The Nynex Foundation and the J.M. Foundation provided the funding that completed the project.

The Center for Universal Design, formerly the Center for Accessible Housing, led by Ron Mace, senior principal investigator, and Mike Jones, executive director, played an important role in supporting the development of this project. The Center provided philosophical and administrative support, assisting with critical marketing and graphics, with organization of the Raleigh colloquium, and with preparation of the resource kit and book display, especially Jan Reagan and Colleen Tarry.

Ray Lifchez, through his teaching, laid the philosophical and moral groundwork for this project. The compelling nature of his writing and his teaching has been an inspiration for many faculty attempting to incorporate more humanistic and inclusive values into their teaching. While his current interests precluded him from participating in UDEP, his presence and influence were felt by many participants through his books and video.

Ron Mace and Ruth Hall Lusher, through their writing and advocacy, provided the intellectual and practical arguments for universal design and lifespan design. Their individual and collaborative work set the stage for UDEP.

The faculty and students who engaged in UDEP courses are the stars whose accomplishments constitute the essence of this work. Their case studies convey the passions, frustrations, and surprise with which they successfully engaged a new way of thinking about good design.

The unsung heroes of this project are the advisors, who have given freely of their time to review proposals, attend colloquia, make site visits to schools across the country, and be a sounding board on issues that needed seasoned perspectives: Robert Anders of Pratt Institute; Dorothy Fowles of Iowa State University; Susan Goltsman of Moore Iacofano Goltsman, Inc.; Ron Mace of the Center for Universal Design; Joe

Acknowledgements *continued*

Meade of the U.S. Forest Service; Robin Moore of North Carolina State University; James Mueller of J.L. Mueller, Inc.; John P.S. Salmen of Universal Designers and Consultants; Robert Shibley of the State University of New York at Buffalo; and Paul John Grayson of Environments for Living. Two others added to the liveliness of the faculty colloquium in Raleigh, North Carolina. Chris Palames gave a charged account of the history of disability rights, which he graciously agreed to have distributed on videotape and to be used in developing the second chapter of this book. Daniel Iacofano, master of facilitation, captured the energy and ideas of the colloquium for posterity through wallgraphics.

Many individuals have contributed to UDEP. Paula Terry of the National Endowment for the Arts played a key role in initiating discussions that led to the NEA's leadership role in universal design. Sylvia Clark, executive director of NEC Foundation of America, and Peter Hawley of the National Endowment for the Arts generously participated in the Raleigh Colloquium. Ruth Hall Lusher of the Department of Justice spoke at the colloquium.

Thankless administrative tasks were competently and thoughtfully supported by staff at Adaptive Environments: Gabriela Sims, Melissa Hammel, Lesli Jo, and Soni Gupta, who played a critical role in collecting the materials for this book.

We especially want to thank the people with whom we share our daily lives. Liliana Welch learned about coloring on the back side of the draft pages while helping her mom become even more appreciative of the value of universal design to children. Earl Ostroff, lifelong companion and supporter, has growing appreciation of universal design.

What is Universal Design?

What is universal design? It is, simply, "an approach to creating environments and products that are usable by all people to the greatest extent possible."[1] The ambiguity of the term *universal design*, according to James Mueller, is its virtue because it provokes discussion. The implication that universal design applies to everyone is another virtue of the term. As Elizabeth Church points out, "universal design implies that 'it' could happen to me" as opposed to "special needs" that are always someone else's.[2] Ralph Caplan adds that "in a rational world you wouldn't have to use it, because that's what design itself would be."[3]

Although a recently coined term, the concept of universal design is not new. Architect Michael Bednar in 1977 noted that the functional capability of all people is usually enhanced when environmental barriers are removed and suggested that a new concept is needed that is "much broader and more universal" and "involves the environmental needs of all users."[4] The term *accessible design* was used in the early 1980s to describe the value of universal design—design for all people.[5] Over time, however, *accessible* and *accessibility* have become synonymous with making environments usable primarily by people with disabilities, losing the more inclusive connotation of making environments understandable to and usable by all people. An accessible building implies that a person using a wheelchair can get into the building, but the notion that the building is convenient to public transportation, has an easily located front door, and provides good directories for wayfinding is usually not part of the image of accessibility that comes to mind for designers. Those features, however, are the essence of a universal design approach.

Universal design is not a euphemism for accessibility. It is not a catchy phrase to make more palatable the requirements of the ADA Standards for Accessible Design. It is a term that re-establishes an important goal of good design—that it shall meet the needs of as many users as possible. *Universal* indicates a unanimity of practice and applicability to all cases without significant exception.[6] Universal design suggests solutions that are capable of being adjusted or modified to meet varied requirements. It is the inclusivity of universal design that makes it cost effective; universal design increases the number of people whose needs are being addressed and it encourages an integrative approach rather than multiple separate solutions.

The need for the concept of universal design emerged through two separate but related movements: the struggle by the disability community to erase the "we-they" dichotomy that allowed designers to marginalize the needs of people with disabilities and the pressure from groups within the design professions for democratization of values through a more pluralistic definition of good design.

Early advocacy and legal efforts by the disability community in the sixties and seventies to make existing public places physically accessible to people with disabilities resulted in the development of numerous architectural features to promote "handicap accessibility"—the ramp, the lift, the larger toilet stall, and the international symbol with its wheelchair user. These devices have provided much needed access and provided potent symbols of separateness as well. Lusher and Mace point out that the hard-won laws to increase educational, employment, housing, and recreational opportunities for people with disabilities "were inadequate as educational media and they reinforced the outdated, narrow view of human environmental needs by requiring a few special features for what was perceived as a few people."[7]

The term universal design was invented in response to a conceptual dilemma that has plagued advocates of barrier-free environments since the passage of the first ANSI standards. How do you overcome pervasive attitudinal barriers when physical barriers can be neatly addressed with a few code-compliance measures? The circular dilemma confounded the disability community's effort to win broad access. The codes, balancing cost and change, established minimum standards, which provided the most basic access, but did little to encourage designers and building owners to consider the benefits of making buildings more accessible to a broad array of users. Some building owners even wondered why they should make their buildings accessible if people with disabilities never used their buildings, overlooking the paradoxical nature of their question.

The second movement, with roots in the same decades, is the loose association of designers and scientists interested in how the built environment meets the needs of its users. Early efforts focused on the functional fit of environments and products to people, resulting in anthropometric and human-factors research. Unfortunately, much of the data that reached designers was based on the average, young, able-bodied male. Other groups pressed for users to have a greater voice in the design of buildings and open space through greater participation in decision-making and through better representation of the diversity of users.[8] Designers and researchers who subscribe to these values have sometimes inadvertently perpetuated the segregation of users by giving specific constituencies, like the elderly, special attention. The study of "special populations" has generated important information for designers on how the environment can meet specific needs, but *special* has become another word for *separate*.[9]

The inherent limitations of design standards, in general, have produced yet another reason for the concept of universal design. Designers, manufacturers, and building officials have pressed for clear, simple specification of solutions for achieving accessibility. People with disabilities found that the reduction of complex variables to single solutions excluded many whose disabilities fell outside the norm. Although extensive empirical research[10] has examined more closely the specifics of how a representative range of people with disabilities access and interact with the environment, an alternative to the prevailing paradigms of *minimum standard* and *exceptions to the norm* has not emerged. Designers have historically tended to interpret minimum standards as maximums, particularly when solutions beyond the minimum might result in higher costs. The codes have also reinforced the notion that design for people with disabilities can be achieved by modification to the norm. Not only does this result in design that segregates, it is also a costly solution.[11]

What is Universal Design?

The passage of the Americans with Disabilities Act in 1990 heralded the opportunity for a paradigm shift. Extending the design discussion beyond the realm of building codes and into the realm of civil rights took the design and building industries by surprise. By framing the issue of access as part of the American promise for equal opportunity, the focus was shifted from the purely pragmatic decision of where to place the wheelchair lift to who uses the built environment and how to provide them with greater opportunities to access places and programs. The broadened perspective created a sense of uncertainty for design decision-makers. Reassurance came in the form of standards that had some resemblance to the earlier code requirements but the new requirements also provided an opportunity for greater creativity and a challenge for designers to think beyond the minimum requirements by introducing the concept of *equivalent facilitation*. To achieve an appropriate equivalent design solution through alternate means requires that designers and building owners must understand the needs of users well enough to make informed judgments and to effectively use the input of users with disabilities.

The positive outcome of the Americans with Disabilities Act is increased consciousness among designers, building owners, and manufacturers about the rights of people with a range of disabilities and more accessible public and private places. The new level of consciousness establishes a teachable moment. By heightening the awareness of designers to a previously marginalized group of users, inclusive design values are more likely to be included in design discourse. The disappointment to some veterans of barrier-free design efforts is the recodification of user needs. People are disabled by situations and attitudes: a designer can meet the letter of the law, follow the details of the standards, and still not create an enabling environment. The possibilities for replacing standards with another paradigm for responsible design may lie in the elaboration of universal design values.

Universal design is also lifespan design. All of us benefit from from accessible places and products at many stages in the passage from childhood to old age. The case for universal design is frequently made by citing national census data and projections. In 1990, 48.9 million Americans had some type of disability and 31 million, one in every eight Americans, were 65 or older; by 2030 it is predicted that one in five Americans will be over 65. While statistics by themselves can be informative, Lusher and Mace contend that arguing the numbers game misses the point. Leon Pastalan concurs, pointing out that by focusing instead on the "context of normal expectations of the human condition, trying to justify the importance of each vulnerable population group becomes unnecessary."[12] Michel Philibert, French philosopher and gerontologist, has proposed that we are at the dawn of a new understanding where aging is defined as a pattern of change throughout the entire lifespan.[13] So designing for children, older people and people with disabilities is not thinking about separate groups of users but a spectrum of human-environment interaction.

Chapter 1

Notes

1. Mace, R., G. Hardie, and J. Plaice (1991). "Accessible Environments: Toward Universal Design." In *Design Interventions: Toward A More Humane Architecture,* edited by Preiser, Vischer, and White, 156. New York: Van Nostrand Reinhold.

2. Mueller's and Church's comments were made at the UDEP Conference, Boston, November 1994.

3. Caplan, Ralph. "Disabled By Design." *Interior Design*, August 1992.

4. Bednar, Michael (1977). *Barrier Free Environments.* Stroudsburg, Pa.: Dowden, Hutchinson, and Ross.

5. Ostroff, Elaine and Daniel Iacofano (1982). *Teaching Design For All People: The State of the Art.* Boston: Adaptive Environments Center.

6. *Webster's Third New International Dictionary* (1981).

7. Lusher, Ruth Hall and Ronald Mace (1989). "Design for Physical and Mental Disabilities." In *Encyclopedia of Architecture: Design Engineering and Construction,* edited by Wilkes and Packard, 755. New York: John Wiley and Sons.

8. Environmental Design Research Association.

9. Kailes, June Isaacson (1984). *Language is More Than a Trivial Concern.*

10. Steinfeld et al. (1979). Two-year project at Syracuse University, the findings and conclusions of which formed the basis for the revisions to ANSI A117.1 described in "Developing Standards for Accessibility" in Ref. 4.

11. Ref. 7, 754.

12. Mace, Ronald (1988). *Universal Design: Housing for the Lifespan of All People.* Washington, D.C.: U.S. Department of Housing and Urban Development, 4.

13. Byerts, Thomas (1977). "Prologue." *Journal of Architectural Education* 31, no. 1.

by Polly Welch and Chris Palames

It is difficult to understand the significance of the term *universal design* without first examining how people who are physically different have been treated socially, legally, and politically in the United States over the course of this century. While designers may not view this history as having bearing on their creativity or being of their making, their work has been instrumental in perpetuating the norms that exclude some people from using buildings, landscapes, and products.

Disability has been made visible in American life primarily as an outcome of military engagement and, therefore, was managed by the federal government in the War Department and, later, at the Veterans Administration. Civilians with disabilities were largely invisible and unaccounted for by government until the latter half of the twentieth century when the social and physical isolation of people with physical and mental disability became the focus of civil rights legislation. Until that time, society managed to keep people who were different out of sight by building institutions such as nursing homes, asylums, and homeless shelters and using statutes such as ugly laws to prohibit from public places people whose different appearance might offend the citizenry.[1] John Hockenberry poignantly captures this social isolation in his description[2] of visiting his elderly uncle who was institutionalized in childhood:

> *As I roll in my wheelchair toward the place where he lives, I understand that my uncle and I share the experience of being different. Our lives are lived in the crawl space between our strangeness and other people's reactions and fears. The instinctive human fear of those who are different has defined both of our lives. The forces that put my uncle away would also place me in a category from which there is no escape. Inside me is the engine that thrashes about, never stopping, always mindful that someday those same forces could decide my fate, claim that I am really helpless, that my life is not worth living, give me a label, and send me away to a place for all those like me.*

Following each of the major wars of this century, the U.S. Congress responded to the needs of returning veterans with rehabilitation legislation in the form of the Smith-Fess Vocational Rehabilitation Act. Enacted after World War I, it was amended in 1943, 1954, and 1965, after World War II, the Korean War, and the Vietnam War respectively, to reflect changes in how people with disabilities were perceived and the availability of new treatment and rehabilitation protocols. In World War I, only about 2 percent of veterans with spinal-cord injuries survived more than a year, but three decades later during World War II, the discovery of antibiotics and more sophisticated medical interventions brought the survival rate up to 85 percent.

Chapter 2

Although the purpose of rehabilitation legislation was to compensate veterans, the Smith-Fess Vocational Rehabilitation Act and each of its amendments brought additional recognition and benefits for civilians as well. In 1943, people with mental retardation were included in the legislation, making vocational training available to them for the first time. The polio epidemics of the early 1950s also brought new attention to the needs of civilians. In 1954, rehabilitation was moved from the Veterans Administration into the new federal Department of Health, Education, and Welfare and funds were allocated for research and demonstration grants. But none of this legislation included any consideration of building accessibility. Its entire focus was on the clinical impairments of people with disabilities and their management.

The first serious effort to address building design as an issue for people with disabilities was a 1958 conference sponsored by the President's Commission on Employment of the Handicapped, the National Easter Seal Society, and the American National Standards Institute (ANSI), a private standard-setting body that called for the development of voluntary standards for the design of accessible buildings. With a grant from the Easter Seal Foundation, these standards were developed by Timothy Nugent at the Rehabilitation Center at the University of Illinois with oversight by a committee of representatives from government, advocacy, health, trade, and professional associations. Published and distributed in 1961 under the title *A117.1 Making Buildings Accessible to and Usable by the Physically Handicapped,* the new standard described "in precise and practical terms, the minimal features required to remove the major barriers that prevent many persons from using buildings and facilities" and became the first scientifically developed design guideline on accessibility in the world. Finally, designers and building owners had available to them specifications for making building elements such as parking spaces, elevators, and toilet stalls usable by people with disabilities. The existence of such information, however, did not result in substantially more accessible buildings; most building owners and designers were unaware of the standards or oblivious to the social benefits of implementing them. These voluntary standards were not enforceable until adopted by a state or local entity, which started to happen in the late sixties and early seventies.

Although an informal group of federal officials had developed an advisory guide for federal agencies on making public buildings accessible during the late fifties, it was not until the 1965 amendment of the Rehabilitation Act that architectural barriers were formally acknowledged by the federal government as an issue. The National Commission on Architectural Barriers was established and three years later issued a report titled "Design for *All* Americans" (ed. italics), which captures the remarkable lack of awareness of American businesses, public officials, and design and construction professionals to the existence of barriers and the standard for their removal:

- In a survey of almost three thousand architects—of the seven hundred who replied, only 35 percent were aware of ANSI A117.1 (1961).

- None of the four major building codes made any reference to architectural barriers or their removal.

- Building industry manufacturers and suppliers were unaware of the existence of standards.

- Public officials believed that there was not enough public interest to develop public programs addressing building access.

The report cited a number of deficiencies in the ANSI standard that diminished its usefulness to designers. The standard did not define the scope of its application—what facility types, what elements of a building, and how many of each element. The standard was difficult to implement because its language was vague and had very few drawings to aid designers in interpreting the information. Just a few years later in 1971, the 1961 ANSI standard was reaffirmed without revision by ANSI and continued in use for another decade as the "pivotal document for the forging of federal and state laws."[3] Confusion persisted for designers because of multiple standard-setting agencies, conflicting requirements, and negligible enforcement.

The National Commission's report concluded that "the greatest single obstacle to employment for the handicapped is the physical design of buildings and facilities they must use." In response to these findings, Congress drafted and passed new legislation in 1968—the Architectural Barriers Act. It is interesting to note some of the issues related to passage of the Act. One of the motivating factors for the legislation was a perception that public funds expended on rehabilitation were a shortsighted investment without removal of architectural barriers. Supporters emphasized the belief that architectural barriers existed because of "simple thoughtlessness" and their removal would occur with education of the public and design professionals. In hindsight, the two-decade delay in achieving full accessibility to both public and private places illustrates the naiveté of this belief.[4] The Act mandated that buildings designed, constructed, altered, or leased with federal funds would comply with standards for accessibility. It established three federal agencies that would set standards—the General Services Administration, the Department of Housing and Urban Development, and the Department of Defense. The Act required two majors amendments (1970 and 1976) before it started to have a significant effect on the accessibility of public buildings.

In spite of significant changes providing people with disabilities greater independence and opportunities for greater participation in American life—federal legislation, medical advances, and developments in assistive technology—changes in public attitudes have followed slowly and primarily in response to educational efforts that have accompanied new laws. The critical factor to real change, according to Harlan Hahn, a professor of political science at the University of Southern California, was that the definition of disability shifted from medical and economic perspectives, which view disabilities from the standpoint of functional and vocational limitations, to a socio-political perspective that focuses rather on the disabling qualities of the environment that limit the possible interactions of people with disabilities.

In this shift, people with disabilities have emerged as a "minority group," oppressed not by their disabilities but by circumstances that can be changed through legislation and political action. A principal dimension of oppression of a minority group is the assumption of biological inferiority by the majority. While other minority groups have managed to disprove this assumption, the visible, physical differences of people with disabilities evokes fearful reactions that perpetuate the notion of subordinate status. Citing *Stigma,* in which Erving Goffman describes people with disabilities as being viewed by society as not quite human, Hahn argues that it is this failure to meet the twentieth-century Western values of physical attractiveness and individual autonomy that permits society to set disabled people apart.[5] For public-policy changes to be effective, the attitudes that lead to the marginalization of people with disabilities must be addressed equally along with functional changes in the physical environment.

The disability rights movement, both in a formal legal sense and in a moral sense, has its roots in the civil rights movement of the 1960s. The Civil Rights Act of 1964, focused in its intent to eliminate racial discrimination, set the stage for a number of minority groups to broaden its coverage and use its mandate to demand equality. The disability rights movement began to be a force and have its agendas recognized in legislation during the 1970s, starting with the Rehabilitation Act of 1973.

The power of that Rehabilitation Act comes from the fact that its language, especially Section 504, echoes Title VII of the 1964 Civil Rights Act. Section 504 was the first statutory definition of discrimination towards people with disabilities. Although it did not have the scope of the Civil Rights Act of 1964 and only outlawed discrimination by those entities that received federal funds, it was a crucial factor in shifting disability issues from the realm of social services and therapeutic practice to a political and civil rights context. The Act survived two presidential vetoes, suggesting that Congress finally understood the social significance of the issues. The Act laid important groundwork for change but did not address implementation; it took four more years for the regulations enforcing Section 504 of the Rehabilitation Act to be issued in 1978.

Three important new concepts emerged during the 1970s—program accessibility, mainstreaming, and independent living. While none of them directly addressed the technical issues of accessibility, each had implications for the accommodation of people with disabilities by organizations that own and operate buildings. Section 504 introduced the concept of program accessibility, which allowed programs to achieve accessibility by being "viewed in their entirety." This permitted some flexibility for compliance. For example, a community program could relocate activities to a physically accessible space in lieu of costly renovations to an existing location. In 1975, Congress passed the Education for All Handicapped Children Act, mandating free, appropriate public education for children with disabilities. This legislation introduced the concept of mainstreaming, ensuring children with disabilities an education in the least restrictive environment—when possible, the same environment as children without disabilities. Public schools throughout the country struggled with barrier removal, in spite of the fact that existing standards did not address accessibility for children. In 1978, federal funding for independent-living services became available for the first time. The independent-living concept, first talked about in rehabilitation circles in the 1950s and 1960s as a full menu of services provided by expert professionals to people with disabilities, was redefined by the disability movement as a self-help empowerment movement to liberate people with disabilities from the traditional concept of dependency, especially in their choice of living environments.

While national disability policy was being rewritten, a social and political movement was emerging among people with disabilities in local communities through local action. The disability movement was reputedly born in Berkeley, California, where the first center for independent living was established in the early 1970s and people with disabilities had their first dramatic confrontations with the federal bureaucracy, in this case the occupation of the Health, Education, and Welfare offices in San Francisco in 1977 and 1978 to force the issuance of the 504 regulations. What occurred in such dramatic terms in Berkeley resonated throughout the country among people with disabilities who had experienced social oppression and the devaluation of personal identity and were looking for a political model for change. The proliferation across the country of independent-living centers, other kinds of disability advocacy organizations, a movement into government by people with disabilities, and the formation of state and municipal offices on disability demonstrated the power of local action and proved to be very valuable in sustaining a political presence during a period of restricted national resources.

Government at the state and local levels moved more quickly than the federal government. While Washington was slow to implement the Architectural Barriers Act, many states adopted the ANSI standard and required compliance for state-funded facilities. By 1966, at least thirty states had access legislation and by 1973, every state except Kentucky had done so. Ten states had expanded jurisdiction to privately funded buildings designed for public use.[6] Enforcement, however, continued to be problematic at every level.

The 1980s were a frightening period for people with disabilities because the prevailing notion that the best government was no government threatened to undo hard-won rights. But the disability movement was sufficiently strong at this point to pre-serve the basic legal structures of disability rights, unlike other progressive efforts such as the environmental movement, which experienced major revisions in policy. In spite of the Commission on Regulatory Relief, the disability movement was successful in opposing attempts to deregulate Section 504 and the Architectural Barriers Act, achieving some bipartisan support and making apparent its potential political power. The groundswell of response from parents had a profound effect on George Bush, who chaired the Commission on Regulatory Relief.

In spite of the no-government rhetoric in Washington, federal administrative wheels kept churning and more standards and legislation were passed. In 1981, the Architectural and Transportation Barriers Compliance Board (ATBCB) first issued its "Minimum Guidelines and Requirements for Accessible Design," but the new Reagan appointees on the ATBCB proposed recision. The MGRAD were subsequently reis-sued in 1982 as a result of overwhelming public comment. These established the basic underpinnings for the Uniform Federal Accessibility Standards (UFAS) issued by four federal agencies: General Services Administration, Department of Defense, Department of Housing and Urban Development, and the U.S. Postal Service. In 1986, the Air Carriers Act was passed indicating that Congress was returning to the business of expanding the rights of people with disabilities to participate in all dimen-sions of society, in this case, the right to air travel.

Two years later in 1988, four things happened in one year. The first, HUD finally issuing its 504 regulations, only eleven years after the model regulation had been issued, was another step in the slow effort to develop standards that would change the physical environment. But the other three events were on the civil rights front, an arena that was critical to a major shift in perspective for people with disabilities.

The Civil Rights Restoration Act was written to repair the damage that had been done to the structure of civil rights enforcement, both by administrative and judicial decisions in the 1980s. The Civil Rights Restoration Act, which was stimulated by a gender-discrimination case, required federal-funding recipients to comply throughout institutions, not just within the funded unit. Important to disability rights, it was the first time that the disability community was accepted as a full partner in the legislative and the lobbying process for civil rights.

The Fair Housing Amendments Act, the prelude to the Americans with Disabilities Act, expanded the protections of the Civil Rights Act of 1968 to include both people with disabilities and families with children. It expanded the scope of accessible hous-ing from that which received public funds to all new multifamily housing with four or more units, both public and private. For the first time, a person with a disability could reasonably expect to be able to seek accessible housing in the open market.

A Brief History of Disability Rights Legislation in the United States

And finally, the first version of the Americans with Disabilities Act went before Congress, crafted not by radicals in the disability movement, but by Reagan appointees to the National Council on Disability. At this time the disability movement, from the conservative to the radical wing of the movement, was unified in the view that what was needed was not a new and better brand of social welfare system, but a fundamental examination and redefinition of the democratic tradition of equal opportunity and equal rights.

In just two years, Congress passed this ambitious legislation and in 1990, President George Bush held the largest signing ceremony in history on the south lawn of the White House, an historic moment for all people with disabilities. The passage of the ADA was to some degree effected by members of Congress realizing their obligation to ensure civil rights to all Americans. The benefits of the ADA extend to a broad range of people by cutting across all sectors of society; virtually every voter will experience positive benefits from the law or know someone who does. Policy makers saw important implications for the next century in terms of managing costs of potentially dependent populations. Demographers project a dramatic increase in the number of people who will live into their nineties. The extent to which their needs can be accommodated through responsively designed environments and assistive technology may save billions of dollars in institutional care, largely underwritten by federal programs. As many as two-thirds of people with disabilities are unemployed, largely due to attitudinal and physical barriers that prevent their access to available jobs. With the national sentiment opposed to long-term welfare reliance and a labor-deficit economy, employment of people with disabilities is essential.

The Americans with Disabilities Act is not only historic nationally but globally as well. There is no other mandate of this scope in the world. Though other nations provide greater levels of support services and assistive technology, the United States ensures equal rights within a constitutional tradition. The ADA has a unique appeal for all Americans because, unlike other civil rights categories such as race and gender, an individual may become a member of the protected class at any moment in his or her life.

Notes

1. Lifchez, Raymond (1987). *Rethinking Architecture: Design Students and Physically Disabled People.* Berkeley, Calif.: University of California Press, 2 n.

2. Hockenberry, John (1995). *Moving Violations: War Zones, Wheelchairs, and Declarations of Independence.* New York: Hyperion.

3. Lusher, Ruth Hall (1989). "Handicapped Access Laws and Codes." In *Encyclopedia of Architecture: Design Engineering and Construction*, vol. 3, edited by Wilkes and Packard, 647. New York: John Wiley and Sons.

4. Hull, Kent (1979). *The Rights of Physically Handicapped People.* New York: Avon Books, 67.

5. Hahn, Harlan. "The Politics of Physical Differences: Disability and Discrimination." *Journal of Social Issues* 44, no. 1 (1988).

6. Ref. 3, 648.

The Universal Design Education Project (UDEP) has a number of precedents, especially in the field of architecture. Although UDEP is the most recent coordinated effort to integrate user needs into the training of designers, it is not entirely new in concept. The impetus for curriculum development in the design fields usually comes from a recognition that factors important to students' competence as practitioners are not sufficiently represented in the courses offered within a program. UDEP differs from other curriculum development efforts in several ways: its focus is a value rather than a skill or specific subject matter; it looks at the issues across multiple design fields; and its premise is that faculty need to invent interventions that are appropriate to their own institutional context rather than teach a course from a packaged curriculum. The search for precedents turned up quite a few courses that addressed human and behavioral issues in design but treated physical ability, size, and age within the existing social constructs of the *elderly* and the *handicapped*, reinforcing stereotypes and segregation that are antithetical to the value of universal design. The organizers of UDEP drew from previous efforts at curriculum change to develop a strategy that would stimulate new thinking and create momentum for change.

In 1975, the Gerontological Society of America (GSA) turned its attention to the application of gerontological research in teaching. Over a two-year period, the Curriculum Development Project funded by the Administration on Aging, under the auspices of architect Thomas Byerts, developed educational materials that would transmit four years of research on aging and environments to design faculty. The purpose of taking the materials into the schools was to prepare future practitioners to design for a population that was growing exponentially and whose needs would be met by a range of building types. The project compiled a source book of thirty research articles on environment and aging and pretested this package and strategies for course development at Ohio State University, the University of Michigan, and MIT. A second round of testing introduced eight more schools to the materials. Teaching case studies from many of these schools were published in *The Journal of Architectural Education*.[1] Several patterns emerge from the case studies: students read only a few of the research materials, finding them theoretically cumbersome and limited in graphic examples; students responded well to input from visiting experts (usually gerontologists and architects, except in one case where students met with older people); and students had difficulty applying the information they received to design-studio problems. Sandra Howell's comments on her teaching experience at MIT are prescient of the UDEP effort fifteen years later.

Despite the critical importance of educating planners and designers in the environmental problems and needs of a growing aging population, sole concentration on this population segment narrows opportunities for illustrating user needs and behaviors relevant to future professionals who will undoubtedly be designing for a range of populations and of settings.... Not all students are psychologically or intellectually prepared to explore human aging. Introduction of materials and methods

Chapter 3

equally appropriate to issues of old and young, workers and retirees and able and disabled, brings the student more slowly into the arena and offers options within a behavioral context.[2]

The aging curriculum that was introduced in the 1970s continues to be taught in many of these schools, typically by the same faculty who helped promulgate the effort in the first place. Several of the schools created research centers devoted to aging and environment, which sustained senior-faculty contributions to the subject and gave greater visibility to the topic in the department or school. The formal dissemination of the materials to a broader constituency never happened and it is now difficult for new faculty to locate a copy of the original materials for teaching, although several interim publications can be found in design school libraries.

In 1994, the AIA/ACSA Council on Architectural Research was awarded a grant from the Administration on Aging to develop new curriculum materials for use in architecture programs, building on the earlier endeavor by the GSA. The Council convened a committee of eight experts on aging and environment to develop a curriculum package, drawing heavily on people who had been involved in the GSA project twenty years earlier. Among the new members, two had an interest in aging as another dimension of designing for people with disabilities. The meetings of the committee occurred after the first cycle of UDEP so Polly Welch, who was instrumental in developing both projects, shared the insights from UDEP with the Aging and Environments Project.

A new package of materials was created with a more critical eye towards what students might read and find useful to their design inquiry. In addition to several by-now-classic articles on aging and environment, the committee suggested expanding the resources to include a list of literature and film that described aging and older people. Also included were some studio design problems that faculty could use directly or reinterpret for their own students. An attempt was made to provide case studies of existing facilities designed for older people. Finding a dearth of rigorous evaluations, the committee instead included as illustrative material projects submitted to an AIA awards program for facilities for aging.

In 1981, Uriel Cohen at the University of Wisconsin–Milwaukee expanded his research on the important distinctions between mainstreaming people with disabilities and barrier-free design by publishing a resource guide for teachers and students of environmental design. He was responding to two distinct problems affecting architectural education: "the lack of a balanced body of information regarding physical design applications for all handicapped people and the marginal treatment given to design for the handicapped in most architectural criteria."[3] His prior work pointed out that most of the focus in mainstreaming children with disabilities into school programs had been in the realm of barrier-free compliance, leaving unaddressed the needs of 90 percent of the affected children—those with non-mobility related disabilities. This was the first curriculum material to raise the subtle and equally important issue of designing for people with sensory disabilities, developmental disabilities, and mental illness. The resource guide contains programmed instructional materials and information resources and continues to be available from the University of Wisconsin–Milwaukee. The materials are still relevant even if the terminology and bibliography are a bit dated.

The most useful precedent to UDEP is the project initiated in 1979 by Raymond Lifchez, professor of architecture at the University of California at Berkeley. With a grant from the Exxon Education Foundation, he initiated an experimental project called "Architectural Design with the Physically Disabled User in Mind." Lifchez states that the goals were to: "develop a reasoned critique of the traditional methods of teaching, propose and test alternative methods that would place clients at the heart of the design process, and enable students to develop skills needed to bridge the gap between able-bodied and disabled people."[4] In a two-year period between 1979 and 1981, approximately 400 people, including teachers, students, consultants, and observers, participated in the project. Lifchez initially included four other schools in this experiment. The Berkeley team pilot tested the curriculum and provided oversight to the four schools. After one term, however, the participation of the other schools was discontinued and Lifchez concentrated his energy and resources at Berkeley.

Lifchez recognized the unintended legacy of the last decade when social sciences were introduced into architectural training without adequate translation. "This dangerous misconception [among design students] about client accommodation as antithetical to creative expression can be dispelled only be teaching students how to be client-conscious and make beautiful buildings at the same time." At best the legacy had created a few design schools where user needs was the primary subject matter in courses such as "Social and Behavioral Factors in Design." Lifchez elaborates that "client accommodation is not merely the third element in design, alongside aesthetics and technology, but is in fact the context within which all factors of architectural design must be placed."[5]

Throughout the project there is an important ambiguity about whether the studios were to teach students about disability or about user accommodation in general. One of the consultants interprets the purpose this way: "Our studio course was a general architectural design studio that emphasized social factors, although many students perceived it as a class in which they were supposed to learn about accessibility by meeting disabled people in the studio. But in fact the central theme of the course was the examination of one's stereotypes and prejudices about people different from oneself: the elderly and children, middle class people and working class people, gays and nuclear families, conservatives and radicals."[6]

Chapter 3

This project also emphasized the importance of exploring the issues of differences in the context of a design studio rather than through lectures on issues, legal requirements, and hardware options.[7] There is an important symbolism to the placement of material in the design curriculum. The design studio has historically been considered the center of design education. Ideas and issues discussed in the studio setting are assumed to be critical to good design; ideas and facts presented in non-studio courses are often seen by students as contextual and, perhaps, discretionary or peripheral to basic design. The Lifchez project lives on in several forms. The Exxon Education Foundation funded the National Center for a Barrier Free Environment to document Lifchez's teaching process as well as reflections by many of the participants in the form of a video called *A House for Someone Unlike Me*.[8] The reflections of many of the people involved in the studio courses—faculty, consultants, and evaluators—comprise the chapters of the book *Rethinking Architecture: Design Students and Physically Disabled People*. Robert Shibley, in reviewing the book, says "this book is much more than a book about course curriculum or even about architecture. Powerful and often poignantly, this work forces us to confront our own vulnerability and recast the issue of human frailty as one that is a universal element of the human experience."[9]

Issues of accessibility in design education were also being addressed at the individual and organizational level. In addition to sponsoring the Lifchez film, the National Center for a Barrier Free Environment sponsored another project, an international design conference coordinated by John Salmen in 1982 at the United Nations—Designed Environments for All People. Hundreds of advocates, practitioners, and educators attended to display and discuss examples of successful accessible design. Many individuals across the country were experimenting and teaching courses that grew out of their own passion and personal commitment to the issues of greater access. One of those educators was industrial designer Mark Harrison. His teaching at the Rhode Island School of Design was an early documented model of universal design education. He routinely taught his students about the complexity of designing tools and appliances by introducing them to the needs of people with limited hand function. His design for the Cuisinart appliance in the late seventies is one of the most frequently cited examples of how understanding the needs of people with a functional limitation can lead to improved design for all people.

Some of these faculty and practitioners were identified by the Adaptive Environments Center and came together in Boston in 1982 for a seminar supported by the National Endowment for the Arts called Design for All People. The conference was an opportunity for faculty already involved in teaching accessible design to become more aware of each other's work and to identify existing successful curricular material for further development. The conference report emphasized the need to "go beyond the codes, and toward more universal design."[10]

Precedents for a More Inclusive Curriculum

In spite of these conferences, there were few other formal efforts at curriculum development related to accessible design during the eighties. When the ADA became law in 1990, its broad scope and requirements for compliance planning became an opportunity for faculty already versatile with accessibility concepts to expand their teaching and contribute to professional acceptance of the new mandate. Some design disciplines needed to make very little adjustment to their curriculum. *Interior Design* magazine surveyed the eighty-eight interior design programs accredited by the Foundation for Interior Design Education Research and found that the majority planned to change very little of their teaching because access standards, anthropometrics, and human factors were already incorporated into the curriculum.[11]

There is little evidence that architecture and landscape architecture educators responded to the new law in terms of formal curriculum. Conference proceedings of the two national design educators' meetings for the three years following passage of the ADA include no papers on the impact and significance of the ADA to the teaching of architecture and landscape architecture. By 1993, there were indications that ADA and universal design consciousness was beginning to permeate educational organizations. The National Institute for Architectural Education, which sponsors student design competitions, developed a competition for a house for Stephen Hawking. The annual design competition sponsored by Otis Elevator specifically mentioned in its guidelines the importance of universal design (even though it was used interchangeably with the concept of barrier-free design). The National Architectural Accrediting Board performance criteria for accredited programs now require that "students should be able to design both site and building to accommodate those with varying physical ability."[12]

Industrial design educators had the advantage of the pilot study conducted at Pratt Institute by Robert Anders and Daniel Fechtner in 1991 to develop a model course on universal design for industrial design students. Funded by the J.M. Foundation, the syllabus emphasizes user-based design instead of object-based design.[13] The project produced two other products that have become useful resources to other design faculty: a design primer and a survey of products and environments that illustrate the principles of universal design.

When UDEP was in its conceptual stages, the organizers drew from one other precedent that had no connection with universal design but represented a successful approach to curriculum development in a design field. The Architecture, Energy, and Education Project was a project initiated by the Association of Collegiate Schools of Architecture with a grant from the Department of Energy in response to the lack of quality teaching materials for energy-conscious design. The two-step process included developing eleven curriculum resource packages and selecting twelve schools to use the materials and evaluate them. The project found that no one type of intervention was found to be most viable: "The intervention must be tailored to the strengths and

Chapter 3

weaknesses of students, faculty and curriculum."[14] This finding became a critical foundation to the philosophical development of the Universal Design Education Project. It was within this context and with these precedents that Adaptive Environments developed its proposal for a universal design curriculum development project.

Notes

1. *Journal of Architectural Education* 31, no. 1 (September 1977).

2. Howell, Sandra. "The Aged as a User Group." *Journal of Architectural Education* 31, no. 1 (September 1977): 27.

3. Cohen, Uriel (1981). *Mainstreaming the Handicapped, A Design Guide.* Milwaukee, Wis.: Center of Architecture and Urban Planning Research, School of Architecture and Urban Planning, University of Wisconsin–Milwaukee.

4. Lifchez, Raymond (1987). *Rethinking Architecture: Design Students and Physically Disabled People.* Berkeley, Calif. University of California Press, 3.

5. Ref. 4, 185.

6. Ref. 4, 98.

7. Ref. 4, 99.

8. See "Selected Videos" in the appendices for availability.

9. Ref. 4, back cover.

10. Ostroff, Elaine and Daniel Iacofano (1982). *Teaching Design For All People: The State of the Art.* Boston: Adaptive Environments Center.

11. Cohen, Edie Lee. "Student Work." *Interior Design,* August 1992.

12. NAAB Criteria #33.

13. Available from the Department of Industrial Design, Pratt Institute, Brooklyn, New York.

14. Shibley, Robert G. and Laura Poltroneri, with Ronni Rosenberg (1984). *Case Studies in the Evaluation of the Teaching Passive Design in Architecture Workbook Series.* Washington, D.C.: Association of Collegiate Schools of Architecture.

by Polly Welch and Elaine Ostroff

In 1990, the National Endowment for the Arts' Design Arts Program and the Office for Special Constituencies (now the Office for AccessAbility) sponsored two key meetings on universal design. The first, in January 1990, examined the possibility of establishing an NEA-sponsored Universal Design Leadership Initiative. The meeting participants highlighted the fact that, in design schools, access issues are taught primarily as code requirements and are not interwoven with the theory and process of design itself. As a result, many people with disabilities are further segregated by designs that are ugly, cold, awkward, and expensive. Changing demographics and new federal laws accelerate the need for a new approach to design. The meeting identified the many constituencies and topics to be included in future thinking about universal design and recommended another, larger meeting to explore further universal design issues, audiences, and options.

In September 1990, the NEA convened a larger advisory meeting consisting of distinguished individuals in the fields of architecture, landscape architecture, industrial design, education, and disability rights to discuss how to educate design professionals and laypeople about "the need and means of taking a 'universal' approach to the design of buildings, public spaces, and products." The meeting provided guidance to NEA in three areas—Professional Practice, Publication and Clearinghouse, and Teaching Design. The recommendations in the latter category urged the NEA to support education by:

- convening design accrediting organizations and discuss how they could evaluate design schools for their inclusion of universal design in the curriculum;

- funding the development and distribution of design problems that faculty from design schools could use for teaching universal design; and

- funding a project to publicize the availability of materials and resource people to whom educators could turn for assistance.

Since that time, the NEA supported several universal design efforts through the competitive grants process, including the Universal Design Education Project and the first international conference on universal design—Universal Design: Access to Daily Living, held in May 1992 in New York City. Subsequently, the Design Arts Program and the Office for AccessAbility secured funding to create a Universal Design Leadership Initiative. The first phase of the Initiative supported marketing and dissemination of an introductory videotape, *Toward Universal Design,* which was produced by the National Rehabilitation Hospital and funded by the National Institute on Disability and Rehabilitation Research and Herman Miller, Inc. Through a cooperative agreement with the National Building Museum in Washington, D.C., the second phase of the Initiative is to research and document exemplary images of universal design from the disciplines of architecture, interior design, landscape architecture, product design, and graphic communication.

In the fall of 1989, Elaine Ostroff of Adaptive Environments submitted a proposal to the NEA for an incentive-based, faculty development program in universal design. The proposal was "a response to the rapidly changing demographics in our society and the extraordinary new accessibility legislation which impacts every facet of the built environment." It proposed to "support the integration of universal design into the post-secondary education of five professional disciplines—architecture, industrial design, interior design, landscape design, and urban planning." The proposal was predicated on the idea that there were design educators already engaged in the teaching of accessible design who, with financial support, could expand their approach to infuse universal design into the curricula of their schools. The proposal emphasized the importance of building on existing precedents in design education and involving people with disabilities and older people as consultants in the studio and classroom.

Ostroff's proposal approach was inspired and informed by Ray Lifchez's work in the late seventies at the University of California at Berkeley. He had introduced consultants with disabilities into the design studio to help students learn about designing for people unlike themselves. Lifchez had planned to export his approach to other design programs but had experienced some difficulty in transplanting the ideas. The proposal by Adaptive Environments, expanding on Lifchez's ideas and values, encouraged faculty to initiate teaching innovations that built on their interests and expertise and that fit within the culture of their department and their university. The proposal also built on recommendations from the 1982 and 1983 faculty seminars, Design for All People, organized by Adaptive Environments. Although the proposal was initially rejected by an NEA peer review panel, Adaptive Environments resubmitted the proposal and in January 1991 was officially awarded funding to initiate the Universal Design Education Project.

It took almost eighteen months to raise the required matching funds needed to launch the project. In spite of the focus on a topic of national concern, curriculum development for design programs in higher education was not a funding priority of most foundations. The search for support revealed that foundations which fund disability-related projects focus primarily on the delivery of services and that foundations which fund curriculum development focus on primary and secondary levels of education. A reaction by a potential funder to the UDEP proposal highlighted the problem that this project proposed to address. A design school dean, asked to review the proposal, told the foundation that design schools already teach this material adequately because it is only a code issue. One foundation responded by suggesting that the professional design organizations should fund the project, like the professional organizations in medicine and law. At last, NEC Foundation of America saw the match between the proposal and its mission of excellence in science, technology, and disability, enabling Adaptive Environments to start faculty recruitment. This support was followed by funding from other foundations.

Nationwide recruitment was made possible by the collegiate design associations providing the project with their membership lists. Two thousand posters announcing the availability of the $5,000 stipends were mailed to over four hundred accredited programs of architecture, landscape architecture, interior design, industrial design, and urban design in the United States. The purpose of the project promoted in the announcement was to "challenge existing values in design education and to stimulate innovation in design curriculum that will lead to the development of products and environments which incorporate universal design concepts." The original plan was to fund, on a competitive basis, projects from fifteen design schools, distributed across the five disciplines.

The application required a fairly detailed proposal, in addition to evidence of expertise in teaching and disability issues. The Request for Proposals included a narrative description of precedents and a bibliography on the teaching of accessible design to help faculty build on the body of work in curriculum innovation. Criteria for selecting proposals included:

- the experience of faculty in teaching accessible design;

- the conceptual approach and who it was intended to impact;

- involvement of people with disabilities and across the age span;

- faculty knowledge of and familiarity with disability and age-span issues;

- dissemination at national and regional meetings of professional associations;

- anticipated impact on department and school;

- evidence of departmental and university support; and

- a plan for evaluating teaching effectiveness.

Forty-five proposals were received from across the country. The largest number of proposals came from programs in interior design, followed by architecture, landscape

Chapter 4

architecture, and industrial design. There were no proposals from urban design programs, so that discipline was dropped from the project. Capturing the inclusive spirit of the project, a significant number of proposals were multidisciplinary, across design departments and across disciplines.

Six of the ten UDEP advisors reviewed proposals and selected thirteen projects to receive full awards: a stipend of $5,000 plus travel to two national UDEP meetings, the initial faculty colloquium and the subsequent final conference. To extend resources to as many faculty as possible, an associate status was established, offering travel funds to the two meetings and access to teaching resources. The associate status enabled more teams to participate in UDEP and thereby broadened the number of students and faculty impacted by this project. Faculty who received awards included professors with accessibility credentials as well as untenured faculty with promising ideas.

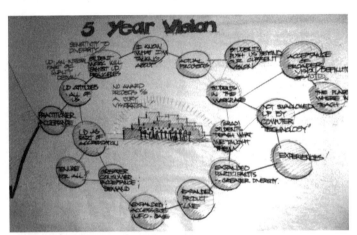

A total of forty-five faculty representing twenty-two design programs comprised the pilot group in the Universal Design Education Project. The proposals represented a range of curricular strategies. Some proposed to teach a single course or studio focused on universal design, and incorporated linkages to other courses to offset the problem of isolating the subject in the curriculum. Some proposed to introduce material to a cross section of a department such as all second-year design students. Others proposed to present material to students at different levels throughout a program. Several projects included community events such as a design charrette, awards program, or symposium that would engage a broad range of people including students, practitioners, and people with disabilities. Two projects undertook development of computer-assisted instruction.

At the Raleigh colloquium, the UDEP faculty, including Ron Mace (bottom), outlined the five-year vision for the project (top).

In the spring before faculty were to implement their proposals, the UDEP staff organized a faculty colloquium in Raleigh, North Carolina. Developed in cooperation with the Center for Accessible Housing at North Carolina State University, the three-day colloquium was both an orientation to the value of universal design as well as an opportunity for networking and brainstorming between faculty, advisors, and project staff. A substantial resource kit was provided to each school, which included four videotapes, a reference binder with reproducible materials on universal design, and an extensive bibliography. Introductory presentations included a video of the precedents in Ray Lifchez's work, slide examples of universal design, and a history of the civil rights legislation that led to the Americans with Disabilities Act. Interactive sessions covered personal reflections on disability, a discussion of the values of universal design, developing working partnerships with people with disabilities, and the politics of change in the university. During the three days, each team was encouraged to develop their planned activities in response to input from colleagues. Daniel Iacofano, co-facilitator of the colloquium, captured the discussions and presentations with extensive wallgraphics. The Center for Accessible Housing created an extensive display of most of the materials in the bibliography.

The colloquium was an opportunity for faculty with similar values about inclusive design to share experiences and ideas that received little support from professional colleagues and institutions. For many participants, it felt like the first time there was actually a critical mass of people interested in universal design, enough to make an impact. "It's the beginning of a movement," said UDEP advisor Jim Mueller.

Before leaving the colloquium, faculty were asked what form of technical assistance and what additional tools they might need. There was unanimous concern about the dearth of visual examples of good universal design, which resulted in a slide collection effort managed by John Salmen, with contributions from colloquium participants. Ed Steinfeld urged that the group use electronic mail to facilitate networking; this launched the creation of an Internet network through which all participants could reach one another. Colloquium participants identified the need to bring greater visibility to their projects within their institutions. Site visits to each school by a UDEP advisor who could give a schoolwide presentation on universal design would be an opportunity for students, faculty, and administrators to learn more about the project. The original plan was for the advisors to act as mentors by telephone as needed. The need for these additional resources stimulated the development of a timely proposal from Adaptive Environments to the U.S. Department of Justice (DOJ), which was soliciting proposals for voluntary ADA compliance. Within two months of the colloquium, DOJ funded support and dissemination of the work of the twenty-two schools, including development of the Internet network, travel costs for a visit by a UDEP advisor to each school, presentations at the annual meetings of the four collegiate design associations, the production of the illustrated case studies, and the final conference for the faculty in Boston at the end of the project.

UDEP Advisor Joe Meade (bottom) participates in a discussion led by Bob Shibley (top) on the politics of change.

The role of the UDEP advisors was critical to the project and represented a major contribution of time and talent by acknowledged leaders in universal design. The volunteer effort by each advisor, especially the visits to each school were very important to and valued by the faculty. These site visits lent credibility and visibility to the project through schoolwide presentations, studio reviews, and meetings with deans and department heads to discuss the importance of the project.

During 1994 and 1995, UDEP faculty and advisors presented their work at the annual meetings of numerous professional organizations:

- Council of Educators in Landscape Architecture (CELA);

- Association of Collegiate Schools of Architecture (ACSA);

- Interior Design Educators Council (IDEC);

- Industrial Design Society of America Educators Conference (IDSA);

- Society for Disability Studies;

- National Association of Minority Architects;

- Environmental Design Research Association (EDRA); and

- AIA/ACSA Teachers Seminar at Cranbrook on Designing for Diversity.

The response to these presentations indicated growing interest in universal design. There continues to be a need to distinguish between the responsibility of schools to teach students about complying with the Americans with Disabilities Act and to teach them the value of designing for all people.

The 1993–94 UDEP faculty.

Receipt of the stipends was contingent on faculty teams submitted three reports over the course of their project. The third and final report summarized what they had learned and became the basis for the illustrated case studies that follow in the next twenty-one chapters of this book.

In November 1994, following the academic year in which the faculty had done their UDEP teaching, Adaptive Environments hosted the final conference in Boston. The conference was held in conjunction with the regional professional trade show of the Boston Society of Architects. Two days of presentations on both the ADA and universal design by national experts from government, advocacy, and practice were followed by two days of debriefing by eighteen of the twenty-two schools. Each school made a formal presentation on what its team had learned. Task groups summarized the collective experience on several issues: using consultants, engaging students through empathic experience, building bridges within schools, communication, and developing criteria for success. The last chapter of this book draws on those discussions in describing what has been learned from this five-year effort.

Chapter 4: The Universal Design Education Project
Matrix of Approaches

School	Participation by discipline (F=Faculty, S=Student)					Required	Elective	Event
	Arch.	Industrial	Interior	Land.Arch.	Other			
Cal Poly San Luis Obispo	F/S		S	S	S		course	student exhibit
Iowa State University	F/S		F/S	F/S		studios and courses		
Kansas State University	F/S		S	S		studio		
Louisiana State University			F/S					conference and charrette
Massachusetts Institute of Tech.	F/S					studio		
Miami University			F/S		F/S	studios and course		conference and charrette
Michigan State University			F/S			studios and courses		
North Dakota State University			F/S			studio		
Norwich University	F/S					studio and course		
Pratt Institute	F/S	F/S	F/S		F/S	studios and courses		citywide teach-in
Purdue University		S	S	F/S		studio	course	
Ringling School of Art and Design			F/S			studios		
State Univ. of New York at Buffalo	F/S	F	S	F				
Texas Tech University			F/S	F/S		studios and courses		
University of Michigan/ Eastern Michigan University	F	F/S	F/S			studios		
University of Missouri	F/S		F/S			studio and courses		Universal Design Week
University of South Florida	F/S					studio	studio	
University of Southwestern Louisiana	S	S	F/S				course	
University of Tennessee			F/S			studios and course	computer tutorial	
Virginia Tech: Interior Design			F/S			studio and courses	graduate seminar	
Virginia Tech: Landscape Architecture				F/S			computer tutorial	

Chapter 4: The Universal Design Education Project
Matrix of Techniques

School	User consultants	Biography	Empathic exercises	Competition/award	Interview	Gaming	Computer modules	Videotape by students	Videotape as document	Other tools
Cal Poly San Luis Obispo	•		•	•	•			•	•	teaching children
Iowa State University	•		•						•	mock trial
Kansas State University	•		•							
Louisiana State University	•		•							
Massachusetts Inst. of Tech.	•		•							
Miami University	•		•						•	
Michigan State University	•		•							
North Dakota State Univ.	•		•						•	
Norwich University			•							body tracings
Pratt Institute	•		•						•	teaching matrix
Purdue University	•		•							
Ringling School	•		•							RIDDLE worksheet
SUNY Buffalo	•	•	•	•					•	full-scale mock-up
Texas Tech University	•		•							entourage figures
University of Michigan/Eastern Michigan University	•		•		•	•				reference sheets
University of Missouri	•		•							
University of South Florida	•		•							
University of S.W. Louisiana	•		•					•		
University of Tennessee	•		•	•	•	•	•			
Virginia Tech: Interior Design	•		•		•					
Virginia Tech: Landscape Arch.	•						•			

Project Case Studies

Educating Others About Universal Design

Team members:

Brad C. Grant
  Associate Professor
Paul M. Wolff
  Professor Emeritus
Michael L. N. Shannon
  Teaching Assistant

Proposal

We proposed to build on the insights and materials from the course that Paul Wolff has taught over the last thirteen years, "Towards a Barrier-Free Environment," to develop a new seminar on universal design. The purpose of the new seminar would be to give students an experiential introduction to the theoretical, social, psychological, cultural, legal, and ergonomic issues related to designing for diverse users.

A critical component of our seminar was to use participatory and collaborative methods, an approach we reinforced by forming a collaborative teaching team with diversity of age, race, and ability. If universal design is responsible design for all people, then the current concept should be expanded to include cultural and gender issues. The seminar would include the active participation of a diverse client and user population, including persons with various disabilities, people across the age span, and people of ethnic and cultural minorities.

We planned the seminar to promote the understanding and application of universal design as an integral issue within the context of the typical design studio at all levels of the curriculum. There would be no special project for this class; the holistic principles of universal design would have to be applied to whatever project was challenging the student in his or her current design studio. The class would be directed at architecture, landscape architecture, and interior design students in their second through fifth years.

A second part to our proposal addressed the need to reach beyond the seminar to expose the issues and principles of universal design to the widest possible multidisciplinary audience of the College of Architecture and Environmental Design, including students, faculty, and practitioners. We proposed a Universal Design Awards Program as an opportunity for students across the school to participate in UDEP. The awards program was intended to promote and reward design excellence in the application of universal design principles.

Activity

We predicated the course on the notion that students would learn the most about universal design if they had to educate others about the subject. The first third of the ten-week quarter gave the class an introduction to universal design—its philosophy, its implications, and specific information regarding people with differing abilities. We developed assignments that would encourage students to explore the ramifications of diversity:

- Interviewing children, seniors, underrepresented community members, or persons with disabilities to reveal their views of the community environment.

- Collecting print ads of "people who are different" as the basis for discussion of advertising stereotypes of age, gender, cultural background, and disability.

- Simulating mobility and sight impairments with wheelchairs and blindfolds.

- Participating in a Department of Architecture event—a diversity panel comprising people with disabilities and people of African American background.

- Wearing colored dots on their foreheads and organizing themselves into similar color groups to discuss issues of difference.

- Taking class field trips to recently constructed buildings around campus to assess the extent to which they were universally designed.

During the remainder of the quarter, students selected audiences with whom to share their new-found knowledge and awareness and developed suitable activities and projects. The necessary research and preparation for this was, in itself, a valuable learning experience for the students. The projects included:

- "Human performance sculptures" that posed in public spaces to promote awareness of discrimination and bring attention to universal design issues.

- Visits to several elementary schools to lead third and fourth graders through a series of exercises illustrating the concept of universal design.

- A slide presentation on universal design to be used in other classes in the College of Architecture and Environmental Design.

- A survey of College of Architecture and Environmental Design faculty to determine their knowledge of and attitudes towards universal design.

- Scripting and production of an educational video on universal design.

- Video documentation of the course, including student projects and evaluations.

We also organized a schoolwide design competition open to individuals or teams of students in all five departments. There was no special project or program. Students could submit their studio projects, showing how they had applied the principles of universal design. Faculty in all departments were asked to encourage their students to submit their final design projects. UDEP grant money made possible cash awards to the top entries. The competition announcement was a very detailed booklet giving an overview of universal design, how its integration into design projects would be judged, and the availability of students in the seminar to give assistance.

After simulating a mobility impairment using a wheelchair, a student explains that a ramp may "look to code" and yet be much too steep for the user.

Outcome

The course was oversubscribed at forty-two students and drew students from four disciplines—architecture, city and regional planning, interior design, and landscape architecture. Originally, the video project had been the only planned product of the class. The larger class prompted the instructors to develop a greater array of hands-on projects. One student in the class was a wheelchair user and a number of others had less obvious disabilities. Sixty-three percent of the students had some personal experience with people with disabilities, and 31 percent had experienced personal limitations in the built environment. Forty percent claimed to be familiar with universal design but only half of those students could describe universal design. Sixty-four percent of the students claimed to be familiar with the Americans with Disabilities Act, while only 6 percent could describe it.

Interviewing People with Different Perspectives. This exercise was designed as a catalyst for class discussions. Students were expected to make informed contributions to class discussions from their notes. The students were assigned to meet with and interview someone very different from themselves. They explored questions about perceptions of the environment and attitudes towards people who are "different." This was an attempt to have students gain an understanding of environmental design issues from perspectives outside of their personal experience. We wanted students to envision the environment from the perspective of children, ethnic minorities, seniors, or persons with varying abilities.

Field Trips. Small groups of students toured two recently built campus facilities to explore the actual application of universal design. They noted numerous well-designed features that promoted greater access. The students were amazed, however, to encounter many examples of unresponsive design in new structures where the concrete had barely cured—ranging from impossible double-sloped ramps to a total lack of privacy options in the changing/shower area of the well-appointed recreation center.

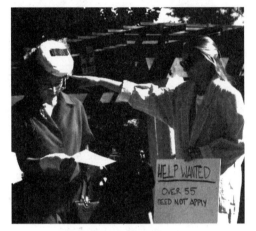

Analyzing Advertisements. We asked students to analyze current advertisements and report to the class how "people who are different" are depicted. This exercise was assigned to get students to explore how our society views or, in most cases, hides people with disabilities, children, seniors, and ethnic minorities. Each student came to class with a print ad or an excerpt from a television commercial with a brief written and graphic analysis. This worked well for class discussions and for several students it was an "eye opener."

Color Dot Exercise. With all students' eyes closed, the instructors placed a small colored dot on the forehead of each individual. The students were then instructed to open their eyes and without verbal communication arrange themselves in groups by dot color. Each student had to rely on others to identify his or her color and to locate the right group. This exercise proved to be a powerful stimulus for a discussion on belonging, identity, and difference.

Several activities had a public dimension and brought visibility to the class and its content:

Human Performance Sculptures. Students developed scenarios to represent the problems of being different that they had explored in class. The scenarios included an elderly person looking for a job, an interracial couple getting married, a person using a wheelchair trying to cross a curb, and an obese person trying to sit in a very small chair. In public places in San Luis Obispo, such as the Mall, the Mission plaza, and the student union plaza, they posed as the characters in these scenarios, similar to street mimes. Leaflets were distributed to bystanders explaining how the human performance illustrates some of the issues of universal design. It emphasized that attitudinal barriers are the primary cause of physical barriers. The public's reaction ranged from being very interested and engaged to

Human Performance Sculptures: *Cal Poly students explore issues of age discrimination (top) and racial attitudes as through the eyes of a blind student (bottom).*

ignoring the students' performance. The local television station featured the group in its nightly news spot.

Elementary School Visit. This was the most successful learning method of the exercises. In order for the students to teach ideas about universal design to young children, they had to understand the issues themselves. They developed several exercises appropriate to children such as a learning-disability puzzle, a blindfolded walk, and class discussions. The grade school teachers and children as well as our students and teachers considered this exercise a great success.

Faculty Survey. A group of students developed and administered a survey to approximately one hundred faculty in the College of Architecture and Environmental Design. The survey was designed to reveal the degree of understanding of universal design. The survey results indicated that our faculty was not very familiar with universal design. There were problems with the survey instrument and method that, unfortunately, compromised the survey. In the future, students would consult with the statistics department to insure proper surveying methods for more reliable results.

Schoolwide Competition. Over thirty students submitted designs in all categories for the competition. This number was far fewer than the number of registration forms received and a disappointment considering the total number of students in the college eligible for the competition. This may be due in part to the fact that students in our department historically have not entered many competitions.

A number of students incorporated universal design into projects they were already working on, including papers for other classes and thesis projects. Others wrote up their critiques of buildings on campus. A majority of the entries demonstrated an understanding of the most obvious issues of universal design. Only the winners reflected the more complete understanding of universal design outlined in the five criteria in the competition program.

The jury consisted of the assistant coordinator of Disabled Student Services, a professor of architecture, and the three faculty for this course. After lengthy and careful analysis of all competition entries, the consensus of the jury was to award no first place, only second and third place, in both the fourth/fifth-year architecture category and the interior design category. Two first places, a second place, a third place, and an honorable mention were awarded to third-year architecture students. The students seemed to have difficulty documenting, representing, and demonstrating their understanding of universal design in the traditional graphic manner of architecture. The

". . . to successfully teach ideas about universal design to young children, [the students] had to understand the issues themselves."

Elementary School Visit:
Cal Poly students conduct a blindfolded walk (top) and discuss universal design awareness in the classroom of third and fourth graders (bottom).

Chapter 5: California Polytechnic State University

written statements describing the entrants' intentions were essential to the jury process. The jury found the design of the "Centro de Cultura" or the "Center for Latino Culture" to demonstrate a design sensitivity beyond physical accessibility. Sounds from a fountain along the circulation path, textured walkways, and a family of entries all contributed to the total idea of universal design. The project also displayed appropriate symbolic cultural ties to the Latino heritage.

We displayed the winning schemes in the College's main office, the usual display area for student work, and in a display of student work for the architecture department's accreditation visit. The competition is worth repeating but needs greater faculty support to make it more successful. The faculty needs to be more knowledgeable about universal design and willing to encourage their students to participate.

Reflection

Following are some of the reflections made by the three course instructors.

On the Value of Having Co-Instructors

The presence of three instructors at each class meeting was an opportunity for interactive dynamics. The different life perspective of each instructor was key to conveying the multifaceted concept of universal design.

A student's critique of the new recreation building on campus observed that the fenced opening allows short people and people using wheelchairs to view the pool below.

Although I had taught a related course, Towards a Barrier-free Environment, for the past thirteen years, I discovered invaluable benefits from teaching with my two creative partners, Brad Grant and Michael Shannon. In class we would frequently discuss, debate, disagree with, or reinforce each other. (Wolff)

We discovered areas of universal design that we hadn't planned and were able to continue with the strong enthusiasm and energy with which we started. We would not have been able to attempt so many activities and course programs without the collaborative involvement of three distinct teachers. (Grant)

On the Course Structure and Participatory Learning

The initial one third of the term was devoted to instructing the class on the perspective, philosophy, implications, and specifications of universal design. During the remaining class time, students were challenged to design projects for audiences of their own selection, with whom they could share their newfound knowledge and awareness. The necessary research and preparation for this, was in itself, a valuable learning exercise for the students. (Wolff)

Several all-class activities were very successful, especially field trips to buildings which display varying degrees of universal design success, even though recently constructed. The ability to see expensive failures, often costing many thousands of dollars to correct, is a valuable tool for a new designer/architect. By far the best group project was the elementary school visits, which we documented on video. I was personally thrilled to further substantiate what most of us know, that the time to change discrimination is early in the lives of a new generation. As a person who uses a wheelchair knows, children have a natural curiosity and not a natural prejudice or avoidance—that is left to their parents. (Shannon)

The emphasis on participatory learning produced some fine projects, which can be used in future classes. Primarily, however, it served to maintain a high level of interest and involvement while encouraging students to design with greater empathy and understanding for the rich variety of human behaviors. (Wolff)

On Universal Design Education

In many ways the concepts and ideas involved in universal design are debatable and can be questioned. It was often difficult to have the class argue both sides of the controversial issues as it can be with other new social/environmental issues. I want, in the future, to create a universal design class that will debate all the issues of universal design. (Grant)

As a person who came back to college after a serious automobile accident in 1987, and has spent five years totally involved in promoting accessibility on many fronts, each class section was also an opportunity to further erase the "line" that separates persons with disabilities from the non-disabled remainder of the world. In a very short time, my wheelchair, braces, crutches or hearing aids were not really thought of as other than the assistive devices they are. In this particular situation, they were some of my strengths and perhaps tended to add a dash of validity to some of the dialogue that became extremely important as the class progressed. It was natural dialogue and curiosity which replaced negative reactions, such as pity and avoidance. (Shannon)

First place winner in the universal design competition (above and facing page).

Evaluation

Students were asked to complete questionnaires after the class as an informal measure of change to help the faculty determine whether the course had increased the students' understanding of universal design and the Americans with Disabilities Act. In response to a question on the impact of the course, students' comments included: "New appreciation for other's perspectives;" "Understanding that universal design has no limits;" "Universal design can be beautiful;" "Better understanding of what to consider to ensure better design decisions;" and "Broader understanding of design for different people and cultures."

Students identified the field trips and the video production as the most effective resources used during the class. They also gave strong positive feedback on the simulation exercises, use of consultants, and games.

It is important to emphasize that this course will continue to be offered—although probably without making the video. It will continue because an understanding of universal design is an essential component in helping to eliminate discrimination in our architecture and because it can contribute to the creation of a more humane environment for the twenty-first century. Universal design means that we will become a less separate, more integrated society; we will be empowered to be

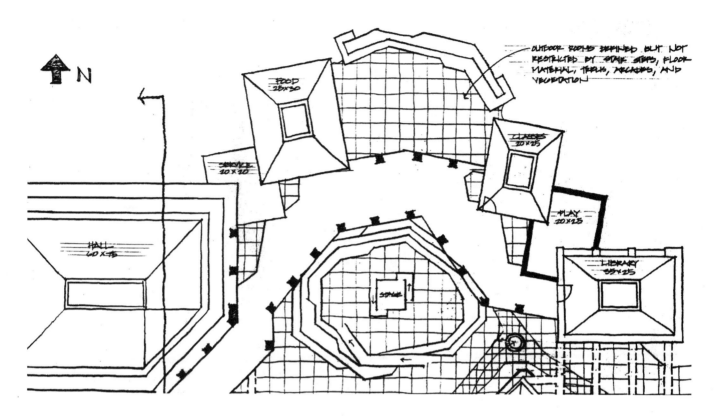

competent in dealing with the physical world; we will be enabled toward greater interaction in the workplace, as well as, social, professional, commercial and recreational settings. This dynamic experiment has shown that just as attitudes influence design, design can also influence attitudes. (Wolff)

Acknowledgements

We gratefully acknowledge the valued contributions of the following individuals: Jerry Burge, Mark Dariz, and Benny Martin, students; Beth Currier, Disabled Student Services; Susan Goltsman, MIG, Inc.; Brian Kesner, professor of architecture; Norm Rogers, media production coordinator; and Kathy Nannula, sign language interpreter.

*One student's
reflections on
the importance of
universal design.*

Through this course,
I came to realize that the only way that I can ever hope to make a change
is to have an idea of what a person
who must deal with physical barriers
encounters on a daily basis.
I had a taste of that reality and
I found it to be an eye opening experience.

I do not know how it feels to be stared at,
to have to spend most of my physical energy to just go from one class to another.
To have both physical and attitudinal barriers placed on me every minute of my life.
To be told that I can only enter a restaurant through the kitchen.
To be excluded from experiences as simple as playing in a park.
To not be given the opportunity to live freely,
to be limited,
to be segregated.

Sure we can retrofit,
we can apply standards,
We might even be able to create aesthetically pleasing designs.
But, we can not forget the users,
because we are all users.
We will age, we might even lose our sight or hearing.
Some of us might use a cane, perhaps a wheelchair.
so, we as designers and planners
must stop taking the ideal 30 year old abled body man as a prototype.
We must stop assuming that building a barrier-free environment stifles
the imagination and creativity
and take it as a challenge.

Perhaps through courses such as this
minds will be opened,
attitudes swayed and ideas generated.
It might create new thoughts,
perhaps it will make people think a little harder and a little deeper.
It might help to bring about unity into our society
But, most of all,
it will enlighten and increase our sensitivity for all the individuals
who might not get around on two legs,
or who use their hands to see, read and speak.
It might just be as simple as respecting all people.

I came to the realization that
sometimes the higher our eye level the lower our outlook
and that at times it is possible to see more clearly when staring into darkness.

Iowa State University – Ames, Iowa
Departments of Landscape Architecture, Architecture, and Art and Design: Interior Design Program

Using Awareness Levels Across Design Disciplines

Team members:

Mark Chidister
Associate Professor
Albert Rutledge
Professor
Arvid Osterberg
Associate Professor
Robert Harvey
Professor
Fred Malven
Associate Professor
Harlen Groe
Graduate Assistant

Proposal

An interdisciplinary team of faculty from three departments proposed to engage all one thousand students majoring in the environmental design disciplines of landscape architecture, architecture, and interior design by infusing the curriculum with awareness modules of increasing intensity. The modules start at the level of Consciousness where students would be exposed to the physical design issues associated with disabilities, move on to Engagement and Accountability, and eventually reach the highest level, Integration, at which point students would apply universal design principles automatically to their design projects. The modules would be infused in several courses in the three departments over the fall and spring semesters.

The teaching modules would be documented on videotapes that could be used as reference materials for improving instruction and for perpetuating the approach with the inevitable turnover of instructors. The videotapes would be formatted to share with other institutions to extend their range of influence.

The faculty working on this project felt strongly that the principles of universal design had to be integrated into multiple courses at different levels and with different intensities to avoid having students perceive that universal design is an optional body of material that is addressed at the discretion of the designer.

Activity

The faculty met initially to discuss how modules and materials might be integrated successfully into the five courses. The strategy was to present the material in as many different venues using different methods to solidly instill the intentions, knowledge, and principles pertinent to universal design. The faculty also requested and received a small instructional development grant from the University to support the involvement of the Iowa Center for Independent Living in offering experiential workshops for design students. A visit from Robert Shibley, the UDEP advisor, was used as an opportunity for a schoolwide presentation on universal design.

Four faculty members taught courses in the fall of 1993 in the departments of landscape architecture, architecture, and interior design. Most of the faculty were able to follow up their fall semester teaching with additional courses in the spring, building on the lessons learned.

The awareness modules were formulated as follows:

Consciousness Level. At this level, individuals become aware of some of the real-life issues of a person with a disability. This level is achieved through indirect exposure by showing selected films such as *A Day in the Life of Bonnie Consolo* and *In a New Light*. Follow-up discussions are conducted to learn how the films may have altered students' thoughts about persons with disabilities. The intention at this level is to begin breaking down misconceptions about people with disabilities and as a result, foster a more accurate understanding of the lives they lead and the barriers they actually face. Results are evaluated through conventional quizzes and exams.

Engagement Level. At this level, individuals experience disability in relationship to the physical environment. This level is achieved through direct exposure, by having each student assume one of the disabilities listed in the Enabler Model[1] thus demonstrating the entire model collectively in the class. Results are evaluated through student diaries and the design of an object/space that responds to the environmental issues raised by the experience.

Accountability Level. At this level, there is conscious application of universal design principles. One vehicle to achieve this level is the comprehensive design of a setting of moderate complexity, with substantial direction from faculty. Results will be evaluated in a mock-trial format, emphasizing the personal responsibility of the designer for satisfying the intentions of the Americans with Disabilities Act (with findings of "guilty" or "not guilty"). Prosecutors, defense attorneys, and members of the jury are comprised of peers who have previously completed this level. Judges are people with disabilities from the community.

Integration Level. At this level, there is automatic application of universal design principles. This level is achieved with the comprehensive design of a highly complex setting, with only modest direction from faculty. Results will be evaluated by means of a formal presentation to a panel of consumers from the community, representing a range of disabilities and age groups. The panel rates the projects on their degree of satisfying the intent of the ADA as well as the broader goals of universal design.

Outcome

LA 284, Introduction to Landscape Architecture (Chidister). Consciousness was the first of four levels of the awareness developed by the faculty. Through the use of videos, lectures, and class discussions, this course focused on increasing students' consciousness of people with disabilities and on the need for designers to be knowledgeable of and sensitive to a wide range of populations. The specific goals of the course were to increase awareness of the widespread presence of people of dif-fering abilities; to begin to understand what it means to be a person with a disability; to be aware of appropriate language when referring to a person with a disability; and to introduce the concept of universal design and the Americans with Disabilities Act.

The instructor attempted to treat the ADA and universal design not as a stand-alone topic but as part of a larger discussion of designing for people who are different from the designer. This includes differences of ability, race, and social, economic, and geographic background. By integrating the material into the discussion of "sense of place," the instructor was able to address the criterion of access in the broadest terms.

At the outset of the semester, students completed a personal profile to help the instructor get to know the students better and to get a sense for how much they knew about the topics that would be covered during the semester. Embedded in the profile were several questions relating to ADA and universal design. Sixty students filled out the profile, which served as a kind of pre-test. Half of the students had prior, first-hand contact with people with disabilities. Almost three-quarters of the students had prior, first-hand contact with an older person. Very few (17%) were familiar with the term universal design. When asked to describe what the term meant, none of the stu-dents were able to define it. Quite a few students (33%)—though still less than half—had heard of the Americans with Disabilities Act. When asked to describe the ADA, most of those who stated familiarity with the ADA were able to convey some under-standing of the term.

The post-test was the exam on this portion of the course that followed the presen-tation of material by two-and-a-half weeks. A review session was held a few days prior to the exam where much of the material was reiterated. Fifty-eight students took the exam. The exam indicated a fairly good ability to recognize definitions of univer-sal design and the Americans with Disabilities Act. For both concepts, a full definition was printed on the examination and students were asked to fill in the concept which the definition described. Almost 90 percent were able to accurately identify the defini-tion of universal design (88%). The same percentage were able to identify the defini-tion of the Americans with Disabilities Act, although only 19 percent used the full, cor-rect title of the act.

The most revealing question was one in which students were asked to assume that they were the project designers of a multi-family housing development and recre-ational area that was designed in the true spirit of universal design. They were asked to state how they would refer to people who cannot walk, see, or hear in a verbal presentation of the project to a client group. The responses, with a few exceptions, were consistent with Longmore's guidelines in *Unhandicapping Our Language*.[2] Students were beginning to use language in a manner that was sensitive to the people involved and many were sensitive to design issues related to people with disabilities, i.e., neither singling out people with disabilities or assuming that people with similar disabilities fall into homogenous groups. The real test of whether any of this material had an impact will come next year as the students prepare ideas for dwelling, educational, work, and recreational environments.

LA 284 was a success to the extent that it contributed to individual understanding of and sensitivity to designing for people with disabilities. The videos used were essential in a course of this type for students to understand and empathize with people who are different that they are. One improvement to make in the course would be to include a well-documented case study of a complex environment that fulfills the goals of universal design. An illustrated case study would help students make the connection between the concept of universal design and its tangible realization.

LA 342, Intermediate Landscape Architectural Design I (Rutledge). This studio is the first of six studios in the undergraduate professional program. It lays significant groundwork in the development of problem-solving skills. The subject of study is typically housing, with emphasis on land analysis, land-use allocation, concept development and articulation, three dimensional space formation, vehicular and pedestrian circulation, and open-space system planning. The studio is an excellent opportunity to form sustaining design habits.

Given the focus of the studio on site-planning fundamentals, the instructors decided to introduce students to universal design considerations and the ADA near the end of the semester when, ostensibly, students had become somewhat confident in their general problem-solving abilities and could benefit more from the introduction of dramatically new information.

The project was an in-town housing development in which social factors were introduced as design determinants, specifically the phenomenon of "neighboring." Students were told to prepare a preliminary design presentation to be made to a representative user group. Nothing further was said about the group. One half-hour before the students were to pin up their work for inspection by the representative users, the faculty casually said, "Oh, didn't I tell you? The representative users all have disabilities."

While this class of students was average in their skill level for this stage in the curriculum, they were considerably above average in maturity and desire to learn. The announcement of the user group was received with stunned silence. The students had stayed up all night preparing to present to a predictable group of reviewers. A relatively unfamiliar group was now at hand, with the exception of the landscape architect who had attended several class sessions as a critic. The students turned quickly to formulating new approaches for presentation.

The group of consultants included a transportation specialist who is deaf, accompanied by his daughter who signed for him; a computer specialist who is blind; the University coordinator of services for persons with disabilities, who has paraplegia and uses a motorized wheelchair; an 81-year-old retiree who lives alone in an apartment; and a practicing landscape architect who uses hand crutches to walk.

The students pinned their work on the wall. They explained their design solutions to individual consultants as the guests circulated through the room. How does one explain a two-dimensional design to a blind person, for instance? "Easy," one student said after the fact, "we used points of the compass as our frame of reference." The discussions were animated. Students seemed relieved at how easy it was to establish rapport. The consultants talked directly about each project in terms of accommodating people with a disability like their own. They seemed interested in the work and excited to be included in the learning process.

Afterwards, the consultants joined the students in a roundtable discussion, sharing general impressions about the work and fielding students' specific questions about disabilities and the design of the environment. One consultant explained why it is dangerous to locate a traffic lane between a parking stall and one's destination. Another described how blind people memorize a site including the utility of landmarks and the disorienting impact of curved or zigzag walkways.

Building on the interest that the students had shown at the studio review, several resources were introduced at the next class meeting. Faculty presented the facts on the Americans With Disabilities Act, introduced the students to the Enabler Model, a paradigm to replace the "average person," and showed two videos. One was on the political history of the disability rights movement as presented by Chris Palames at the UDEP Faculty Colloquium and the other was *Taking Part: A Workshop Approach to Collective Creativity* by Lawrence Halprin, showing interns in his studio experiencing disabilities prior to designing a public space sensitive to the needs of people with disabilities.

Two weeks remained in the project. Students were asked to incorporate their insights from the presentation experience into their work and to prepare a sheet demonstrating how their plans addressed at least one aspect of universal design. Expectations were modest but the results are good documentation of what students learned from their initial exposure to universal design.

Students demonstrated notable sensitivity to universal design notions in the final work. Most came forth with at least one substantial feature, albeit a response to the ideas verbalized during the preliminary session roundtable. But the students were definitely engaged by the approach; the shock effect made an indelible impression.

Chapter 6: Iowa State University

ArtID, 465 Interior Design Studio (Malven). Using the first three levels of awareness teaching modules (Consciousness, Engagement, and Accountability), this studio tried to mainstream universal design for upper-division interior design students who had not previously focused on issues of universal access and use. The intent was to integrate universal design principles into most aspects of practice, rather than being viewed as add-on requirements or a code-compliance annoyance. Universal design was one of several current issues that were researched and layered onto other design considerations. Other issues included health, safety, and socially responsible design concerns. A major educational goal for this course was to establish student accountability and documentation for design research and design decision-making.

The instructor assumed that the senior students had sufficient background with universal design principles to start at the Accountability level. To verify the students' background and to set the stage for a larger-scale project, the students were divided into small teams on the first day of class and given a two-week-long sketch problem—the design of a small entrance lobby for a county hospital. Each team was assigned an environmental component on which to focus in developing its concept. The teams were required to use the P.A.Th.Way.S. method[2] or similar technique for documenting their accountability. The results of this sketch problem indicated that only one out of the ten groups actively addressed universal design issues. This required a course adjustment to integrate components from the first two modules (Consciousness and Engagement levels) into the course. As a result, the faculty decided to include sophomores and juniors in these teaching modules so they would be prepared for the Accountability level by their senior year.

Subsequent class meetings addressed the Consciousness level by showing the students a video, *Designing Environments for Everyone* by Lawrence Halprin, and by having the students discuss its contents. Lynn Paxson, a faculty member in architecture, presented an overview on the importance of dealing with socially relevant issues. Students visited Green Hills, a local extended-care and assisted-living facility in Ames, to interact with the residents and staff.

Students moved on to the Engagement level by assuming disabilities in an experiential workshop, "Welcome to My World," led by the executive director for the Central Iowa Center for Independent Living (CICIL). Students had the opportunity to experience several disabilities (sight impairment, dyslexia, limited use of limbs, speech impairment, mobility limitations, and hearing impairments) and interact with the president of CICIL, who has quadriplegia, in a lively question-and-answer session.

During this time, students were working as teams on Phase I of their design project, the research and development of a program document. Two facilities were used for this project: a unit for people with dementia and an assisted-living program in a wing of the county hospital, used in the initial sketch problem. In Phase II students, working in teams of two to three people, spent five weeks working on developing a design concept for their project. This project required the comprehensive design of a setting of moderate complexity and required substantial direction from faculty.

The major critique session included a variety of jurors: representatives of the hospital and the Ames Alzheimer's support group, faculty with elderly parents in assisted-living or dementia-care units, interior design faculty, architecture faculty who actively work in the health care/aging area. This four-hour session was videotaped. It was clear that the application of universal design principles, as well as other legal requirements and social concerns, were not sufficiently or consistently integrated into the design concept solutions.

Four team projects that were generally strong but contained serious problems were selected as examples for the Accountability level teaching module. A mock-trial format was used to emphasize the personal responsibility of the designer for the impact of design decisions, satisfying the intentions of the Americans with Disabilities Act as well as codes and other areas of professional liability. This simulation was based on the Moot Court used at Arizona State University.[3]

During the next class the Story County sheriff (a graphic design faculty member) appeared to deliver summonses to four interior design teams requiring them to appear in court at the next class meeting. Each summons was for a different complaint, including one for failure to comply with Americans with Disabilities Act. Prosecutors and defense attorneys were named in each summons so that every student was involved in a case. When the sheriff left and the students recovered from their shock, the moot court procedures were explained and the remainder of studio time was used to prepare both sides for the trial. One faculty member acted as advisor to the defense and the other faculty member acted as advisor to the prosecution.

For the trial, a large room was organized with tables for the defense and prosecution, a witness stand (red chair), a table for the judge, and chairs at the back of the room for visitors. The larger group of students not playing the part of the defense or prosecution acted as the jury. The court was called to order by the bailiff, the judge in a black academic robe appeared, and witnesses were sworn in using the design bible, *Time Saver Standards for Interior Design*. Students had been encouraged to use expert witnesses from the college and community and several faculty served in this capacity. The proceedings were videotaped.

After the mock trial, students refined their designs, bringing considerable energy and involvement to understanding codes and issues of social responsibility. Some totally revised their projects. At this point students were working at the Accountability level, consciously applying universal design principles, health and safety standards,

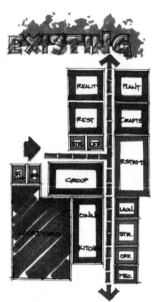

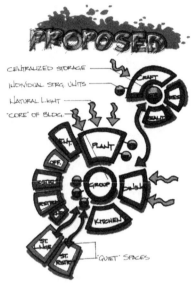

and other issues related to program requirements. About two-thirds of the students elected to complete this final phase of the project individually; the other third of the students continued in design teams and developed refinements, details, and some working drawings for their entire project. The semester culminated with a two-hour informal critique of the projects, which was videotaped.

The mock trial was an excellent active learning technique. Students felt that they understood their legal as well as moral responsibility after preparing for and going through the trial process. They felt that some of the citations would be better placed after they had done more developed drawing and drafting, but agreed that they had a heightened awareness and interest in the issues, including the ADA and universal design. The faculty agree that the extensive use of guidelines and code books in the final two weeks is evidence of the students' increased sense of accountability.

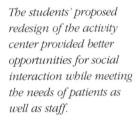

The students' proposed redesign of the activity center provided better opportunities for social interaction while meeting the needs of patients as well as staff.

The approach of using modules provided flexibility within the studio to adjust to the students' level of knowledge. After the first sketch problem, it was clear that the first two levels must be addressed before achieving the third level of accountability would be possible—even though the students were seniors and supposedly had been involved in barrier-free design in previous courses.

Arch 240, Materials and Methods (Osterberg). This required course in the technology area (currently taught by Bruce Bassler, a professor with extensive experience in architectural practice, teaching, and research) is an introduction to common architectural materials, their physical properties, and their integration into light construction subsystems. The prerequisite for the course is completion of the pre-professional program and admission into the professional program. Because the course covers building codes, it provided an excellent opportunity for Arvid Osterberg to lecture on the subject of the *ADA Accessibility Guidelines* (ADAAG) and universal design to raise consciousness and provide indirect exposure to the need for universal design. He showed parts of two videotapes: one provided by the UDEP project and the other made in conjunction with Osterberg's detailed study of the Iowa State University campus to determine the deficiencies of 150 buildings and exterior spaces (parking, routes of travel, building entrances, etc.), as defined by ADAAG.

After the lecture, student teams of two were assigned specific locations in and near the College of Design for analysis in relation to ADAAG. Each team was required to measure and record ADAAG deficiencies using sketches and notes on a form that was specifically prepared for the exercise. Overall reaction to the exercise by students and their instructor was quite positive. Consciousness (level 1) was raised and Engagement (level 2) was vicariously achieved through hands-on measuring and scrutiny of the ADAAG standards. Accountability (level 3) was achieved throughout the evaluation and grading of the students' drawings and notes.

Architectural design studios. Several architectural design studio projects that included issues of human needs relating to universal design concepts became opportunities for the UDEP faculty to provide informal input. The videotape *Toward Universal Design* by James Mueller was shown on several occasions. At the beginning of one design studio project taught by Lynn Paxson, students were required to complete readings from *Rethinking Architecture* by Raymond Lifchez and other selected publications.

Overall reaction to the integration of universal design concepts into architectural design studios was positive. However, results thus far have not been consistent from one studio (and instructor) to another. Consciousness (level 1) was raised in some studios through the use of videotapes, readings, and discussions. Accountability (level 3) was also achieved to a limited extent, through comments made by students and faculty members during project reviews, and by the evaluation and grading of the students' designs and drawings. However, overall accountability was difficult to measure, because of the high number of students and faculty involved at various levels of architectural design in the curriculum.

Four faculty members—Rutledge, Osterberg, Malven, and Dorothy Fowles—pursued the integration of universal design principles into their spring semester courses.

LA 343, Intermediate Landscape Architectural Design II (Rutledge). This studio was offered in the semester immediately following LA 342 where the ADA and universal design considerations were introduced by "shock effect." Most of the same students were involved. In contrast to LA 342, which addressed primarily large-scale site-planning problems, LA 343 focused upon small-scale problems and design detailing.

The underlying idea of this studio was to discourage the notion of universal design as an obtrusive add-on; rather it was stressed as a creative challenge. "No, it is not an option. You will meet the five-percent minimum grade requirement. Think of it as an adventure."

A small park on a sloping site between two commercial buildings was to be designed as a place to stop as well as a place to move through. On-grade access was to be provided to the commercial buildings approximately halfway into the park.

Grades could not be steeper than 5 percent. The most obvious solution—to zigzag the full length of the park several times in a series of narrow hairpin walks—would not be permitted for one simple reason: the results would be a totally utilitarian construction at the expense of everybody's aesthetic sensibilities. Moreover and most important, such a self-conscious treatment was viewed as an offense to the dignity of persons with disabilities. The design goal was to have a sensitively integrated scheme. Students were instructed to treat the site as one sculptural unit, handling the grade requirements with a butter knife as opposed to a blunt machete.

To reinforce the necessity of a maximum of 5-percent grade, the studio was equipped with two wheelchairs. Students leaving the studio space during the studio period had to use a chair to go to the bathroom, get a Coke, meet a friend, and buy drafting supplies at the in-house college store.

The class turned out some of the finest design work that has been produced by students at this level, including many "personal bests" as well as a number of exceptional, goose bump–generating pieces.

Most of the students in the class, having been through the "shock" orientation to universal design during the first term, took to meeting the 5-percent requirement as a matter of course. Having met the requirement with classy results increases the possibility of them automatically taking a universal design posture in professional work to come. In comparison, another studio at the same level did the same project. They were urged, but not required, to meet the 5-percent grade standard. Most did not.

A student who had both studios wrote of his landscape architectural internship with the U.S. Forest Service during the subsequent summer. His first task was to suggest ways of making facilities comply with ADA standards. Interns from other schools responded to the assignment with varying ways of saying "Huh?" The ISU student went easily to work.

ArtID 167, Interior Design Foundations (Fowles and Malven). This introductory studio course for all interior design students is the only applied studio taken by students prior to their screening for selective admission into the Interior Design Program. As such, it is an ideal opportunity to expose students to universal design issues. This influenced course planning in several ways. The course is charged with helping clarify the students' understanding and functional definition of their proposed field of study; in this case, the facilitation of individual rights to access and use of the built environment as an inherent responsibility of the design professions. Activity and success related to universal design intentions was cited as a probable source of professional gratification, positive identification, and satisfaction with the field.

A stated objective of the course was an awareness of fundamental human-factors concerns in interior design—with an emphasis on universal access and use. Each assignment stated the expectation that the students' consideration of universal design issues must be evident in the final submission. Two projects included universal access and use as priority project goals. Although universal design was a stated priority for only two of seven projects, juries for all projects were instructed to address important access and use issues. Universal design came to be seen as the student's implied responsibility.

The Americans with Disabilities Act and ADAAG were given particular attention. All students were given a copy of ADAAG, and selected sections were highlighted for coverage by examination. One class session was devoted to the refinement of a small-scale public amenity (a public telephone) by careful examination, interpretation, and application of the ADAAG. Although the faculty gave regular attention to universal design throughout the semester, four key activities were pivotal in establishing student sensitivity to the issue.

In the first activity, held during the third week of the semester, all students participated in simulations of several disabilities, staged by the staff of the Central Iowa Center for Independent Living in the College of Design building. Students participated in one of several disabilities:

- Simulating a sight impairment or sight loss. Using goggles and glasses that fogged and/or distorted vision or blindfolds, they negotiated the building with the assistance of peers and identified problems such as high-contrast lighting and low-color contrast.

- Simulating loss of fine motor control. Using tape to immobilize their hands, students attempted to perform manual tasks, including the operation of a variety of building controls and hardware.

- Simulating loss of mobility. Students navigated the building using a conventional wheelchair, stopping to use features such as elevators, drinking fountains, public toilets, and fire-stair landings.

The session attracted an unusually high level of student participation and enthusiasm. Students engaged in personal and group experimentation beyond the basic parameters established by CICIL. Evidence of the success of the session was the students' voluntary adoption of similar simulation techniques to explore the universal design requirements of projects later in the semester.

The second activity consisted of a walking tour of significant campus interiors. While the purpose and emphasis of the tour was on technical, operational, and aesthetic subjects, two Iowa State University students, non-designers who use wheelchairs, agreed to accompany the students on the tour. The perspective of these two students proved to be highly effective in establishing universal design as an appropriate "overlay" for discussions of many other types of design concerns.

For their third project of the semester, students were asked to redesign a small vestibule in the centralized student lounge and information center called The Hub. The space included a public telephone that was poorly designed for use by any user but was particularly ill-suited for people using wheelchairs and other mobility aids. The small size of the space and the unavoidable demands of the dysfunctional telephone forced students to deal with technical criteria related to universal design. After participating in a highly structured analysis and redesign of a conventional public telephone using ADAAG criteria, students applied the process independently to the student-lounge project.

This project reinforced the students' understanding of universal design as a priority issue through first-hand experience: their use of the phone and other features of the project site while using a wheelchair. Their confidence in dealing with universal design was bolstered by successful use of minimum technical standards, such as the ADAAG. And they were able to recognize universal design as a source of creative insight. This was achieved by encouraging use of functional features as driving influences on broader aesthetic and technical decisions.

The final project of the semester focused on conceptual design of a large-sized motor home (recreational vehicle) suitable for use by an aging adult population. The project was a joint project of Iowa State University and Winnebago Industries of Forest City, Iowa. Criteria included accommodation of the broadest possible range of potential owners and users. Compliance with ADAAG was encouraged as one way of achieving more accessibility. A tour of current motor homes at the manufacturing facility reinforced the idea of universal design as a priority issue. This gave students a chance to evaluate issues of universal access, use, and safety in a setting for which such goals may previously have seemed unwarranted. The unconventional, automotive nature of the project caused students to explore problems less commonly encountered in building interiors—slight level changes, unusually compact functional areas, requirements for multi-functional space use, and problems of restraint while in motion. From discussion, it was clear that students were developing an ability to generalize solution concepts and apply them across differences in setting types—specifically, they were able to apply building concepts to a vehicle and vice versa. This project increased the students' awareness of the designer's role as an agent of change. This was reinforced when students witnessed the enthusiasm with which industry sponsors greeted concepts that might better adapt their product to the growing market of aging users with functional limitations.

The semester demonstrated the value of initiating students' exposure to universal design at the earliest possible moment in their professional development. The previous semester's work with senior interior design students would suggest a degree of "unlearning" is sometimes required before upper-division students can begin to internalize universal design issues. Introduced in the students' first semester, universal design concepts seem to supplement, rather than displace, other elements of the student's value structure.

Beyond forming a basic sensitivity to universal design, several freshman participants in this project came to understand universal design processes as potential tools for creativity. This rather sophisticated view seems to offer the promise of even higher levels of attainment among upper-division students in the very near future.

Evaluation

While no formal evaluation was conducted of the courses offered during the 1993–94 academic year, the teaching of universal design continues, definitely a measure of its importance. It is interesting to note that continued teaching of universal design has not been actively promoted by the UDEP faculty coordinator, instead, interest of faculty is due to the recognition of its success over the last year. Overall reaction to the integration of universal design concepts into design studios continues to be positive. However, accountability is difficult to measure because of the number of students and faculty involved. Consciousness has definitely been raised at all levels, and is becoming increasingly evident in design problem statements and interim and final design reviews. The next step to integrating universal design concepts into the curriculum is by enhancing existing design elective courses.

Initially, we had hoped to measure outcomes to see if the different approaches used actually changed students behavior and attitudes over time. We found, however, that over the course of one semester or even one year, we did not have enough information to know the impact on students beyond the particular course or course experience. To understand long- term impact and change of design values, students need to be tracked over a two- or three-year period through a series of courses in order to measure how much change actually occurs.

Reflection

One of the strongest aspects of the project was the sharing of ideas, by the five faculty members involved, at the conceptual stage early in the semester. The UDEP grant was a catalyst for bringing the five of us together to engage in focused discussions about universal design. We were able to freely exchange ideas with each other on a common ground. The sharing of our pedagogy regarding common goals and views towards universal design helped each of us by reinforcing our individual commitment to it. There was a tendency, though, for us to burn out when it became progressively more difficult for the five of us to get together as the year progressed. We also saw that our focus of attention shifted from developing learning modules to providing a breadth of exposure to universal design concepts.

The awareness levels developed by the faculty team for UDEP (Consciousness, Engagement, Accountability, and Integration) is now impacting curriculum development in the three participating disciplines, architecture, landscape architecture, and interior design. It is also impacting the development of the interior design curriculum, not just the inclusion universal design issues, but also the examination of how students learn and how faculty can change how students design.

The five faculty members involved in UDEP have come to regard the levels model as being very useful. Each time a course is planned and organized, the awareness levels are used to examine and analyze the starting point of students, the intentions for the course, and the appropriate conceptual level for bringing material into the classroom. Awareness levels are also helpful in identifying strategies that can be pursued by faculty to achieve the next highest level.

Use of the levels model also made us realize that no one course can adequately address universal design issues. The diversity of experiences that is needed to achieve all four levels requires multiple reinforcement. This cannot be accomplished in one course. A specific course devoted to universal design might become a cornerstone for an understanding the subject, but there also needs to be a broader exposure to the subject throughout the student's education.

We discovered that some students whom we had expected to have knowledge of universal design did not and that seniors do not automatically have the ability to work at level four, Integration, simply because they are seniors. Instead, they need to work their way through each of the four levels. Since seniors also had to start at the Consciousness level, fast-tracking them through the succession of four levels was difficult and not totally satisfactory. We believe the levels approach will have more positive impact on students when they are exposed to the first level during their first year.

We learned that shock treatment regarding universal design, such as surprise jurors with disabilities and mock trials focussed on universal design issues, can have a profoundly positive, and potentially lasting, impact on students. We found that consultants are very useful to the process, but faculty members need to be careful not to wear out their goodwill. Videotaping consultants' comments might be an appropriate technique for repeated use of consultant input with other classes in subsequent years.

The five faculty members involved in UDEP would like to see our cross-disciplinary effort continue. The project has been a catalyst for understanding that the nature of design is fundamentally the same for the disciplines of architecture, landscape architecture, and interior Design. UDEP has been a stepping stone, not just for increasing awareness of universal design issues, but also for understanding the nature of design and our pedagogical approach towards it.

We believe that our greatest contribution to UDEP was the development of a conceptual framework involving increasing levels of awareness. Other modules and pedagogical approaches developed at other UDEP schools can now be examined as to where they best fit according to the levels model.

We have concluded that universal design should not be put on a pedestal or be treated as a distinct subject area. Instead, it should be integrated throughout the curriculum. To accomplish this, we need to muster the support of more faculty, so that the progression of levels can be built into the curriculum and universal design ideas become a standard of practice.

Acknowledgements

We would like to share credit for this undertaking with the following colleagues: Robert Harvey, professor of landscape architecture; Bruce Bassler, associate professor of architecture; Alan Michelson, associate professor of art and design; Lynn Paxon, adjunct assistant professor of architecture; and Harlen Groe, graduate student in landscape architecture. We are also grateful for the consultation and assistance of: Jeff Bensen, landscape architect; Robert Jeppesen, executive director, Central Iowa Center for Independent Living; and Joyce Packwood, coordinator, Students With Disabilities, Iowa State University. We would like to acknowledge Iowa State University for its award of an instructional development grant, providing additional funding for this project.

Notes

1. The Enabler Model can be found in Steinfeld et al. (1979). *Access to the Built Environment: A Review of the Literature.* Washington, D.C.: U.S. Department of Housing and Urban Development, Office of Policy Development and Research. Available from *HUD User,* Publication #660.

2. P.A.Th.Way.S. method is a five-step design process that emphasizes a clearly defined rationale for decisions in solving design problems. P.A.Th.Way.S. stands for Problem Definition, Analysis, THeory, Ways, and Solution and is used in teaching interior design classes at Iowa State University.

3. DiCicco, D.B. and S.C. Reznikoff (1992). *Moot Court: Demonstrate and Evaluate Design Competencies.* Research Resources: 1992 IDEC International Conference Proceedings, 21–24.

References

Halprin, Lawrence (1984). *Designing Environments for Everyone.* Videotape. Washington, D.C.: Landscape Architecture Foundation.

Longmore, Paul and Diane B. Piastro (1988). *Unhandicapping Our Language.* Available from Cryptography, P.O. Box 454, Long Beach, CA 90809-0454.

Breaking the Myth of Modernism

Proposal

Kansas State faculty proposed an interdisciplinary, multifaceted approach to teaching universal design values and strategies. This approach assumed that to understand lifespan design, students would not only need to acquire knowledge, but also to reinforce the application of that knowledge in studio, including peer recognition of highly aesthetic universal design responses. Three activities were proposed: the creation of resource modules for use in class, a Universal Design Awareness Week, and an awards program for excellence in universal design.

The project was implemented differently than it was originally conceived due to limited funding and changes in faculty responsibilities. Universal design was integrated into the syllabus of one section of the first-year design studio by a faculty member who was relatively new to the issues. The original UDEP faculty grantee, Lyn Norris-Baker, served as a mentor and advisor to the project. The first-year studio was selected because of interest from its faculty, the ability to involve students from all four professional curricula, and the importance of introducing a universal design philosophy as early as possible in the students' course of study.

Activity

The first-year design studio enrolls students who intend to pursue architecture, landscape architecture, interior architecture, and interior design. Students pursuing any of the first three professional curricula are in the College of Architecture and Design; those pursuing interior design are in the College of Human Ecology. Twenty-nine students enrolled in the studio section. Universal design was not mentioned prior to studio enrollment.

Universal design concepts were introduced in the spring semester studio, which is an introduction to serving human needs through design. The students have already had a semester of basic design principles. The spring semester studio includes two design problems: a chair design and a pavilion design, based on fragments from Modern Movement architects.

The studio was team-taught by two faculty and a graduate assistant. The faculty were particularly well-suited to teach a pilot section on universal design. One is the coordinator of the Year I Studios for the College; the other has served as the KSU campus architect, working extensively on campus accessibility issues. The UDEP faculty grantee served as a resource person and visiting critic.

Team members:

Madlen Simon
Assistant Professor
Lyn Norris-Baker
Professor
Lawrence Garvin
Professor

Chapter 7: Kansas State University

The chair design problem helped introduce the basic philosophy and concepts of universal design.

The educational objectives for the first-year studio are to explore fundamental topics, including spatial definition, spatial order, massing and form, envelope and enclosure, and interaction of color. The projects also provide opportunities for addressing related issues such as design decisions and the factors that influence them; design archetypes and precedents; significant buildings, landscapes, and interiors and their designers; design processes; and work habits, attitudes, and values. The first problem, designing a chair, is shared by all first-year studios, taught by nine faculty and two graduate assistants. The second project, designing a pavilion, is often approached differently by each instructor. The challenge was to adapt these existing problems to incorporate universal design concepts. The instructors' strategy was to allow students to explore design issues without specifically requiring consideration of universal design, and then requiring students to reconsider and re-investigate their projects with universal design in mind.

Universal design concepts were introduced into the first project, the design of a chair, near the end of the three-week project. Each student was asked to design and build a full-scale cardboard model of a chair to suit his or her requirements. The review of these chairs initially focused on the ways in which each chair fit the unique needs of the designer. The faculty then introduced a variety of different users into the review process, including people who were young, old, large, small, and disabled with respect to the environment. These consultants sat in the chairs and discussed their reactions with the students. The intent of this portion of the studio was to heighten awareness of and sensitivity to "the other" as well as the self as user, and to highlight the philosophy and basic concepts of universal design.

For the remainder of the semester, students worked on a problem that had previously been used for studios in Year I. It was developed from a sequence written by Madlen Simon and her colleagues at Temple University in 1992 for a first-year studio program coordinated by Professor Judy Bing. Students were asked to design a pavilion incorporating a fragment from a well-documented piece of Modern architecture. The pavilion was expected to accommodate a variety of simple indoor and outdoor spaces where individuals, couples, and small groups could gather and socialize. The program did not define specific requirements for these spaces. Students were asked to complete drawings and construct a model of the pavilion for review. No specific expectations about universal design were mentioned in the first phase of the project. The final phase was an opportunity for a universal design "intervention and re-investigation."

Outcome

Chair Problem. Designing and building a cardboard chair is a hands-on, full-scale experience in which each student explores his or her own particular needs for dimension, comfort, function, and aesthetic pleasure. After the class reviewed the chairs for how well they fit their designers, a group of guests arrived to re-review the chairs.

The guests included a woman with visual limitations and her infant son, a seven-year-old boy, a ten-year-old girl, a woman with mobility problems due to severe arthritis, an older woman, an obese person, and a very tall male college student. They circulated through the studio trying out chairs and discussed with students how the various designs facilitated or hampered their own sitting experiences. The guests responded enthusiastically to the wide range of solutions the students had generated. Their criticism covered a range of needs outside the personal experience of a vigorous group of nineteen year olds. The guests were sensitive to issues such as proportion, height, back support, back angle, presence of armrests, stability, and suitability for various tasks performed in the sitting position. Unlike faculty, they tended to emphasize the good attributes rather than the deficiencies.

The majority of the students were interested in learning more about their chair designs. Only one student appeared completely resistant to learning from this situation. He insisted that his chair was primarily a visual object and not designed to offer comfort to himself or to anyone else. The guests were particularly interested in the aesthetic properties of the chairs, which reinforced for students that universal design includes aesthetic experience as well as functionality and accessibility.

Guests of different ages, abilities, and sizes helped review the usability, comfort, and aesthetics of the students' chair designs.

Pavilion Problem. For the remainder of the semester, students were asked to design a pavilion in a park-like setting that provided a variety of indoor/outdoor spaces in which individuals, couples, and small groups could sit. The pavilion project was divided into three phases: extending a building fragment into a pavilion; researching and documenting the four houses that served as sources for the fragments; and re-investigating the design, using the perspective of universal design. The first phase of the problem statement was to engage in analysis and manipulation of historical precedent in a variety of media, using four fragments of houses designed by architects from the Modern Movement. Since the program had been developed for other educational objectives, none of the houses was chosen with universal design criteria in mind. The four houses were:

Chapter 7: Kansas State University

- Frank Lloyd Wright's Goetsch-Winkler House

- Rietveld's Shroeder House

- Louis Kahn's Esherick House

- Richard Meier's Shamberg House

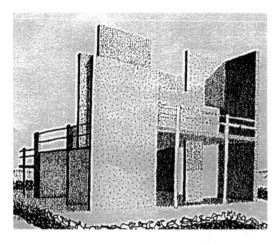

Students developed a project based on a fragment of Modern architecture, and then re-explored the project to incorporate universal design.

The first two weeks were spent introducing students to the concept of design language and, specifically, four different languages of form-making. They were given plans, sections, elevations, and axonometric views of a fragment of one of the Modern houses. This phase had an element of mystery because students were asked to extrapolate a whole from a part, a system from its elements, a language from a phrase—with no other information than the fragment drawings. Students worked in teams of two, making model studies in different materials and exploring how the fragments could be manipulated using the basic design principles introduced in their first semester.

Having gained some understanding of the elements and ordering principles of each design language, the students designed pavilions by extending the spaces of their fragments into new forms, using the language of the fragment. This strategy of investigation distanced the student from designing by personal preference and separated the activity of form-making from the association of familiar images with familiar activities. This problem served as a jumping-off point for beginning students entering a new world of possibilities. At the conclusion of the design phase, students moved into a research mode. Working in four teams of five to seven members, they documented the houses from which the fragments were drawn as another means of understanding the design languages.

The formal introduction to universal design principles came after students had completed their designs for the pavilions. Paul Grayson, UDEP advisor, gave a slide presentation illustrating how universal design can be applied to design. The students seemed exceptionally attentive and interested in the presentation because of its coincidence with a lecture by Japanese architect Hiroshi Hara. Grayson showed a number of examples of universal design from Japan.

After the presentation, students participated in an informal review with Grayson to consider how well their projects responded to the concept of universal design, an impetus for students to recreate their pavilions. At the end of the session, we introduced the next phase: to transform the pavilion models to incorporate principles of universal design and to promote accessibility as an aesthetic experience. Students were asked to focus on "entering" as an activity important both functionally and symbolically to the building as a whole. This exercise gave them the opportunity to evaluate critically how well the language of Modernism supports universal design, and how this design language might be reinterpreted. The students clearly were convinced of the value of universal design principles, as evidenced by their effort to identify many alternatives to monumental stairs, multiple level changes, pipe railings, and other icons of Modernism.

Paul Grayson critiques a student's pavilion from a universal design perspective.

The students were, however, highly resistant to the idea of changing the models into which they had poured so much time, energy, and ego. Eventually, even the most resistant of the students began to modify their models. Some of the designs improved significantly as a result of applying new principles. As students focused their attention on the range of different modes by which people enter buildings, they produced more clearly delineated building entrances. By the conclusion of this phase of the pavilion project, students were no longer claiming that "you could slip into the building anywhere," but had clearly defined the entrance as an event in the experience of the pavilion.

Dee Strickland, working with Frank Lloyd Wright's Goetsch-Winkler House, had designed a pavilion that relied on a flight of stairs for access to the second floor, lacked a primary entrance, and suggested no preferred route to the stairs. After Strickland overcame his reluctance to tamper with his finished model, he added an elevator adjacent to the stair and redesigned a balcony to become an entrance canopy that shelters visitors. Improving the entrance in keeping with Wright's design language gave Strickland's pavilion the frontality it had been lacking.

Shirley Beaner's pavilion, using a fragment of the Rietveld's Shroeder house, featured a stair that wrapped around and up to the second level. Beaner considered replacing the stair with a ramp and was shocked to discover the length of ramp required to reach the second floor. Like Strickland, Beaner chose to offer options for vertical circulation, so she provided an elevator in addition to the stairs.

This exercise in rethinking requirements, redefining goals, and redesigning a product was useful to students in forming their understanding of the design process. It helped students accept the model as a process tool rather than a precious product. The most popular response to the universal design challenge was to add an elevator. A few students incorporated ramps into their designs, but generally experienced difficulty in dealing with the length required. Some students worked with railing safety and others dealt with wayfinding issues in terms of paving and floor materials. All of the students approached the problem by trying to retrofit their designs. None of them extended the rethinking process back to the *parti*. Perhaps the students needed more time for this phase of the project and perhaps should have been required to return to schematic design to address universal design criteria.

At the end of the pavilion design exercise, on completing their model revisions, all students participated in an exercise in which they took turns using a wheelchair. Teams of students navigated, assisted, and observed as they made their way around the College of Architecture and Design, across the street to the K-State Union, through the bookstore, cafeteria, restrooms, and back to class. Limited time precluded simulating other disabilities in this studio, but other opportunities exist in upper-level courses for such simulations. When the students returned to studio, three guests arrived for a review of the redesigned pavilions: the Tylers (a former police officer who uses a wheelchair and his wife) and the director of Disabled Student Services. The co-instructor for the studio, who had been campus architect when ADA was implemented on campus, also contributed an important perspective to the discussion.

After an hour of firsthand experience using a wheelchair, students were keen to talk and we had the most productive group session of the year. The direct physical experience of limited ability seemed to help the students internalize what had heretofore been a set of external ideas. This meeting evidenced tremendous progress in students' understanding from the initial experience of "otherness" in the chair project. We had been concerned that we were setting up a situation in which there would be tension between students and the Tylers. Instead, the students responded well to the consultants, who were able to help them translate their new experience into programmatic and design considerations in relation to the pavilion models.

Several resources made available to us as UDEP participants were very helpful. In addition to providing critiques of students' pavilion designs, Paul Grayson's visit provided an opportunity for a public lecture and for meeting Human Ecology faculty members who are developing a universal design educational facility. The lecture coincided with a required course for Year V students in architecture and interior architecture so that faculty and more advanced students were able to attend and benefit from his visit. Faculty and graduate students had informal opportunities to interact with Mr. Grayson at lunch and dinner. The UDEP impact was further extended through the UDEP resource kit, particularly videos, which were used in the studio and in both the professional practice and the environment and behavior classes in the fall semester.

Reflection

Should we have introduced a wide range of client needs at the outset of the project or focused on a particular client or user group as we entered the design process?

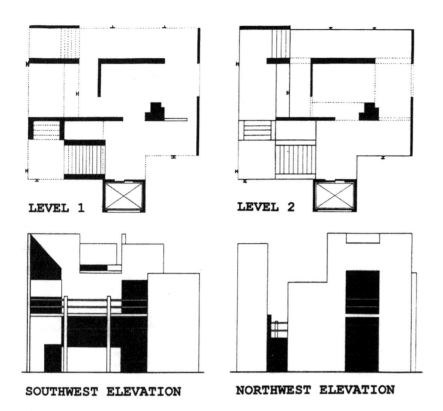

LEVEL 1   LEVEL 2

SOUTHWEST ELEVATION   NORTHWEST ELEVATION

Shirley Beaner's Pavilion:
Universal design thinking led Shirley to create an entry sequence leading to a choice of elevator or stairs for second-level access.

By doing so, we would have missed an important step in the learning process. The concept of otherness may be understood best if presented in relation to the self. Designing for oneself gives the designer a necessary measure against which to understand the needs of others. The chair exercise helped students understand their own needs in relation to the range of human needs. In the initial review of the chairs, the students observed that the elasticity of young bodies compensates for design deficiencies in the chair. The reviewers, however, required a closer fit between their physiological characteristics and the chair. The students learned that users are a varied group rather than a uniform entity. This experience also focused students' attention more clearly on the specific functions of each part of the chair.

This sequence of exercises introduced design students to the aesthetic of Modernism, a language of form that is loaded with cultural and political meanings. The concept of universal design offered a new opportunity to critique Modernism. The Modern Movement standardized the client and idealized human form, as exemplified by Le Corbusier's Modulor Man. Where Modernism promoted uniformity, universal design celebrates the diversity of real life. Modernism was an exclusionary discourse; universal design is inclusionary.

The wheelchair experience might have been incorporated into the pavilion project earlier and expanded to include other kinds of physical challenges. The experiential learning could have reinforced Grayson's presentation about the need for flexibility and accessibility in the environment. Our timing worked well, however, because the wheelchair trip gave the students a common ground for discussion with the Tylers. Mr. Tyler clearly appreciated the students' receptive attitude and willingness to discuss their experiences, such as being looked down upon at the information counter, traveling out of one's way to use an elevator, entering a building by the service entrance, and encountering inaccessible restroom facilities. Over the course of the discussion, the students' comments shifted from describing the difficulties they encountered to expressing their feelings about the experience. One young man's description of his helplessness in the men's room was a particularly poignant reminder that design can make the difference between dignified self-sufficiency and frustrating dependency.

Very little of a design professional's work takes place on a clean slate. Most design work consists of intervention in an existing environment. The heroic forms of modernism often fail to accommodate universal design goals. As our culture learns to appreciate diversity, our government has mandated equal opportunity in the environment. An important task facing designers today is to create eloquent architectural language that can give expression to the range of human needs.

Reviews with consultants helped translate the students' simulation experiences into programmatic and design considerations.

Lyn Norris-Baker, the UDEP grant recipient who had planned to implement the proposal, reflects on her modified role and the outcome of the project:

This studio was my first attempt to teach universal design "indirectly" by working with another faculty to integrate universal design issues into existing problem statements. As a resource person/visiting critic, I worked primarily behind the scenes, with only periodic interactions with the students in the studio. The selection of a first year studio including students studying for careers in a variety of design disciplines allowed us to introduce universal design concepts at a formative stage in students' philosophies of design, which both Madlen and I felt was important. If these concepts are introduced later in students' programs of study, their design philosophies and approaches to problem solving have become more established.

The existing curriculum shaped the idea of a "re-thinking, re-design" approach, although it would probably not have been my first choice had I been structuring the studio problem myself. It was more successful than I initially hoped, because allowing students to design first "for themselves" highlighted the kinds of preconceptions they brought to the design process. This concept was developed further when they reconsidered their pavilion designs that had been created using a fragment of a Modern house, representing a movement that focused on idealized human needs, rather than the diversity that exists in reality. Thus many students confronted their own and other architects' less-than-universal design approaches. The re-thinking/re-designing aspects of the studio also provided great opportunities to teach them about the nonlinear nature of the design process. In retrospect, more time was needed to encourage students to really reconsider their responses, and not simply to adapt them using a retrofit approach.

> *"An important task facing designers today is to create eloquent architectural language which can give expression to the range of human needs."*

The visit by the advisor, Paul Grayson, was a great asset to the studio in terms of engaging students in talking about universal design and presenting them with excellent exemplars. Our students have a strong interest in Japanese architecture (fostered by a summer studio opportunity as well as lecturers), which enhanced the students' responses to Paul Grayson's presentation. The participation of the user groups in reviews and the experiences of disability made an impact on the students, but being able to have more continuity in these experiences would have made an even stronger statement. It also was clear that just discussing universal design issues and having the diverse user group review the chair project was not as powerful as having to deconstruct and redesign a project. It will be important to continue the emphasis and reinforcement of universal design concepts with these students throughout the remainder of the curriculum.

Evaluation

Students completed pre-test and post-test questionnaires prepared by the UDEP sponsors. Of the resources used in the course, students found the consultants and the simulation exercise most useful to their understanding of universal design.

Many of the students, as evidenced by their evaluation comments, found that the course had changed the way they view the built environment.

I now understand that universal design does not mean designing for the handicapped. It is designing for the convenience of everyone.

Now that I am aware of the different aspects of universal design I will always look to incorporate them into my design projects.

Universal design is for all people, not just the handicapped, and it can be integrated in the design with few changes to the intentions of the design.

As an architect, I need to be constantly aware of the entire public and respect everyone's abilities, and not discriminate either consciously or unconsciously.

I now look at designs of everything in a very different way, one that looks at all needs.

Acknowledgements

We gratefully acknowledge participation by individuals who generously gave their time and energy to the studio: UDEP Advisor Paul John Grayson; and community and university members who represented user interests, Robin Bruner, Ryan Bruner, Pam Evans, Irene Harlan, Laura Harrison, Gretchen Holden, Janet Schanbeck, Lewis Tyler, and Vicky Tyler.

Raising Awareness through a Universal Design Symposium

Faculty coordinator:

Nikki Joan Spencer
Associate Professor

Proposal

Louisiana State University's proposal for its involvement in UDEP was to develop and teach a four-part workshop that would expose students to universal design issues through interventions occurring over the course of a semester. Due to limited funding, the proposal was condensed into a single symposium. Initially, the topic of the symposium was to be the *Americans with Disabilities Act Accessibility Guidelines* (ADAAG). After the UDEP colloquium in Raleigh, North Carolina, the topic of the symposium was expanded from code compliance to the value of universal design.

Activity

The twelve-hour symposium was held during the first week of studio sessions in spring semester 1994 and was attended by over one hundred interior design students and faculty from LSU, as well as a number of local and regional design professionals.

The symposium's stated objectives were:

- Raise awareness among participants of the impact of design decisions across the lifespan.

- Build a vocabulary and conversancy with universal design issues as well as an attitude directed toward positive change.

- Develop a process of design response incorporating issues inherent in universal design.

Outcome

The first two sessions of the symposium were primarily informational and experiential. UDEP Advisor James Mueller opened with a keynote address and exercises for the audience that introduced the concept of universal design and demonstrated the validity of universally designed solutions. During his presentation, students began to internalize the challenges and identify usable solutions in the designed environment. Participants' were encouraged to expand their definition of potential users of design to include people with a variety of impairments.

Chapter 8: Louisiana State University

I realized that many different types of people can be associated with (but not defined by) the term handicapped...not just those who use a wheelchair. I realized that I have people with disabilities in my family and that I am disabled, too, by the environment, based on the broadened definition of universal design. (Interior design student)

The second session provided an orientation to and explanation of Title III of the ADA and the ADAAG. During this session participants began to understand the legal requirements for compliance.

Through discussion and expansion of material presented in the first session, participants were challenged to move beyond the restrictive attitude of simply "meeting code" to the potential for designing across the lifespan. Students' reflections at this point indicated the beginning of a paradigm shift—moving the problem from "them" to "us," away from "it's someone else's problem" to "what can I do as a designer?"

Environmental obstacles are not only challenges for someone with an impairment but for everyone. We as designers have created barriers in the built environment, now we should use good design to remove them...successful designs should work well for everyone! (Interior design student)

The third and final session of the symposium consisted of a design charrette in which teams analyzed real-life situations, synthesized their findings, and developed design responses that reflected universal design issues. Student teams conducted on-site interviews with several building users who have physical and visual impairments. Working in conjunction with student consultants, each team was asked to document existing concerns and develop a proposal for change. In addition to learning from the consultants with impairments, students had an opportunity to simulate a number of mobility, strength, visual, and auditory limitations during the course of the site survey.

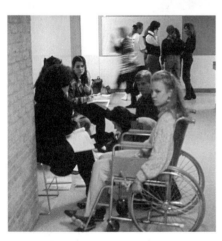

Expectations were realized when the students' proposals went beyond code compliance and responded to the challenge of universal design. The participants were very positive about the charrette experience. Mental, physical, and emotional engagement and relating their observations and suggestions to a consultant for validation were important experiences that reinforced the reality and importance of the universal design concept.

Student participants at the design charrette.

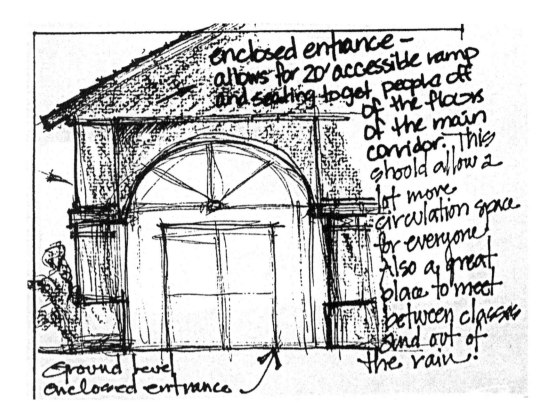

Student's sketch of proposal for change at the entrance to Allen Hall.

During the 'simulation' I realized that Allen Hall could not accommodate and support the activities of anybody...but especially people with disabilities. There were design flaws and obstacles for every user. The charrette exercise made a difference in the way I approach a design solution...incorporating concern for all users into my proposals for change. (Interior design student)

Evaluation

The impact of the symposium was visible over the course of the semester. Design responses in studio projects reflected increased student awareness and an understanding of universal design issues. In addition to results of pre- and post- symposium questionnaires, journal entries were monitored in several studio courses for reference to the symposium's effect on design projects. Project evaluations at mid-semester and final reviews were informally monitored for universal design content.

Based on the evaluation of semester project outcomes and verbal presentations, each of the symposium's objectives was realized to some degree: vocabulary, awareness of universal design as an issue, and its consideration as an integral part of the design process. The ongoing challenge is to continue emphasizing the concept that "good design is universal design" in studio solutions.

The assignment of an experienced advisor, access to vocal advocates, availability of a variety of audio-visual materials, and a sense of "mission" were essential components to organizing and implementing the symposium.

The Bridge to Universal Design

Proposal

MIT's proposal began with a description of the entrance to the institution. This served both to highlight the importance of reaching students who live and work in this environment and to introduce the mechanism through which the project would unfold.

MIT's front door is the entrance at 77 Massachusetts Avenue. Entering the building first requires ascending a long flight of stairs—a climb that is physically demanding, and no doubt quickens the pulse and increases one's blood flow. One arrives in the lobby of Building 7: the size of the lobby, the amount and quality of the light within, and especially the reverberation of the large space are all physical aspects of the experience of entry—an experience intensified by the exertion of the climb. While the experience of entering this building will have different effects on different people, the building and its entry seem to take themselves quite seriously, and the person who has made the climb and walked through the doors will have little doubt that this is an important place. Just as this passage is an important feature of the building's architecture, it is one that is changed or denied to anyone who cannot make the ascent, or whose sensory perception is different.

Len Morse-Fortier has a daughter with Down syndrome. His personal experiences motivated him several years ago to include an exercise on accessibility in his Introduction to Building Technology course. The exercise asked students to spend three hours using a wheelchair, making their usual MIT journeys. Although cast as a technical exercise, the instructor expected students to acquire more than simply a practical understanding of technical issues. They did. In addition to the assigned observations about ramp slopes, handrails, curb cuts, and sight-lines, students commented at greater length and with deeper feeling about the emotional aspects of their experience—expressing feelings of vulnerability, dependence, and exclusion.

Morse-Fortier and Reiter proposed to increase the number of students being exposed to universal design by introducing students in the Level I studio, both undergraduates and graduate students, to the physical and physiological aspects of architectural experience through experiential exercises and analyses of place experiences. Two daylong faculty workshops were proposed to give the Level I faculty opportunities to confront the issues and develop appropriate strategies for engaging the students.

Team members:

Leonard Morse-Fortier
Assistant Professor
Wellington Reiter
Assistant Professor

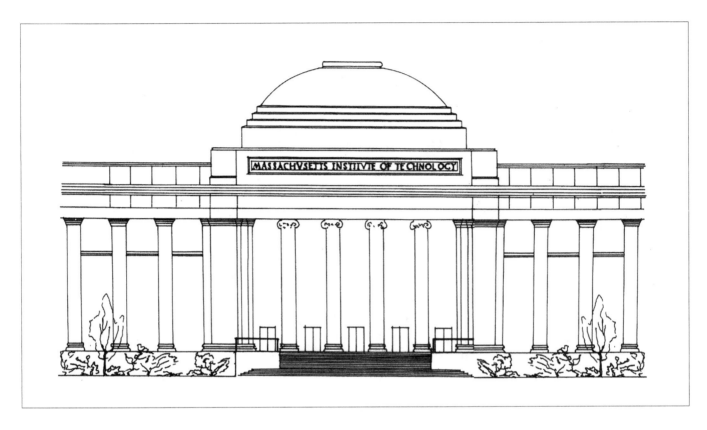

MIT's front door, the entrance at 77 Massachusetts Avenue.

Activity

The first project in the Level I Studio, titled "Axis and Access," was executed in the 1993 spring semester. Students were asked to consider the architectural image most frequently associated with the campus of MIT, the imposing Beaux Arts portico at 77 Massachusetts Avenue. The passage through this temple-like facade represents "entry" into MIT at both the practical and ceremonial level. Yet for some in the MIT community, the ritual of mounting the stairs, weaving in-between the huge columns, and passing through the brass doors is impossible, witnessed only secondhand. Students were asked to provide an architectural response that acknowledges the entire community of users.

Students were asked to address the following questions:

- Is an MIT experience minus the daily passage through the primary threshold of the campus necessarily less than, equal to, or possibly greater than the same set of circumstances with access? Why?

- Could you quantify in detail all of the sensory components that constitute the process of entry into this or any building? Based on what experience?

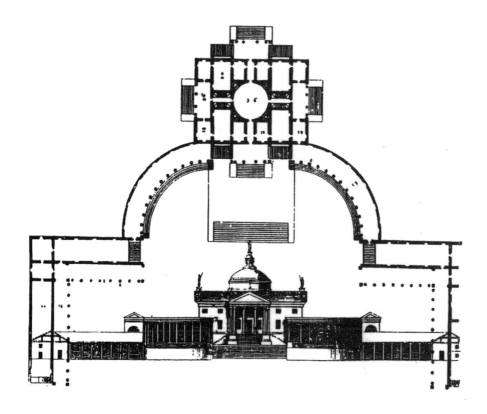

- What are the metaphoric and symbolic aspects of entry? What is a threshold? A door?

Palladio as a reference for the design of access.

The answers to these questions have ramifications not only for people with disabilities but for architecture itself. Frequently lost in the stylistic or theoretical discussion of contemporary architecture is the bald fact of its existence and our daily interactions with it.

Students were also asked to reflect on whether the typical stair/ramp duality is an architectural necessity or an ad hoc response to societal (and now governmental) demands for equal accessibility. Are there other possibilities that would diffuse the idea of two discrete paths? Is only one route a worthwhile objective? Should this issue be played out on the primary facades of public buildings where many other concerns are also competing for attention?

Following the UDEP colloquium, we made plans to integrate the topic of universal design into MIT's Level I studio in the 1993 fall semester. As Reiter was coordinating the studio for the fall semester, it seemed logical to include universal design as the unifying theme. Unfortunately, changes in faculty responsibilities combined with some faculty resistance made the universal design theme impossible. In one case, a faculty member had already developed the studio problem around a different theme, and in another case, the faculty member refused outright to weigh accessibility as more important than any other "practical" concern, and commented that all such constraints were inconsistent with the pedagogical aims of that particular studio.

We developed a new proposal to offer a special exploratory course over MIT's Independent Activities Period in January 1994. We proposed a four-week, intensive course in which students would revisit their fall-semester studio project with an eye toward identifying barriers and their causes. In part, the course description read:

This course is not a clinic on how to adapt a building design to meet the requirements of the ADA. It is a design studio that explores the issues of access and inclusion and introduces the principles of universal design into the design process. The ideal outcome is not a building design that can be adapted to meet the ADA, but one that so fully includes and accommodates individuals of all abilities that it needs no adaptation at all.

No one signed up for the course. Many architecture students use the IAP to serve unpaid internships in local firms, an investment towards securing future employment. Nevertheless, we were disappointed.

We persisted for one more semester. In spring 1994, Reiter taught a studio on "The Inhabited Bridge." This project explored a unique urban circumstance, the design of a new bridge over the Seine in Paris connecting the new colossal Bibliothèque de France and the opposite bank, which features Frank Gehry's recently completed American Center plus a vast contemporary park now under construction. A bridge at this location is a virtual certainty, a great deal of attention is being paid to the idea, and the studio had the potential to play a role in shaping the definition of the program. As the need for the bridge is born as much from ceremony as necessity, the bridge is more than just a simple crossing.

As part of the development of the project, we invited consultant Larry Braman, an architect who uses a wheelchair, to spend an afternoon in the studio. He shared with students his ideas about architecture, access, and circulation. Unfortunately, he was unable to be present for final jury review of the projects. From the final review, three projects were selected for further development. This development will take the form of streamlining presentation graphics, providing high quality reproductions, and supporting the inclusion of the projects in the final exhibition of competition entries at the Pompidou Centre.

Outcome

The initial project dealt with the classical design of the entrance to MIT. As background for dealing with the implications of this problem, the students were asked to attend a roundtable discussion with a variety of members of the MIT community for whom these issues are a fact of everyday life. The visiting panel of consultants was a particularly effective component: Gail, who has a sight impairment and a guide dog named Laura; Paul, who is blind and uses a cane to navigate; and Scott, who uses a power wheelchair. Each panelist discussed buildings and access, confusion and clarity. Paul commented that he loved architecture, that several of his friends are designers, and that he welcomes the opportunity to discover the "idea" of a building. Scott, talked about the issue of access and dignity, and told a story about taking his girlfriend out to dinner. The students empathized with the feeling of trying to impress someone when the restaurant has to let you in through the kitchen. Gail joked about training Laura to find attractive men. Overall, the consultants came across as people first; their disabilities and the effect of these on their daily lives emerged through their stories. Because the consultants were assembled and seated before the students arrived, the students did not actually see how these particular folks get around until after the discussion.

This experience with the consultants was overwhelming for many students. We were surprised by the anger that they expressed. The anger seemed to stem from a frustration that the built environment could be so cruel, but also from self-criticism: as design students, they were frustrated by their own lack of awareness. The level of emotional engagement suggested that the students would be likely to incorporate the principles of universal design in their design work. However, the effects of this experience seemed to wear off rather quickly.

Over the course of the studio, students became very interested in the experiential aspects of access. In response, we revised the requirements to exclude the proposal of a built "solution." Instead, students were instructed to focus on the experiential aspects of access, and to present their conclusions in any medium. Consequently, the products of the experience included pamphlets, recordings, drawings, and essays. One presentation included a recording of the background sounds together with a narrative of the journey from the student center across the street, up the stairs and into the building. Other, irreproducible work included a percussion piece reflecting the intensity of the experience. Overall, student work was creative and diverse. Nevertheless, the exercise was separate from the mainstream of studio design and seemed marginalized.

Fully one year later, we incorporated the ideas of universal access into the mainstream of a design studio and the results were much more gratifying, but paradoxical as well. The program of the "Inhabited Bridge" was a museum for the twenty-first century.

Inhabited bridge proposals for Paris, France.

The project required a synthesis of engineering, urban design, public space, and museology. A detailed basswood model of the site was created by the class and a high level of presentation quality was established as a result. All reviews were conducted in a juried format and were almost exclusively provided by outside visitors. The pace was brisk, the criticism pointed, and the atmosphere in the studio very positive. Student work included drawings and models at various scales and degrees of architectural resolution. Collectively, these models reveal the paradox alluded to above, and reflected upon below.

Reflection

For our initial exercise on "Axis and Access," the results were gratifying, but the subject became marginalized. Although universal access had been addressed within the studio, it was isolated from the mainstream studio design work. The students were sensitized and enthusiastic, but the problem was too sharply focused and, therefore, marginalized. A full year later, in search of a better way to introduce the subject into the studio, we were much more successful. A graduate level studio engaged the topic of universal design through a semester-long project, designing an inhabited bridge. Although not explicitly directed at the issue of accessibility or the ADA, this design problem lent itself to discussions of universal design by virtue of its site, building type (a pedestrian bridge), and focus on the idea of public space. Although this approach was in direct contrast to the investigation of accessibility from the previous year, we chose it purposely.

In the course of developing the Inhabited Bridge studio, we felt that to segregate the issue of accessibility from the general design problem would marginalize the issue and miscast opportunities as burdens. Therefore, the subject of accessibility was woven into the list of concerns along with many others with which the students were required to grapple. One of a number of guest critics, consultant Larry Braman, provided architectural criticism inextricably coupled with his unique perspective on access. As a direct result of our attempts at seamless integration, the evidence of the studio (models and drawings) may look suspiciously disinterested in the specifics of accessibility. The work looks very much like the production that one would normally expect from such a program and site. What this points out, in our opinion, is the limitation of the media and not the seriousness with which the students concerned themselves with the issue. Upon first glance, and without the benefit of the give-and-take that was the daily hallmark of the studio, it may be hard to decipher the works as being particularly attentive to the concerns of people with disabilities.

First, of course, these projects were not developed to a level of detail that could engage accessibility on an ergonomic level except in terms of access for wheeled vehicles. Because of its public nature and scale, however, together with the possibility of wheelchairs, the project admits strollers, roller-blades, and luggage dollies (train stations on either side of the river provide one excuse for making the crossing). As the designs are further scrutinized, it may be possible to see that attempts to create a fluid connection across the River Seine revealed themselves in the actual pedestrian avenues, the various sight lines, and the formal expression of connection. In many cases, the grade changes on either bank were handled with great ingenuity such that an unimpeded, or even better, an inviting threshold was created without distinction for shoes or wheels. This occurred, we believe, because the emphasis of the studio was on the nature of the public realm and concerns of inclusion of all types of people—both visitors and residents, economically privileged and homeless, able-bodied and disabled.

Our efforts in this studio were successful. However, that success must find its way into the culture of our school, and this will not be so easy to accomplish. Our exercise reached fifty students. In the recent studio, there were nine students. We hope that the visibility of the projects will enhance their reputation with the rest of the students, and we plan to meet with the entire studio faculty to discuss how universal design principles can be more fully included in the curriculum.

In closing, the following ruminations by Morse-Fortier emerged while grappling with the difficulties of integrating universal design into design teaching:

Most design studios do not develop projects beyond basic massing and formal issues, so the ergonomic issues of accessibility are largely irrelevant. Counter heights, door hardware, and the finer aspects of universal design are meaningless at that scale. In the typical architectural design studio, the only apparent accessibility issue involves wheelchair access and stairs. By not acknowledging the large population who have reduced ability, the issue of accessibility becomes marginalized. The number of persons in wheelchairs seems small, and the perceived importance of accessibility is weighed against the risks of breaking with architectural tradition. Tradition usually takes precedence.

Building placement, level change, vertical separation, and even stairs themselves are important components of architecture that also pose potential barriers to accessibility. It is hard to imagine the US Capitol Building without its front stairs, or on a smaller scale, MIT's entrance to Building 7 without its own ceremonial threshold flight. These formal features appear to clash head on with the formal implications of accessibility, and so it is understandable that the discourse on design considers the argument for accessibility to be intrusive.

Presently, the architectural palette includes level change as a tool for delimiting space. Unlike ceiling level shifts, color, texture, or even lateral shifts and partial walls, stairs and the level changes they announce read clearly in plan. Student designers are trained to develop their proposals in plan, and plans are submitted for design competitions and for presentations to clients. Attempts at describing architecture in experiential terms often fail when considering a proposal for unbuilt architecture. Our ability to "experience" the proposal depends upon our ability to infer from its plans something of the experience it promises. If that experience relies on moves outside of our traditions, or outside of what plans can convey, then we are unable to "see" them, and the building proposal is likely to be judged a failure.

When the ADA became law, like so many other laws, it was placed in the category of difficult real issues that may interfere with the design studio pedagogy. Structural considerations and energy issues have traditionally been accommodated by designers after the fact, considered to be unimportant to basic design or aesthetics. Accessibility, too, has been left until the end. Design proposals are reviewed as they approach their final refinements. If accessibility issues are introduced, they require a de-facto renovation or retrofit of the proposed scheme. By postponing discussion of accessibility until the final stages of design development, the barriers are embedded in the fundamental objectives of the design, and the introduction of a new value—accessible design—threatens the design proposal. Clearly, it is important to understand how barriers are introduced to be able to address accessibility at the earliest stages of design.

Acknowledgements

This project owes a debt of thanks to the following people, whose work, help, support, and encouragement provided whatever success was achieved: Consultant Larry Braman; Advisors Polly Welch and Elaine Ostroff; the MIT students of Level 1 and Level 2 studio; and for their individual contributions, Mike Reid and Noah Greenberg (Palladio), Chih-Jen Yeh, Winston Lim, and Robert Benson (bridge designs).

Infusing an Interior Design Program with Universal Design

Team members:

Barbara Flannery
Assistant Professor
Ken Special
Assistant Professor
Roberta Null
Associate Professor

Proposal

We proposed to infuse our program with the concept of universal design by implementing two different strategies. First, we would specifically incorporate universal design into studios and courses at every level of the program. All students in the program would be exposed to universal design by the end of the academic year and would re-encounter the concept in at least one course in subsequent years.

Second, we proposed reaching across academic levels, disciplines, and campuses by hosting a one-day universal design conference and one-day design charrette, and by creating a universal design resource library for students.

Our teaching objectives were twofold:

- To increase students' sensitivity to the "whole person," an approach to age-span and disability issues that gives equal consideration to social, psychological, and physical factors; and

- To make students aware of the full range of disabilities covered by the Americans with Disabilities Act, including mental, cognitive, and physical, and of the individual variability within a given disability.

Our notion was that these strategies would break down students' stereotypes through access to information, repeated exposure to issues, and opportunities for application in design. This approach is consistent with the concept of repetition, continuity, and progression set forth by the Foundation for Interior Design Education Research (FIDER), the accrediting body for interior design programs.

Activity

Six courses—five studios and one lecture course—were modified to include universal design issues. First-year students were introduced to the "whole person" approach to design in the introductory studio. Sophomores, who already have a required lecture course on design and human behavior that includes units on cultural diversity, the elderly, and the ADA, explored application of universal design through a class project.

Chapter 10: Miami University

Universal design was also incorporated into the junior and senior studios with progressively higher expectations for understanding and application. Projects at the upper division included designing recreational vehicles and a recreational community for people of differing abilities and across the lifespan; designing a retail space that conformed to the ADA; and a futuristic project that looked at both present and future technological advancements affecting design. In a multi-story design project at the senior level, one of the partners in the client firm was a wheelchair user.

During fall semester we also hosted a one-day conference on universal design followed by a one-day charrette incorporating universal design into the redesign of a university-owned conference center that was inaccessible.

Our objectives for these two events included the following:

- Involve students and faculty from several schools, representing a variety of disciplines.

- Include many users with different perspectives.

- Have multiple perspectives represented by national and regional speakers at the conference.

- Encourage students to apply their knowledge of universal design to a real design problem that included interior design, architecture, landscape architecture, and product design components.

- Stress the value of interdisciplinary approaches to universal design concepts, including access to a broader range of specialties and areas of expertise, access to a broader range of user needs through involvement of users, and the creation of better design solutions.

We involved potential participants, including faculty, users groups, and students, early in the planning process, which seemed to increase their investment and interest in the project. We found that they, in turn, recruited others to take part. Involving users in the project was an important objective for our project. We contacted on-campus student disability organizations and, as a starting point for community-wide user groups, Independent Living Options, a local organization in Cincinnati.

In deciding where to hold these events we had to accommodate the activities as well as to assure accessibility. We had two very different activities to accommodate—a conference and a charrette. For our mini-conference, we needed auditorium seating with enhanced sight-lines; for the charrette, we needed a classroom with movable tables and chairs, well-equipped with media (rear-screen multiple projection, sound amplification, VCRs, etc.). Access to the building from parking areas had to be considered so that equipment and individuals could easily enter and special parking permits could be obtained, if needed.

We debated whether to hold our charrette activity at the actual site—a university-owned log cabin used for retreats and small conferences. Because the space was off-campus (posing transportation problems), small in size, and inaccessible (which is why we selected it for the subject of our charrette design process), we decided that it was not an appropriate location for the charrette. Because the space was inaccessible, we also decided not to conduct a site visit that would exclude some people. Instead, we took slides and photographs and made a detailed videotape of the space. These materials, as well as building plans, were available to participants during the charrette.

We selected three national speakers for the mini-conference based on their expertise and the balance they would bring to the program. They included Robert Anders (our UDEP advisor) of Pratt Institute, Joe Meade of the USDA Forest Service, and Eleanor Smith of Concrete Change in Atlanta. We used regional speakers to fill out the program and provide additional perspectives in various areas of universal design. Most speakers also served as facilitators or judges during the charrette.

All participants received an information packet including: city and campus maps, an agenda of activities, participation certificate, evaluation forms, information about Miami University, handouts provided by speakers, a bibliography of universal design resources, and Title II and Title III highlights. We carefully considered how many universal design resources to include, and decided to be selective. Our criterion was to include things that were easy to read and directly usable for the charrette. For example, we did not include the complete version of Title II in the packet; instead we selected a summary article that charrette participants could understand more quickly.

This university-owned retreat and conference facility was the focus for a one-day design charrette.

Coordinating communication at an event for one hundred people involves everything from signs to audio-visual needs to sign language interpreters. We took communication a little further. At the beginning of each day we presented an overhead of that day's agenda. At the registration table, we had a large map showing the schools in attendance to enhance communication between participants from various universities. In the lobby we set up a browsing table with universal design literature.

Universal design literature was available for browsing by conference participants.

Our goals in marketing were to maximize diversity in participants, encourage representation from a variety of schools, let potential participants know about the quality of the planned events, and focus on activities that would be both fun, educational, and result in successful universal design solutions. We aggressively marketed the events well in advance using a variety of techniques with a variety of potential audiences.

We marketed to our own students by involving them in the planning process and by encouraging early commitments from them to participate. An upper-division student from our interior design program went to all studio classes to talk about the events, ensuring that all majors would know about the events. We found that having an enthusiastic student promote the events was an excellent complement to faculty efforts and increased student participation. We also tied into presentations by universal design speakers at the American Society of Interior Designers (ASID) Student Chapter meeting one week before the events to foster interest in and momentum for the universal design conference and charrette.

We also marketed to colleagues and students in other disciplines at the university by preparing a brief written announcement and invitation for students that focused on the events' appeal for nondesigners. We developed a poster promoting the event and got permission to post it across the campus; we contacted the university news bureau to cover our events and to write a description for publicity; and we put both a pre-event announcement and post-event story in the student newspaper.

Attracting a broad group of people from outside the university was very important. We contacted area disability organizations to invite members and to encourage participation. We were quite successful in this regard, and the several users at the events who served as resource people proved to be a strong point in participant evaluations. We marketed to non-student design groups by sending large mailings to members of the regional professional ASID chapter and to all interior design alumni within a 100-mile radius. We marketed to other schools in a multi-state region using personalized posters for each school and establishing a contact person at each school. We found that it was very important to have repeated contact with the participating schools.

We actively sought sponsors and donations to meet our budget. Herman Miller donated universal design templates (which also made students aware that these items are available) and Knoll donated architect scales. We also got sponsors for awards, including Miami University t-shirts, drink squeeze bottles, and monetary awards.

Outcome

Curriculum Enhancements. Students in four courses during fall semester were engaged in learning about universal design. Because we wanted to expose students to universal design principles in a direct way early in the program, we introduced several activities in the Design and Human Behavior course at the sophomore level. Students completed two questionnaires on universal design and persons with disabilities, drew themselves with a disability encountering a barrier, and assessed two environments for accessibility from a whole-person needs approach. Three weeks of lectures were devoted to disability and lifespan issues.

Many students, when asked about what they would consider to be disabilities, were able to list a wide range across all categories: sight, hearing, cognitive, and mobility. They did not, however, reflect that breadth of knowledge in the in-class assignment to draw themselves with a disability confronting an environmental barrier. Sixty-four of eighty-six drawings (74 percent) showed a person using a wheelchair, and the most common barrier was steps. Time was spent in class discussing the range of disabilities beyond mobility impairments. One reason for the heavy use of the wheelchair image may be the predominance of the wheelchair icon as a symbol of disability on signage.

The project assessing the campus and community buildings for appropriateness of use by people with a variety of disabilities increased student awareness and was a useful precursor to students' projects in the upper-division courses.

Studio courses at the first-year and upper-division levels focused on the specifics of the ADA, the technical and graphic considerations of universal design, and a job site visit to interview a university employee with a disability to receive firsthand information on interior design issues. Through these experiences, students were exposed to situations that many had not, up to this point, given much consideration. The final presentations of design studio projects, on the whole, reflected a marked increase in student awareness of the importance of universal design—both in their drawings and their presentations.

Conference and Charrette. For a 48-hour period in November 1993, in Oxford, Ohio, over 100 people came together to explore universal design. Participants included students, design practitioners, and persons with disabilities who served as consultants. Students from eight schools in the region attended. During the charrette, on the

Consultant input was critical to the quality of the final project solutions.

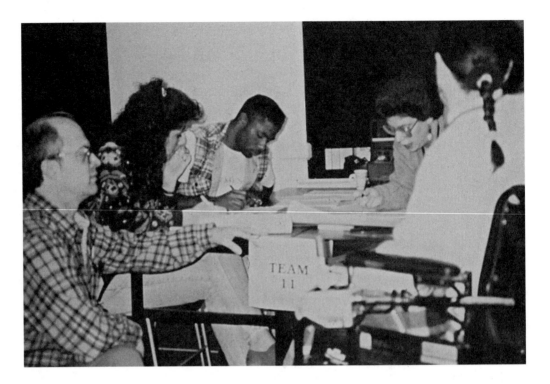

second day of the conference, each of ten teams produced a design solution to the charrette problem. Each team included students and at least one facilitator. Consultants served as facilitators to the teams and as floating advisors, moving from team to team to provide resources. This "floater" approach allowed each team greater access to people with a range of disabilities. The mini-conference and charrette sparked a great deal of discussion, particularly at the closing session of the charrette. New perceptions, awareness, and surprise at the depth of design considerations for universal design were topics of discussion.

The charrette design teams had a mix of academic levels (first-year, sophomore, junior, and senior), majors (design and non-design), and schools. Each team decided how to present its work, with the caveat that students rather than facilitators should make the actual presentation.

Facilitators' assistance to the design teams varied according to the individual's style and personality. Some fully participated in the development of the design solution; others served only as resources. One vocal facilitator presented the group's work despite the explicit instructions.

We developed evaluation criteria against which design solutions were to be judged and gave them to the design teams at the beginning of the charrette. The judges fine-tuned these criteria and allocated points to each project.

According to the judges, the uniqueness of the winning team's design solution was, in part, in the introduction to their design. The team focused on the design concept, including a description of the feeling and atmosphere of the space they created. By giving considerable detail to the solution in the form of detail drawings, a floor plan, and a site plan, the team greatly enhanced the judges' understanding of its design intent.

We documented the event for publicity and grant purposes. We used a combination of techniques including videotaping the entire mini-conference and selected portions of the charrette, as well as taking slides and photographs of both events. To facilitate later display, each team mounted its work on two foamcore boards. Having participants complete evaluations was also part of our documentation. Since our event was two days long and some participants attended only one day, we color coded pre-test and post-test evaluations to allow us to easily separate them and to minimize participant confusion. In addition, we felt that it was important to acknowledge all event participants, and not just teams that won awards. Certificates of participation were given to all attendees.

Charrette team at work.

Reflection

The approach of infusing universal design concepts across the curriculum is one we feel was successful and we will continue. Because we talked about universal design in a positive and frequent way, student enthusiasm for the design conference and charrette was increased. We feel that many students have embraced the concepts of universal design wholeheartedly, seeing universal design as an important and creative challenge. They will continue to do so as practitioners in the future.

The winners display the results of their successful collaboration.

We learned a great deal from hosting two back-to-back events. Our experience and insights are presented in a separate paper on organizing design events to teach universal design.

The inclusion of consultants on the design teams in the charrette was invaluable. They added a dimension that was both necessary and appreciated by the students who participated. We cannot imagine running such an event without the consultants and intend to include more consultants in studio projects in future courses.

In the future we would assign a student/staff-person liaison to each speaker. We felt that the conference would have proceeded more smoothly

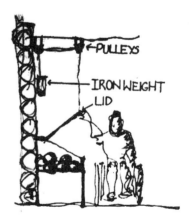

Detailed graphics enhanced project presentation.

if a single person had been assigned to take care of each speaker's needs, including confirming audio-visual requirements and travel arrangements. Although staff-intensive, having personal assistants for each speaker would avoid miscommunications and oversights.

Securing the services of a sign language interpreter should have been done well in advance of the event. Since we had not used a sign language interpreter before, there were several surprises for us in the process. It seemed logical that access for participants who are hearing impaired would be provided through university resources in the same vein that physical access is provided. We found out after budget planning that we would be responsible for the cost of the interpreter. In the end, our division contributed to the cost on a one-time only basis.

Because the event was long, more than one interpreter was needed. Interpreting is intensive work and interpreters need to take breaks. We were fortunate to have a gracious interpreter who carried on despite the lack of backup. We also learned that lighting the interpreter is critical during slides and other audio-visual presentations where room lighting is dimmed. By providing the interpreter with an agenda and description of media, she would have been able to identify unique requirements.

Making a parking plan well in advance is critical. Ground transportation became a serious problem because of the lack of accommodation by the university and the design of newer model cars. We were surprised to learn that lift-equipped university vans could not be used for a university event. They were available only to Miami University students for the purpose of attending classes. Even though they would not be in use at the time we needed them, we were unable to make special arrangements for our event. One speaker who used a wheelchair could get into a large two-door car with a bench seat because of the wider door openings and seat configuration. However, there are no two-door cars in our university motor pool, nor were any available at local rental agencies.

Evaluation

While pre-test and post-test data were collected for the design conference and charrette, different evaluators were used in the various classes. Questionnaire results from classes indicated that students were aware of the Americans with Disabilities Act and had differing levels of understanding of universal design. We administered one questionnaire with a series of true-false questions (N=134) and concluded that the instrument was not particularly useful in assessing student knowledge. An open-ended questionnaire (N=98) that we developed was more informative because we were able to see that there was a great deal of variation in student knowledge and interpretation of issues of universal design. Our questions included:

- Have you heard of the Americans with Disabilities Act? If so, what do you know about it?

- What conditions are considered to be disabilities? How many people with disabilities are there in the United States?

- List five of what you would consider to be the most important goals for designing for people with disabilities.

- What specific design criteria do you already know about for designing for people with disabilities?

- What is universal design?

- What are the goals of universal design?

At the conference and charrette we were concerned about getting all participants to fill out evaluation forms. We stressed their purpose and importance several times throughout the events and still had a relatively low response rate. Our numeric evaluation results were based on asking participants to evaluate the two days on a five-point scale, with zero indicating "poor" and four indicating "excellent." The mean score for the mini-conference was 3.6, with twenty participants responding. The mean score for the charrette was also 3.6, with thirty-four participants responding. In spite of low response rates, we feel confident that both days were successful. The few negative comments primarily focused on time issues, such as starting on time and allowing more time for team interaction and the presentations at the charrette.

In the written evaluation, two things were consistently rated as positive by the participants. The first was the quality of the speakers. All three national speakers were extremely well-received, with participants commenting on what they learned, the excellent presentation styles, and the beneficial use of visual material. The second consistent comment was the success of including people with disabilities as speakers, resource people, facilitators, and judges. Many participants commented on how much they learned, how helpful it was, and that it was enjoyable.

Chapter 10: Miami University

The following comments, in many cases reflecting the views of several participants, are drawn from the open-ended questions on the event evaluation forms.

This should be required of all design students. It's a great way of making people aware. I hardly knew anything about ADA until yesterday. It has totally changed my outlook about design, in a positive way.

The best part of the charrette was the opportunity to work with students from other institutions, with physically challenged persons, and other professionals.

Even though this is a conference type experience, the reality of "stress" was still present. This time, it was positive stress!

The best part of the mini-conference was being able to work with different people and get input from different professionals, the subtleties that you usually don't think about, and becoming more aware.

I got to learn lots of stuff from many different people. I got a chance to interact with students from other schools and see how they do things. I learned so much about universal design—we are exposed to it at school but only briefly and in a limited amount.

Keep doing things like this. It gets info out to students. There is so much I learned this weekend!

After several months of post-event reflection, we continue to believe that this event was significant in its impact on participants—students, professors, professional designers, and user groups.

Acknowledgements

We would like to thank the following individuals and firms for their participation and immeasurable contributions: Consultants and Facilitators—Bob Anders, Suzanne Carney, Marcia Cassidy, Owen Cooks, Bernie Dahl, Gail Dellapiana, Dan Depetro, Dianne Dunn, Caroline Everington, Dorothy Fowles, Dixie Harmon, Jane Hughes, Susan Jackson, Laura Kelly, James Landa, Daria Mauer, David Matthews, Lisa McPherson-Corbett, Joe Meade, Wayne Meyer, Wendy Olmstead, John Peaslee, James Postell, Liz Sanders, Eleanor Smith, Alan Weir, Sheila Zwelling; Staff—Katie Heintzman, Angie Schuckmann, Mike Smith, Andrea Turner, Becca Wanzo; and Sponsors— Creative Crafts; Kinko's; The Miami Co-op; Pizza Hut; The Shriver Center Bookstore; Singer Wallcovering; Snyder's Camera Art & Gift; Subway; Ward's One-Hour Photo.

Michigan State University – East Lansing, Michigan
Department of Human Environment and Design

Embracing Universal Design at All Levels of the Curriculum

Team members:

Roberta Kilty-Padgett
Associate Professor
Lily DeLeon
Visiting Assistant Professor

Proposal

In Michigan State University's FIDER-accredited four-year interior design curriculum, barrier-free design has been a component of courses since long before the adoption of the Americans with Disabilities Act. During the 1992–93 academic year, in response to this Act, guest speakers were brought into many of the courses to help students identify the differences in the new requirements and the impact on design practice. In 1993–94, the faculty wanted students to move beyond code requirements and embrace the larger concept of universal design. The Universal Design Education Project (UDEP) at Michigan State University focused on expanding existing curricular and course content related to teaching universal design to specifically include issues of mental and cognitive disability.

A note must be made about terminology. At Michigan State University the terms *disabled* and *disability* mean incompetent or disqualified. These are considered medical terms rather than civil rights terms. The preferred terminology for a person with a disability is *handicapper,* which denotes equal opportunity and equality in competition. Rather than referring to a person with a disability, the term "characteristic" is substituted, as in "visual characteristic." While this usage is not accepted nationally, nor consistently even in Michigan, students learned that terminology differs by state, region, and nation and that they should use terminology appropriate to their audience.

Four objectives were identified for implementing this project. One was to introduce the concept of universal design in courses at all levels, while building the information base according to subject matter sequencing. This meant that interior design faculty, in addition to the co-investigators, had to make a commitment to include the concept in their courses as they deemed appropriate, which they did. They also had to be able to access universal design information provided by Adaptive Environments. The second objective was to develop and test instructional methods and materials in design studios. The third was to document the process of integration, and the fourth was to evaluate the impact and effectiveness of the approach, thereby facilitating replication and improvement. The investigators did not want students to perceive universal design application as a limited, one-time exercise, but as an ongoing, integral approach to all their projects and to their work in professional practice.

Chapter 11: Michigan State University

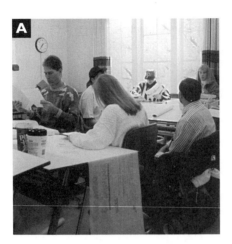

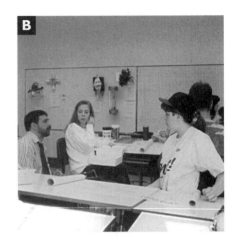

Activity

When dealing with innovation, it is difficult to know beforehand how and where to introduce new ideas and techniques most effectively. Four courses were initially targeted for integrating universal design across all levels of the curriculum. Three of the courses were taught in the fall semester of 1993: HED 150, Interior Design Drafting (for freshmen and sophomores); HED 342, Human Dimension and Interior Space (junior level); and HED 442, Interior Design Residential and Contract I (senior level). HED 840, Design Analysis and Programming (graduate course), was taught during the spring semester of 1994.

By its own momentum, this project perpetuated itself. When fall semester ended, the investigators expanded the project in succeeding courses: HED 352, Interior Design Synthesis II, where the residential context progressed into the commercial/contract realm; and HED 452, Interior Design Synthesis III, in which students pursued the design development of projects begun in HED 442. Only the four initial courses are described in this chapter.

In the drafting course, HED 150, the concept of universal design was introduced along with the application of code requirements. In HED 342 and HED 442, new content included issues related to people with mental and cognitive characteristics in commercial and residential-living situations. Seniors had previously taken the human dimension course without the content on people with cognitive characteristics. In HED 840, students examined existing facilities for their use and meaning. The universal design concept was integrated into both the programming and evaluation components. In all four courses faculty administered a pre-test and post-test questionnaire, developed by the UDEP sponsors, to document changes in awareness.

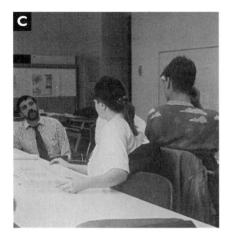

Anticipating that students might have difficulty accepting handicappers' participation in the studio, the investigators had planned to have students take lecture courses on universal design before the studio encounter. This was not possible prior to teaching the studio courses in the fall semester of 1993. Students knew at the beginning of the term that handicappers would be present in the studio and discussions about terminology and the meaning of universal design preceded the handicappers' involvement. However, it takes time for people to overcome their initial discomfort. Body orientation and eye contact are behaviors that can only be learned in the presence of others.

Consultants were an essential ingredient to the project and included handicappers and people with expertise in various characteristics. Selection of consultants was aimed at representing a number of characteristics, including mental and cognitive. Curriculum development proceeded in consultation with a representative from Michigan State University's Office of Handicapper Services, with members of its Student Advisory Board, as well as with the University's Retiree Service Corporation, Office of Veterans' Affairs, and the director of Michigan's Council on Developmental Disabilities.

The co-investigators divided the teaching responsibilities, and each monitored a part of the curriculum for course content continuity. Both worked on developing for faculty use a centralized information source containing universal design guidelines. Interior design faculty cooperated by sharing course syllabi and project descriptions. They turned to the co-investigators for universal design materials.

Interior design student explaining her bathroom layout to a consultant.

Outcome

HED 150, Interior Design Drafting. This is an architectural drafting course. Its objectives are proficiency in mechanical drafting and architectural lettering; understanding the various building components and how spaces are organized efficiently for human activities; and some barrier-free and life-safety codes. Starting in the fall semester of 1993 and continuing into spring semester, the course emphasized universal design for the first time. Teaching responsibility in both semesters was shared with graduate teaching assistants, who were also introduced to the universal design teaching strategy.

The first assignment integrated the students' new knowledge about universal design into lettering exercises, by interpreting information extracted from UDEP resource materials. For an assignment on line weights, students drafted annotated scale drawings of facilities such as ramps and toilet rooms. To learn about metric and English scales, students drafted a complete residential floor plan for a wheelchair user and detailed a bedroom space for two wheelchair users. An exercise tracing different views of a wheelchair sensitized students to the importance of circulation clearances and turning radii. Consultants did not participate at this level.

The pre-test, administered at the first class, indicated that most students were able to define universal design. The definitions show a range of understanding as to what universal design is:

Design that places cupboards, sinks, electric outlets, and knobs at heights convenient to most anyone.

Design that must have certain numbers and types of barrier-free units—as in hotels, apartments, etc.

Design based on the majority of the world comforts.

Design to benefit all people, accommodating different needs for different people.

Design that is able to change/adapt to meet needs.

[Design] that can be enjoyed by everyone, handicapper or not.

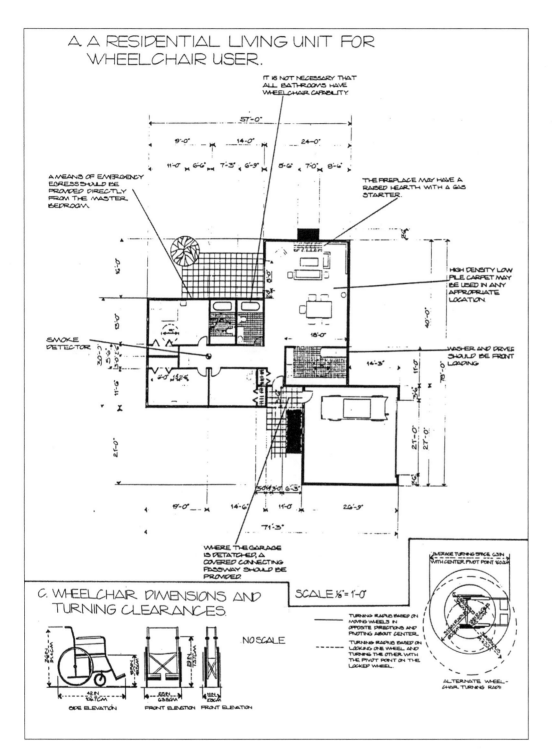

Residential living unit for a wheelchair user by an interior design student enrolled in HED 150, a beginning-level class.

In the post-test, students demonstrated their broader understanding of universal design:

The right of disabled persons to have proper needs fulfilled in all spaces.

All buildings that are not residential have to be handicapper accessible.

Student tests dimensions and construction of manikin prior to assembly.

Most significant was the students' new awareness of the rights of handi-cappers to use facilities and their realization that barrier-free access must be in public spaces as well as residential settings. The cyclical process of exploration, evaluation, and redevelopment in design problem solving required the students to develop solutions that uniquely combined aesthet-ics with accessibility.

Although some students found lettering exercises tedious at the begin-ning, they considered the exercise to be very informative, particularly regarding graphic symbols to indicate barrier-free access, space planning, and furniture arrangement. Students' acceptance of repetitive lettering and drafting practice grew as the course progressed and discussions made its relevance clear. Students incorporated project materials in their reference files as examples of an expanding graphic vocabulary.

HED 342, Human Dimensions. Taught in two lectures and one studio meeting per week, this junior-level course addressed ergonomics and anthro-pometrics. In the studio, students designed either a domestic food preparation and dining area or a bedroom and bath area incorporating universal design values. In the first part of the studio project, students worked cooperatively and individually to ana-lyze the needs of a family group whose statures represented the 97.5 and 2.5 per-centiles—a 58.7-inch female and a 74-inch male. Each student identified and addressed two additional characteristics for which to design.

Following initial exploration of anthropometric data, the students completed awareness exercises and developed their first design solutions with consultant input. They constructed scaled working manikins representing the range of users and partic-ipated in several empathic experiences. Students were not permitted to scrap their first solutions. Instead, they re-evaluated and transformed their designs in response to new criteria that emerged from the empathic experiences and from critiques. Working in teams, students evaluated their decisions, critiquing clearance and reach patterns, equity in privacy and group accommodation, sequence and frequency of use principles, and, to some degree, cost. They used a scroll format to facilitate idea generation and communication and constructed foamcore models to test solutions.

Consultants played an important role in the critiques and students responded to their presence with appropriate presentation devices such as tactile models and drawings.

Final revisions were a team effort. While unusual, this was done so that students would learn to apply the graphic ideation process in a group context and to make the logistics of model making workable within the studio setting. At the final critique, students presented selected projects and consultants evaluated the scroll closures for universal fit.

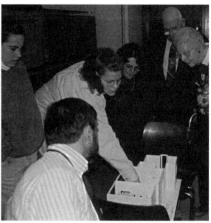

Student explains a residential design proposal in model form to consultants.

One of the objectives of this course was to dispel students' stereotypes by introducing them to people with cognitive characteristics. The investigators consulted Gerry Mutty of the Michigan Council on Disabilities for advice. He advised against taking students to an institution. The most positive approach, he suggested, would be to invite specific individuals to the classroom and asked them to relate their personal experiences and how the physical environment is problematic for them.

Prior to input from people with cognitive characteristics, one of the junior class design teams became interested in development of a time-out room. While the actual practice of providing a time-out room is a rare occurrence, used only in unique situations, the students' interest in designing a time-out space persisted, even after hearing a presentation on cognitive characteristics and meeting the consultant. In the process, students learned important design considerations, including striving for simplicity rather than complexity, providing restful spaces in terms of visual and acoustical attributes, and providing order, whether or not the solution is a separate space.

Consultant tests a universally designed scroll closure.

Students in this course were required to keep a journal about their empathic experiences and their interactions with consultants. Excerpted from a wealth of material are the following entries:

Our group used the green glasses today to give the effect of tunnel vision. It was very hard to see. We found that textural surfaces helped us and it helped when there was a change in the texture and great color change. People either ignored us or were extra nice, such as the girl at the counter in the Union store. She placed the candy in Sarah's hand rather than on the counter. It was especially hard to figure out which candy was which. We also used the ear plugs to resemble deafness. The sound was muffled and we only understood bits of the sentences....

Section of kitchen and dining area was rendered with puffy paint to make it tactile.

I also used the wheelchair. I never realized just how hard it is to manage in one. My arms were killing [me] from trying to get up the many slopes and ramps, and it was hard to keep a straight-line. It takes a lot of confidence and arm power. People treated me differently. They got out of my way and ignored me like they didn't want to be near me or just smiled. The bathroom was very hard to use, another place you need upper body strength and arm strength....

After weeks of interacting with client representatives, I feel I am much more sensitive to the needs of people with disabilities. It amazes me how by lowering shelf heights, or towel bars, or changing the direction of a door swing, designers can accommodate a higher percentage of people. This project is teaching me to think a new way. Normally, I would design an area and accommodate someone like me —my comfortable reach, heights.... I know now that "me" isn't average or normal. I need to broaden my scope. I like this project because it is challenging my thinking. The representatives are very helpful in starting my thinking. The smallest suggestion or problem can make such a difference in a design.

Lighting has an impact on one with a cognitive characteristic. A good mechanism to have are dimmers to control brightness.... Also having the living space organized in a manner where things stay the same so people with a cognitive deficit will not feel uneasy with things out of place and not know where things are. Also color coordinating is very helpful. In the house there also needs to be sound control. Excessive sound creates a problem and becomes overwhelming.

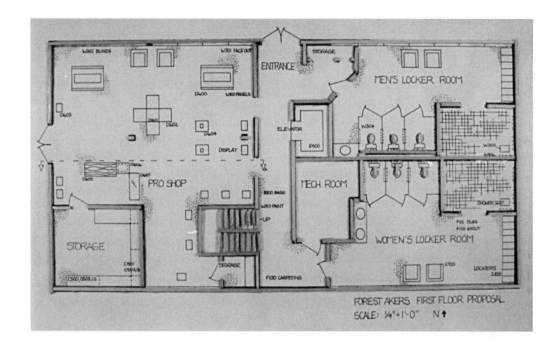

Tactile floor plan prepared by a senior student using balsa wood to cue consultants with visual characteristics.

HED 442, Interior Design Residential and Contract I. This lecture/studio class emphasized programming and schematic development within a universal design framework. It was an excellent vehicle for determining how well students would apply the universal design concept while incorporating new information on mental and cognitive characteristics. People with cognitive and visual characteristics were guest speakers.

The end product for this course was a program document including design schematics. Students' projects included a broad range of facilities: residential (bed and breakfast) facilities, commercial spaces including restaurants, an ecclesiastical project, health-care facilities, museum and exhibition spaces, and offices. Each student team kept a weekly log for effective project management.

Three design exercises supported development of the program document. Students were asked to set themselves up as ten-person design firms. In approximately thirty minutes, they developed a design philosophy using brainstorming and role playing. Another assignment had students develop a corporate logo for their small design teams of three to five people. Each team was required to design a symbol that would represent the design team's image and would act as a locational device. Among other requirements, the design had to have a strong three-dimensional component that could be read easily through touch alone. Each design had to be enhanced by a sound that captured its essence. When these were played at the presentation, the consultant with a visual characteristic was able to easily recognize and comprehend two of the ten sounds.

Chapter 11: Michigan State University

In the first oral presentations, students were only partially successful in communicating to the consultant with a visual characteristic. The first problem students encountered was how to describe their work explicitly rather than pointing to drawings and saying "over here" or "over there." Students learned to present using compass points—north, south, east, and west—to describe visual materials in an imageable way, to prepare tactile floor plans, to have problem statements printed in Braille, and to key drawings sequentially in a tactile manner. The students' goal became presenting their materials in a way that the person with a visual characteristic would receive information at the same time as others.

About halfway through the semester the investigators distributed the following question: "Please describe the concept of universal design as you see it. Has it changed since your experience in HED 342 last year? Has it changed since the beginning of HED 442?" In the responses, one senior of the twenty-five students responding still equated universal design with barrier-free design. The remaining twenty-four responses indicated an understanding that universal design includes all people. Eight students clearly stated that their concept had changed since the previous year. Seventeen stated it had changed since the beginning of HED 442.

Working model for logo in HED 442 combines symbols for the design process, elements of classicism, and a human figure that rotates through battery operation. It is accompanied by the sound of a ticking clock.

I see the concept of universal design as designing for the general public which includes people of all sizes and with all characteristics. My outlook has changed in that now universal design is not an option, it is a necessity. One should not even question it—they should do it automatically....

Last year I learned the basics of universal design. To me, it is simply making an environment usable for all people. I love the idea. It just makes so much sense. I guess I can understand how current professionals may turn their noses up at universal design because it seems so constraining to them—having all sorts of new clearances and considerations to abide by—it's more work. But what about all of the people that past designs have disabled because they couldn't use a space to its full potential? We were constraining ourselves. Universal design isn't about making things more difficult to design. It is about making things more simple to use....

I guess the thing I've learned most this semester is how very necessary it is that we listen, and hear, what people say about being disadvantaged by one's environment. Many new considerations have been added to my mental library. What people want to be addressed as. What they need to be able to get full use from their surrounding environments. I never thought about cognitive characteristics and how drastically a space could affect someone with a cognitive characteristic. That real-ization was very exciting for me. Also, one of the biggest problems I have is when people (design students) make such an issue of handicapper accessibility. It is important, I agree, but it is so overstated right now. It isn't an additional, "special" consideration—it is the norm… designing for everyone….

HED 840, Design Analysis and Programming. This graduate-level course covered programming methodology for generating and collecting data to determine design requirements in facility planning and management as well as design analysis to determine congruence between people, environment, and process. Students examined existing facilities in terms of use and meaning.

Consultants did not participate because actual facility users were available to meet with students. The graduate students applied universal design concepts in structured assignments. They used analysis methods such as observation of physical traces and human activities, focused interviews, photo documentation, and archival research. Students evaluated an existing facility from two perspectives: a personal viewpoint regarding building access and wayfinding, and a comparison of the facility to a set of criteria, in this case the Americans with Disabilities Act Accessibility Guidelines (ADAAG). This enabled students to appreciate some of the problems posed by physical barriers and to recognize the range of possible solutions while providing them with a systematic approach to analysis.

They also developed environment-behavior hypotheses, based on the intent of the ADA legislation, thus moving beyond code requirements. In the last assignment the students used nonparticipatory observation techniques and met with a number of actual users on-site over a period of time. On the post-test questionnaire, six out of seven students explained universal design and the Americans with Disabilities Act appropriately.

Consultant Participation. Eight people with specific characteristics, ranging in age from thirteen years old to mid-eighties, were consultants to classes during the year. One consultant had a cognitive characteristic. Five consultants had mobility characteristics and used assistive devices ranging from wheelchairs to walkers. The two consultants with visual characteristics had different kinds of experiences: being without sight since birth and losing sight over time. Two consultants had auditory characteristics.

People with particular expertise also served as consultants to the classes, including a lifespan coordinator for an intergenerational center, a cardiac rehabilitation specialist, and a social worker whose child developed seizures during infancy. A graduate of Michigan State University's interior design program who is a practicing interior designer,

Thirteen-year-old consultant discusses her personal experiences negotiating the environment with interior design juniors.

advocate, and specialist in barrier-free design attended lectures and studios at the junior and senior levels. Her summary of the experience included the following:

As I conversed with the students, I felt very proud of their enthusiasm for what I had considered... as a student, "criteria for a grade requirement." Even though barrier-free and the human scale was encouraged... I did not have the same excitement that has been conveyed and projected as I visited the classroom. At first I thought maybe the excitement was biased when I would converse with students, since I was in the classroom and possibly the comments would be slight. However, as the semester progressed, it was obvious to me that the motivation was within the students, and I have not heard of one negative attitude. If only everyone had that enthusiasm.

The consultants stimulated the students to ask questions about how well different environments worked for them as individuals. They were able to reach the students on a personal level, developing rapport within an open atmosphere. Even though consultants may not have felt they could contribute very much in terms of design, as their classroom experience expanded, they realized the depth and value of their knowledge and contributions. They were eager to continue with the project during spring semester. The thirteen-year-old was very nervous at being in a college classroom. She overcame her initial apprehensions when the students put her at ease, and they thoroughly enjoyed working together.

Consultants learned to project themselves into the spaces designed by students. An elderly couple in their eighties was so excited to be involved that they voluntarily took measurements at home to give students accurate sizing information. During junior critiques, a consultant with a mobility characteristic and one with a visual characteristic worked well as a team. At times one consultant's recommendation was contradicted by another consultant. Each consultant provided guidance by identifying the problem and the need, but resolving the conflicts was left to the students. An example was hard *versus* soft flooring in the kitchen area. What would facilitate easy movement for the wheelchair user might simultaneously become hazardous for the person with a visual characteristic when spillage occurred. Some spirited interaction with a consultant left one student remembering for life how to lay out a shower for wheelchair users. This consultant enjoyed attending classes so much that he preferred being in the classroom to being in his office.

During fall semester the seniors seemed hesitant to engage in conversation with the consultants on a voluntary basis. During spring semester work sessions with consultants, scheduled in twenty-minute blocks for groups of three to five students, seemed to facilitate communication. It was not possible to objectively measure an increase in the amount of interaction between seniors and consultants during spring semester, but evidence of increased awareness appears in the work of some students. The fact that all independent-study requests came from seniors seems to demonstrate that the universal design concept touched a number of individuals who recognized its value and wanted to enhance their own experiences prior to graduation.

Juniors, however, seemed transformed by their contact with consultants, as evidenced by this typical journal entry:

> *I feel very fortunate to have been able to communicate and brainstorm with our client representatives. I feel like I'm getting closer to actually designing something that has purpose and could actually be used.*

During the final critique in the junior class, the faculty asked the students whether to keep the consultants. The answer was a resounding yes.

Reflection

It is clear to the investigators that experiential learning is an effective technique for educating prospective designers about universal design that directly benefits everyone. For the investigators, this experience was the most rewarding in their twenty-year teaching careers. Surprisingly, the job of teaching took care of itself. The students and consultants taught each other more effectively than an individual faculty member could.

The investigators believe that without user involvement in the design process and without the examination of human performance in the physical environment, the students' level of awareness, understanding, and sensitivity as well as their sense of commitment could not have developed so quickly. When student assistants met with the UDEP advisor, they cited consultant participation as the most valuable aspect of the courses. In the future, bringing consultants in for group sessions during lecture time would encourage more equitable student-consultant interaction.

Faculty also participated in the focus courses, attending guest lectures and student presentations. One faculty member who said she was uncomfortable speaking directly to handicappers appreciated being able to attend critiques and learn from the consultants.

To integrate universal design into the curriculum and professional practice, the support and commitment of people outside academia is also needed. A pool of

"...experiential learning is an effective technique for educating prospective designers about universal design..."

"field" experts and user/clients who can enrich the teaching-learning experience is an indispensable resource.

Although the co-investigators had intended to develop a matrix of suggested project categories as vehicles for teaching universal design, they realized very quickly that universal design applies to all projects in addition to all people. Their focus changed from trying to design problems that emphasized the concept to demonstrating that the concept applies to all projects. In an ideal world, universal design would not have to be called out. Project parameters were specifically designed to incorporate universal design criteria without labeling them as such. The investigators structured the universal design content to gradually develop in complexity appropriate to design studio levels.

The co-investigators proposed to evaluate the effectiveness of these curricular strategies. Pre-test and post-test questionnaires were administered to participating students, consultants, and faculty, comparing levels of knowledge and awareness, opinions regarding quality of experience, and the significance of courses in contributing towards social-responsiveness. Human subjects' approval was required prior to implementation of this project. Questionnaire responses are being analyzed. The data would appear to support what is evident from the students' design work: students' awareness, knowledge, and sensitivity to the needs of all people have grown from this experiment.

The investigators are reviewing the content of lecture and studio courses to document the degree to which universal design concepts are being incorporated over four successive semesters. Student projects in specific courses are being analyzed for content to track participating students through upper design courses, to analyze the degree to which their design solutions apply universal design concepts learned during the experiment period, and to determine the success of the current teaching approach compared to the year preceding the experiment.

Three Projects for Teaching Universal Design Concepts

Faculty coordinator:

Shauna Corry
Assistant Professor

Proposal

A primary objective of interior design educators is to sensitize students to current issues that will have a lasting impact on the profession. By exposing interior design students to real-life situations and exploring innovative solutions, educators can successfully prepare students to meet the challenges of the working world. Universal design is such an issue.

The purpose of this project was to develop and implement universal design teaching units in the course content of the second-year design process studio. Five units were proposed, one to correspond with each phase of the design process—research/programming, conceptual design, schematic design, design development, and documentation. Each unit would address the issues of lifespan design through a humanistic and holistic approach.

The challenge of this project was to integrate issues and concepts of universal design into the curriculum at an early stage in the students' development. As this project did not receive full funding, I tried to introduce and reinforce the concepts of universal design while completing the existing course requirements.

Activity

Universal design was introduced in the first sophomore studio course, Design Process 1. Fourteen students were enrolled; the focus of the semester was residential design. This is the first environmental design course for interior design students. In their freshman year they focus on abstract two- and three-dimensional design problems and drafting skills, but do not engage in designing built environments.

The course description reads: "Application of design theory and process to analyze and design environments. Emphasizes programming, schematics and design development." The two most important course goals were "to understand and apply functional and human factors to interior environments" and "to develop an awareness of and sensitivity to the theory of universal design."

A series of three major projects were developed to focus on one or more of the course goals. Projects varied in scale and consisted of residential spaces. Each project emphasized universal design and the students were asked to address this concept in all phases of their projects.

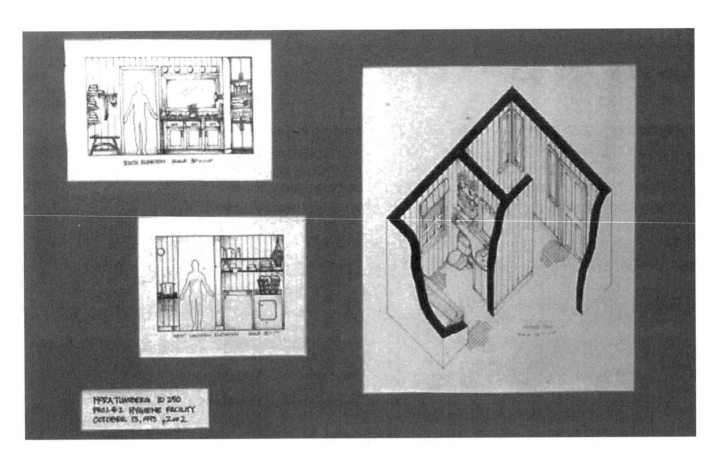

Detailed elevations of a family bathroom shows design sensitivity for a client who has a sight impairment.

Project 1: Analysis of a Problem Environment. This introductory project required the students to combine and apply their knowledge of anthropometrics, proxemics, and ergonomics by analyzing a problem environment on the campus or in the Fargo-Moorhead area. Each student chose a problem environment, one which he had experienced and found to be uncomfortable. The students analyzed the environments for how people experienced the space in terms of function, accessibility, ease of use, circulation, patterns, zoning, materials, and aesthetics. The students were then asked to redesign the space according to the needs of the users.

Project 2: Hygiene Facility. This project focused on residential planning with an emphasis on universal design and the design process. The purposes of this project were: 1) to study and research ergonomics and anthropometrics in a family bathroom; 2) to introduce students to working with a client and designing to meet that client's needs and wants; 3) to introduce students to clients who have sensory impairments; and 4) to introduce them to all phases of the design process. The students selected a client and conducted research on that client's disability. The designs that developed were very sensuous and creative spaces.

Project 3: Lake Cabin Final Project. The students were required to design a living space for a client with a mobility impairment. Consultants with disabilities were used extensively in this project: the consultant with multiple disabilities visited the studio four times during the course of the project.

In addition to the projects, the students made two field trips: one to a residence that was designed exclusively for two people with mobility impairments and another to Easy Street, a rehabilitation center in St. Luke's Hospital. They also participated in a sensitivity training workshop. Resources from the UDEP Colloquium were extremely helpful to the instructor in preparing lectures and to the students as design tools.

Outcome

Over the course of the semester, the students were introduced to and interacted with eight consultants with disabilities and a family member of one consultant. They also attended a seminar on growing up with a physical disability. The consultants included an elderly couple; a couple with mobility impairments, both of whom use wheelchairs; a man who has a sight disability; and a woman who has mobility, speech, and hearing impairments and was accompanied by her father.

The consultants generously gave their time, shared their experiences with the class, and critiqued each student's work. The students were, at first, hesitant and uncomfortable around the consultants. After spending time with each other and asking questions, the students, the instructor, and the consultants developed good working relationships and friendships.

The students initially expressed some concerns about communicating with two of the consultants who had speech and hearing impairments resulting from brain-stem injuries. The students asked to work with other consultants, people with whom they felt they could communicate more easily. At the seminar on growing up with disabilities, the students had spent time with three college students who had mobility impairments and felt these individuals would be easier to communicate with. I felt it was important for the class to be exposed to a wide range of disabilities and did not recruit additional consultants. It is obvious from the student evaluations that in the end, working with the selected consultants proved to be one of the most rewarding experiences.

Evaluation

According to the course evaluations, the students enjoyed learning about universal design and felt that by focusing on the concepts of universal design they were able to develop valuable skills that will enhance the environments they design. It is apparent

The consultants were a valuable asset to the studio.

from the post-test that student awareness of and sensitivity to universal design issues increased. The following comments are from the UDEP questionnaires:

It helped me realize how limited by our surroundings we can be, and how effective design can enable people of all abilities to use and enjoy a space.

That effective universal design provides a functional and comfortable space, not only for those with physical impairments, but for all users. It is not a hindrance, but rather an asset to any project.

Universal design is unique and opens a whole new realm for design. I think it opens up new possibilities instead of adding restrictions.

Noticing that although [a built environment] may look fine, it may not work at all, and as this is a democratic society, so should design be.

When asked "What about this course did you think was most valuable in helping you to learn?" on college course evaluations, the students replied:

The person-to-person contact with disabled people to understand their feelings and abilities so that our understanding and knowledge for designing increased.

Universal design and sensitivity training.

Meeting with consultants and lecturers.

Participation in UDEP has been a positive experience for the students, the consultants, and myself. This project brought together people on the NDSU campus and in the community who had not been aware of the resources and skills each has to offer. This successful project strengthened student awareness of universal design and fostered community, faculty, and student interaction.

Acknowledgements

The successful completion of this project was greatly influenced and enhanced by the following participants: Jack Mckeever, Barb Mckeever, Alan Peterson, Shirley Friend, Harry McCallister, Chuck Robienou, Shirley Robienou, UDEP Advisor Paul Grayson, Project Director Elaine Ostroff and the Adaptive Environments Center staff, and the sophomore interior design students—Barb Allrich, Misty Baird, Amy German, Carrie Hamre, Dana Jablinske, Fran Kurowski, Jenn Llewellyn, Cathy McCarter, Ryan Perala, Allan Ressler, Dee Schmidt, Rachel Strum, Nora Tumberg, Anita Weinmann, and Mary Zipf.

Experiential Exercises for Teaching Universal Design

Faculty coordinator:

Elizabeth P. Church
Assistant Professor

Proposal

Norwich proposed to integrate universal design into a design studio and seminar course for third- and fourth-year students that would focus on housing issues, in particular, shared housing for older people. A two-day design charrette would be the focal point, involve local designers and consultants, and generate multiple solutions for a real client. The focus of the project was modified in response to minimal funding and teaching assignments. Instead, universal design was introduced in the Human Issues class and the concurrent second-year design studio.

Activity

All of the second-year architecture students at Norwich University participate in a required lecture/discussion class entitled Human Issues in Design. In this class, students are introduced to a wide range of topics including, but not limited to, how culture influences the built environment, sign/symbol/meaning, wayfinding, anthropometrics, ergonomics, and universal design.

The concept of universal design is woven into the fabric of the Human Issues course with a straightforward agreement between the students and myself that all people should be able to enjoy and participate in the designed environment. The topic of universal design, the specifics of code issues and products, and developing an understanding of needs specific to certain groups are initially addressed from several points of departure: a lecture on universal design with slides; a video showing of either *Passion Fish* or *Waterdance;* readings from *Design Intervention* (Preiser, Vischer, White); a reading of Ray Carver's short story "Cathedral"; and an introduction to the *ANSI Guidelines* (American National Standards Institute). A design studio is run concurrently with the lecture class. In the studio setting, universal design was addressed throughout each student's design process as they addressed the design problem.

Outcome

To supplement formal presentations on the topic, I asked the students to participate in experiential exercises that, I believe, they are more likely to remember than conventional lecture/discussion and read/test formats. In one of the initial exercises, students compared themselves to historic representations of human form. With one student lying on paper on the floor, another traces the outline of her body onto paper. This exercise is designed to promote students' awareness that their dimensions do not

Students complete an exercise titled "Am I a Renaissance Man or Woman?" in which they compare their own size and shape to da Vinci's and Le Corbusier's ideal human forms.

fall readily into da Vinci's perfect human form, the well-known depiction of a man whose outstretched body is contained within a circle and a square. In the second half of the exercise, students tried to fit themselves into Le Corbusier's Modulor Man—using the proportions he established from the Fibonacci series. The outcome sought for in this class is the students' recognition that there is no single formula for predicting or accommodating human dimensions. The students also became aware that da Vinci and Le Corbusier, as well as many other designers and thinkers, have tied their design to the idealized dimensions and form of a very small population, those figures who fit into the geometric or numeric formula supported by a particular theoretical stance.

In another exercise, I borrowed four wheelchairs, four walkers, two pairs of crutches, and four pairs of blackened sunglasses from the University's Nursing Division and gave the students a short orientation on how to use these items. Although these second-year students sleep in their dorms, eat in the cafeteria, and attend classes outside the architecture building, they essentially live in the studio. By making this equipment available during the evening hours when these students are most likely to be relaxed and open to experiment and play, I offered these healthy, able-bodied, nineteen-year-old students a chance to personally discover the issues of universal design. The only caveat I placed on the use of the equipment was that neither the equipment nor the users should come to any harm; otherwise, the students were free to roam the building and the campus. When I arrived in the classroom, students regaled me with stories of who got stuck going from here to there, who could not get to his dorm room, or who won the race around the quad.

To insure that all students had an opportunity to experience the use of the borrowed equipment, I developed an in-class exercise requiring the students to travel in and out of various buildings on campus using the equipment, collect information from each of several locations, and record their findings.

Comments from Students Wearing "Blind-Sunglasses"

Being blind was a great experience—it sharpened my other senses so that I could tell when the ground surface changed, when people walked by, and the smell of food. I relied heavily on the edges of pathways, like curbs or bricks or grass, to get myself here and there.

Carpets give no clues by texture like the tile floors do. I got around fairly easily without the use of a stick—when I was in the architecture building—because I know my way around. I guess what I learned most was to keep layouts simple and easy to "read" with a stick, because chances are there is no visual memory.

Comments from Students Using the Wheelchair

The wheelchair was very tiring to me, especially since Sara and I had to travel way out of our way to get to Cabot Building. The wheelchair was a pain to be in because even just a step or threshold of 3" or 4" high is hard to maneuver over. Doors are also hard to get through because they are so heavy and handles are so high up. Even some of the slight ramping was a pain inside because it was carpeted.

Uphill sucked, as did the elevator in Cabot. It was very narrow and didn't stop flush with the floor. Also you become endangered of losing fingernails in the spokes.

The main difficulty I experienced in the library was interfacing with the person behind the desk.

In general I decided that the campus is not handicapped accessible. A handicapped person would have to be a Special Olympics athlete to negotiate this campus.

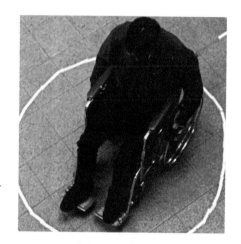

Bathroom is large enough if I'm alone.

The wheelchair is fun, but I wouldn't want to be in it forever.

In conjunction with the lecture course, second year students had a studio problem to design a Museum for the Senses. This fictional museum was to provide visitors with an experience—educational or experiential—of each of the five human senses. When the studio assignment was given, the students had just begun their journeys around campus with blindfolds, crutches, and wheelchairs, so they were in the habit of altering their perceptions of what once had been familiar to them—the campus. To encourage students to draw from their own sensory abilities, I assigned several exercises that stimulated heightened use of their senses. In one exercise the students were blindfolded while listening to a passage of music, smelling various objects, touching highly textured objects, and tasting food. Then they drew one of the sensory experiences. In another exercise the students visited the site of the project and drew a sensory map that was neither representational nor cognitive. Rather,

Students performed a series of tasks from turning within a five-foot diameter circle to navigating across campus.

A "sensory observation map" recording a student's experience of the sense of hearing at the location of the studio project: The Museum for the Senses.

the map, called a "sensory observation map," was intended to record how each of the senses influenced or was influenced by the site.

Reflection

Since all architecture majors are required to take the Human Issues class and I have included this technique in the class for three years, the "Experiencing Disabilities" exercise has become a bit of a tradition in the department. This year, as I watched students navigate their way into a five-foot diameter circle taped on the floor of the architecture building's foyer, I overheard many more advanced students recalling memories of their own experiences doing the same exercise. The campus's compact layout results in many people bearing witness to the travels of students with blindfolds and wheelchairs, a form of residual learning for others on campus.

The level of engagement by the students in both the universal design exercises in the Human Issues course and the Museum of the Senses studio problem was gratifying. From my experience with the exercises in the Human Issues course, I feel that the students' experiential participation was more effective than classroom discussions or a guest with disabilities recounting anecdotes from real life. Likewise, the Museum problem called on the students' ability to isolate and think about each of the senses, and consider each sense, in and of itself, as an opportunity to explore, learn, communicate, investigate, navigate, and be the focus of primary design decisions.

14 Pratt Institute – Brooklyn, New York
Collaboration between School of Architecture and
School of Art and Design: Departments of Industrial Design,
Interior Design, and Communication Design

Teaching the Teachers

Faculty coordinator:

Brent Porter
Associate Professor

Team members:

Bruce Hannah
Professor
Margaret Leahy
Associate Professor
Joe Roberts
Associate Professor
Daniel Fechtner
Physician

Proposal

The faculty at Pratt Institute proposed to take the idea of curriculum innovation beyond the walls of their own institution. By conducting a series of teach-ins, building on the 1960s precedent for responding to a crisis situation, they could address the urgent need to raise the level of public understanding of universal design and to share important information. Calling the effort Teach the Teachers, the faculty planned to build on the curriculum materials for teaching universal design that they had already developed in a previous year through funding from the J.M. Foundation.

The teach-ins would allow both faculty and consultants with disabilities to communicate their unique insights and experiences directly to those who need it most—the teachers—thereby having the greatest impact on the long-term education of our nation. Materials would be jointly prepared by faculty from five fields and five consultants with a range of disabilities.

At the teach-ins, participants would receive a matrix of available resources and an educational "tool kit" representing a range of interdisciplinary contributions from Pratt faculty. The teach-ins would be limited to twenty-five participants and be repeated to include as many teachers as possible from institutions of higher education in the New York City region.

Activity

In the winter and spring semesters of 1994, two teach-ins were held at Pratt, the second event building on the lessons from the first. One of the primary purposes of the teach-ins was to engage participants' imaginations in the issue of universal design and to encourage their use of the concept and available resources in their classroom teaching. Each teach-in was a mixture of presentations by faculty and people with disabilities who had specific expertise on some aspect of universal design, interspersed with videos and slides illustrating the virtues of accessible design.

The faculty team invited professional colleagues with disabilities to be consultants and to contribute to all aspects of the activities, from initial event planning to "taking a walk" on campus and within buildings. Denise Ann McQuade, coordinator of the New York City Transit Authority's Office of ADA Compliance and the person who was instrumental in bringing about the city's disability code, has mobility difficulty and uses a wheelchair. She has been an activist for independent living for twenty-four years. David McFadden, curator of Decorative Arts at the Cooper-Hewitt Museum, has a walking impairment and provided the team with his broad expertise in design, publishing, and confronting New York City everyday. Stanley Wainapel, medical director of Adult Day Services for the Jewish Guild for the Blind and associate professor of Rehabilitation Medicine at Columbia University, has a progressive vision impairment. He helped the team understand the gulf between designers and the medical professions. Milda Vizbar, an accomplished artist and advocate for muscular dystrophy, has difficulty walking. She was invaluable in reminding the team and the teach-in participants that dialogue must be expanded between designers and people with disabilities.

The first speaker of the teach-in, Bruce Hannah, "jump started" the dialogue with remarks entitled "Questions Designers Should Ask." Why design something that can't be used? Why say something that can't be heard? Why write something that can't be understood? Why draw something that can't be seen? Why build something that is inaccessible? Why construct something that can't be climbed? Why paint something that is invisible? Why sculpt something that can't be felt? Why bridge something that can't be crossed? These are questions that had arisen during the planning stages for the teach-in and reflect the collective voice of students, faculty, and professionals.

A brief overview of the Americans with Disabilities Act gave all participants shared knowledge of the federal law. A presentation of images, called "Looking for Mr. Grab Bar," illustrated good, bad, and indifferent examples of universal design that came from a yearlong search for teaching materials. Examples of elegant products that work for diverse users were drawn from a universal design course offered the previous year in the Department of Industrial Design (see photos on the facing page). Other speakers were persons with disabilities who gave firsthand accounts of daily encounters with the built environment, further illustrating the need for new solutions.

Outcome

Faculty from six academic departments worked together to produce the teach-ins, a major accomplishment at any school. These individuals are continuing to work together to propose additional campuswide efforts in the next academic year and to introduce materials into their own departmental curricula. The consultants played an important role in keeping the focus on users. Although the faculty probably needed an opportunity to come together to solidify their goals and directions, consultant Milda Vizbar reminded her fellow team members that the central goal should be to bring those with disabilities together with designers in as many ways as possible and as often as possible.

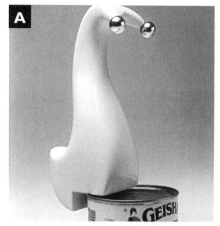

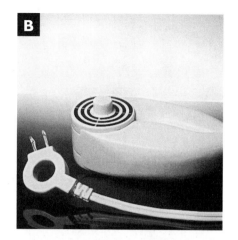

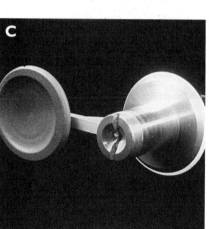

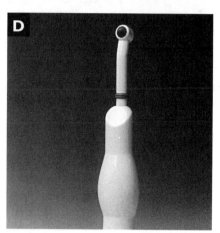

Universally designed products: *(A) light grip rechargeable can opener by Mark Zaininger; (B) travel hair dryer by En-Bair Chang; (C) door handle/ lock hardware by Lutz Sauvant; and (D) oral hygiene device by Benson Kravtin.*

The preliminary task of creating a poster to advertise the teach-in became a unpredicted opportunity for the organizers to confront the tension between design and universal legibility. After many weeks of deliberation about the graphics and language, the result for the initial mailing was appealing to designers but frankly was not well-received by participants with disabilities (part of the poster is reproduced on the following page).

The high-gloss, white and orange poster, designed to command attention, produced glare for people with visual impairments. The deliberate overlapping of phrases on the poster was intended to draw people's attention to the role of graphics. Instead, people had difficulty reading the poster. The multiple layers of letters—large and small, light and dark, receding and advancing on the page—intended to convey multiple meanings and even contradictions, was not understood. One of the consultants, the physician with a visual disability, explained to the team that the terms used by designers did not have the same meaning to physicians who treat people with visual impairments. He noted that because the orange and white color did not offer enough contrast, as red and white color would, the lettering was unclear.

The poster for the initial mailing was orange, white, and black with a high-gloss coating. The visual acuity was intended to be confrontational.

The teach-in events attracted fewer faculty than had been expected. Many of the participants were people who already had some awareness of universal design. Nondesign staff participated and added a breadth that was instrumental in expanding the resources to be used in future teaching. Many faculty who did not attend have design practices as well as teaching responsibilities and cited the attention they already give to universal design in their professional work.

Some faculty hold a strong resistance to universal design but the team found that attitudes are changing. It was particularly difficult to attract faculty from other colleges and universities in the city, which had been part of the proposed aim. Some of these institutions are developing their own programs in universal design. Further, the professional associations in which faculty are members have conducted extensive workshops, lectures, and their own versions of teach-ins in the New York City region. In fact, Pratt's Center for Advanced Design Research (CADRE) assists professional and trade groups in organizing training sessions for designers on universal design.

The shift at the second teach-in, directing the focus toward students as well as faculty, was in response to suggestions from team members and faculty who participated in the first teach-in. The belief, confirmed by student participants, was that teachers were more likely to engage the material if they felt pressure from students who were informed of the importance of universal design to their future as designers. The large collection of videos that had been examined by faculty for the first teach-in were excerpted to introduce students to the extensive resources now available on the Pratt campus.

The second teach-in changed its strategy slightly by introducing a charrette, a hands-on activity that gave designers an opportunity to experience buildings and outdoor spaces accompanied by a person with a disability. By specifically orienting the activity to students, greater participation might be achieved. Over 190 students and faculty attended. At least three faculty brought their classes, integrating the charrette into their design studios.

"Taking a walk" through the campus gave students the opportunity for candid exchanges with persons with disabilities. Based on the practice of Stephen Valentine, a Pratt professor who uses simulation of disabilities in his design course, participants in the second teach-in were asked to re-experience everyday environments. Participants took turns as escorts or as users with disabilities similar to what was done in Valentine's class. According to the nature of the actual or imagined disability, participants responded to encountered environments. The escort or escorts reacted to the response of the participant with disabilities and vice versa. When roles are reversed, the dialogue is enriched. For example, Dr. Wainapel, who is visually impaired, became an escort and led a participant around Pratt's Main Building, based on his degree of localized sensitivity and feedback at the moment. Milda Vizbar, who walks with difficulty with a cane, "took a walk" outdoors and noted the absence of benches located along sidewalks and the difficulty of finding and using those that did exist.

Students take turns simulating blindness and being escorts in the heart of Manhattan.

Visually Impaired Users Meet Visual Professionals. *A comparison of how designers and people with low vision define the elements of graphic design (prepared by Dr. Stanley Wainapel and Mary Salstrom).*

VISUALLY IMPAIRED USERS MEET VISUAL PROFESSIONALS

Those who have cataracts, diabetic conditions, macular degeneration, retinitis pigmentosa, glaucoma, hemianopia or myopia.	Those who are artists, designers and architects.
Major criteria.........(non-magnification issues)	.................(may include scale shifts for effect)

1. ILLUMINATION

    amount of light available and the evenness of light

1. ILLUMINANT, ILLUMINATION, VOLUME, SURFACE and FILM as five "modes of appearance":
ILLUMINANT: light source; sunlight or artificial light
ILLUMINATION: quality of being lighted by an illuminant
VOLUME: three-dimensional
SURFACE: two-dimensional
FILM: skyward, sky-view

2. CONTRAST

    high or low contrast (cannot see low contrasts) and the affect of the distance between colors on the light spectrum; the greater the distance between colors --those approaching blackness and whiteness-- the better.

    SATURATION: saturated or unsaturated; brightly saturated may be better if letters or figures on a dull background which does not produce glare.
SIMULTANEOUS CONTRAST
    affect of one color on a second color may be experienced if broad "contrast" difference
FIGURE - GROUND
    figure in relation to its background; darker background with lighter letters or figures is better for visually impaired.

2. CONTRAST

    degree of difference between the "*Inherent attributes*" of "hue," "value" and "intensity;" i.e.
HUE: redness, blueness or yellowness or pigments; for light, red-, blue- or greenness
VALUE: whiteness or blackness
INTENSITY: dullness or brightness; includes SATURATION
SIMULTANEOUS CONTRAST:
    property of all colors in which one color is influenced by a second color next to it, on it, or around it
FIGURE - GROUND
    figural relation to background

3. GLARE or GLOSS

    (goal for minimum glare and gloss; ex.: less shine on a surface; matte finishes; low gloss varnish on piano, furniture or paintings; use of non-reflective glass; and avoidance of mirrored surfaces

3. GLARE as result of GLOSS "ATTRIBUTE" (goal may likely be minimum glare)
GLOSS (artificial shine) among the "*Geometrical attributes* "* which include.
LUSTER (natural shine), TEXTURE, IRRIDESCENCE, VIBRATION, SPARKLE, FLICKER, REFLECTION, MIRRORED REFLECTION
*affect of movement as well as relationship between angles of the light source, the object's surface and the eye (See Hunt, *Measurement of Appearance*.).

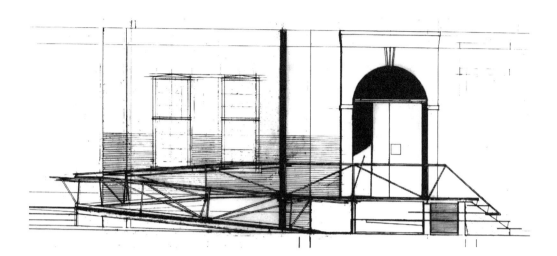

Louis Cespedes' proposal for a new ramp prepared during the charrette.

The consultants with disabilities had a strong effect on the student participants, especially in the Taking a Walk exercise. One student proposed a deconstructivist ramp for the entry to Higgins Hall, home of the architecture department. Another wrote an article in a student newspaper expressing his frustration with the low turnout of faculty: "But, where were the rest of the faculty? They were invited to attend, free, and that included lunch. I wonder how much they know or care about universal design." A fifth-year architecture student conveyed his growing awareness of the inaccessibility of much of New York City with a drawing in which lower Manhattan is shown as unreachable canyons, mesas, and buttes. This is an example of the use of "image mapping" as a consciousness-raising, emphatic exercise in which the student expresses personal imagery, imagination, prejudices, or level of understanding by means of sketching.

Two outcomes from the teach-ins have the potential to reach many faculty across the city who might never have been able to attend a teach-in. First, the two teach-ins inspired the organization of the Pratt Universal Design Resource Center where faculty and students can borrow videotapes, slides, books, and other written material on the subject. The Resource Center is not an actual room but rather an entity representing the cooperation between such existing resources as the Pratt Library, CADRE, and the Multi-Media Center, which is part of METRO, a film co-op shared among two hundred New York City regional colleges and universities. Faculty have suggested titles and assisted in procuring materials. The lending policies already in place at Pratt support continued advances in media communication concerning universal design and the sharing of vast resources among cooperating institutions and campuses in the metropolitan area.

Second, what began as the development of a bibliography of films, plays, poetry, and literature that address universal design, is leading to questions within the School

Dickson Leung's "Manhattan as inaccessible canyons, mesas, and buttes."

of Liberal Arts and Sciences on language and writing concerning universal design. At the first teach-in there was discussion about the correct terminology to use in classes throughout the Institute. As Professor Richard Perry put it, "We usually examine vocabulary which comes out of context, but with 'universal design' the language defines the context." To this end, how we write about universal design may indicate our prejudices, misinformation, or learning. In the fall 1994 semester, some team members formed a creative writing workshop for "keeping a journal" to examine the past year's activities concerning universal design.

Evaluation

While no formal evaluations were done, Pratt received a number of responses from participants. One student had the following insights about the teach-in.

The results were shocking: most buildings are inaccessible to the physically handicapped, and what few accommodations are provided, such as elevators and ramps, are more or less dysfunctional. Even more surprising was the reaction of the students: instead of general apathy some people may expect from us, what we received was some very constructive criticism and even a few well thought-out solutions to the problem of accessibility.

One student submitted a design for a ramp leading from street level into Higgins Hall, the architecture building about to undergo renovation. Some other students worked collectively to design suspension ramps that could connect the mezzanine levels of Higgins Hall to main floors. These efforts, combined with allocation of funds which are actually available for just these purposes, would make for a much more education-oriented environment, one in which your concern is which class you want to take, not which classes you are able to get to.

Stephan Klein, a faculty member in interior design, attended both events and described the important and difficult questions raised in his mind about the cultural politics of universal design.

The question is, where do you go from here?... What happens when Universal Design isn't good for business? How is Universal Design being transformed, how is it being used, as all phenomena are when they enter the public sphere?

How will Universal Design effect aesthetic values? Will we need to change our values? Or, is a Universal Design aesthetic already being used to sell our products and places even when these are not really universally accessible?

What are the limits to "Universality?" The definition of disability is, like most other definitions, socially and historically influenced. As such, it is constantly changing and under constant negotiation by conflicting interests. How is it changing? Is Universal Design being used to simply maintain a status quo (despite its claims) or can it be a force for significant social change? Is there underlying conflict between an association of Universal Design with Modernism's claim to universality and its failure to create a socially just world?

Does Universal Design conflict with the notion of diversity in design? And if so, does it align itself with a "reactionary" rather than a "radical" Postmodernism (to paraphrase Hal Foster)? Does Universal Design represent a challenge and an opportunity to bring diverse groups together towards meaningful social change? How can Universal Design raise consciousness? Are we creating a Universal Design "canon?" If so, what is it? Is this good or bad? Does this process really keep the disabled marginalized, defined as "other," disempowered and unable to participate in the process of change?

Acknowledgements

The following individuals participated in planning and conducting two teach-ins and other activities: Consultants—David McFadden, curator of decorative arts at the Cooper-Hewitt Museum; Denise Ann McQuade, coordinator of the New York City Transit Authority's Office of ADA Compliance; Dr. Stanley F. Wainapel, medical director of Adult Day Services for the Jewish Guild for the Blind and associate professor of rehabilitation medicine at Columbia University; and Milda Vizbar, artist and muscular dystrophy spokesperson; Technical Consultants—Danae Loran Willson, assistant director of Pratt's Center for Advanced Design Research (CADRE); and Stephan Klein, Ph.D., head of Pratt's Luce Fund.

Purdue University – West Lafayette, Indiana
Department of Landscape Architecture

Engaging Universal Design Program-wide

Team members:

Bernie Dahl
Assistant Professor
Frank Dunbar
Visiting Professor
Rachel B. Ramadhyani
Student Assistant

Proposal

Our objective was to implement a three-tiered approach toward universal design education in the landscape architecture program:

- Create and implement a course in universal design awareness and application that is a centerpiece of education for the design departments on campus.

- Integrate universal design application across the existing landscape architecture curriculum.

- Export universal design awareness and application to other parts of the landscape architecture profession through the existing landscape architecture internship program.

Activity

A pilot version of an eight-week, one-credit course entitled "Design for Diversity" was offered during the second half of the fall 1993 semester. Although the course was planned and supervised by faculty from the landscape architecture program, an attempt was made to attract students from the various design curricula at Purdue.

The course consisted of a series of two-hour lecture and discussion sessions that featured Purdue faculty and guest speakers with expertise in various aspects of universal design. All of the lectures had required reading, either in the form of class materials or as handouts brought by guest lecturers. The presentations were videotaped as a resource for future use. Several of the speakers had disabilities and students found their insights particularly illuminating and challenging. In-class discussions sprang both from the content of these lectures and from assigned readings.

In keeping with the philosophy that universal design must not be viewed as separate from other design activities, the landscape architecture faculty attempted to incorporate these concepts across the existing curriculum. A template for making the necessary changes to syllabi was given to faculty in the form of a faculty guidebook prior to the fall 1993 semester. The guidebook made suggestions for incorporating universal design concepts into each course in the program.

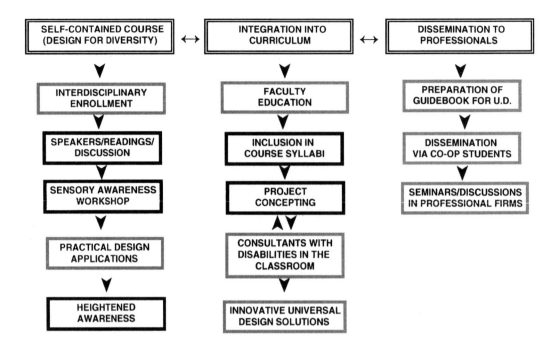

To meet the goal of exporting universal design to the larger professional community, a *Co-op Guidebook for Universal Design* was planned. The guidebook would accompany student interns (those who have completed the junior sequence) in their yearlong co-op employment positions in both private and public design offices. Faculty anticipate that the presence of the students and the suggestions detailed in the *Guidebook* will lead to discussions and seminars within these work settings and that the philosophy of universal design will be spread throughout the profession.

Outcome

As the centerpiece of the project, the Design for Diversity course was very successful. The eight-week course was offered to all the design departments on campus and any student already taking a full courseload was able to add the class mid-semester without paying additional tuition. Eighty-five students registered for the class, including two interior designer majors, six graphic design majors, and two product design majors. The balance of the class was landscape architecture majors. Enrollment by nonlandscape students proved to be relatively low and more vigorous attempts at campuswide outreach will be undertaken in future years. Landscape architecture faculty not only encouraged their students to enroll in the course, but attended the lectures themselves.

The series of guest lectures offered within the course was successful in meeting the main objective of the class, which was to stimulate awareness of the need for universal design application. Students were particularly engaged by speakers who themselves had significant disabilities and could demystify topics that are ordinarily taboo in our culture.

The lectures were complemented by a sensory awareness workshop, in which teams of two students simulated disabilities and followed a pre-scribed route around the campus. One of the students used a wheelchair; the other wore special glasses to simulate legal blindness. The five different routes were purposefully selected to take student teams through a range of easy and difficult experiences. Afterwards, each student reflected on the experience by answering the following questions:

Consultant who is blind demonstrating tactile appreciation of sculpture during Design for Diversity course.

- What was your initial reaction to assuming an artificial disability?

- What was the most difficult or frustrating about using a wheelchair?

- What was the most difficult or frustrating about being visually impaired?

- What architectural barrier was the most bothersome?

- Did you encounter any attitudinal barriers? Explain.

- Did this experience heighten your awareness of disabilities? If so, how?

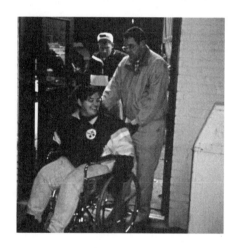

Student using a wheelchair accompanied by faculty simulating blindness as part of a sensory awareness workshop.

Most noticeable in students' comments is a new awareness and better understanding of individuals with disabilities. In many cases, the language used in their comments reflects a "we" rather than "they" approach. It appears that rapid changes in attitude can be achieved by placing temporarily able-bodied persons in the position of those who experience the physical environment differently.

The sensory awareness workshop, which many students viewed as a conceptual turning point during the Design for Diversity course, evoked the following comments:

I felt alone. It was so frustrating being left out of conversations while our group was deciding on which way to go. It felt like they didn't even see me, and I was the one who was blind.

I suppose the two biggest [frustrations] were that I was unable to go where I wanted, how I wanted, and someone had mapped out certain places I could go. I was unable to use the bathrooms in many buildings. That's not just frustrating but embarrassing.

The most important part is not to be made to feel 'special.' If you are able to easily use the entrance [in] the same manner that the rest of the public uses [it] you are not made to feel estranged.

I feel you cannot design for disabilities until you experience it for yourself. In my experience [with the workshop] there were countless things that I never would have even considered otherwise.

I think that the saying, 'Put yourself in my shoes' is really a shocking statement because you actually have to put yourself in the position to see what type of responses you get from people and also what barriers you would encounter.

All in all probably the most frustrating barrier in a [wheel]chair is simply that the minimum has not been achieved. What I mean by this is that it would be one thing if it were a rough ride somewhere, but most places it is virtually impossible to get to—even if it's signed.... By being able to design through the eyes of those who are physically challenged I feel that it does not detract from my design abilities because it simply makes the design stronger and able to be used by a greater number of the population.

I think I realize now that minimum acceptable standards are not necessarily good or easy or even comfortable.

Throughout our life, we will not always be as able-bodied as we are now, and perceptions of people with disabilities need to change within ourselves so that we will be prepared for our own disabilities.

Students also commented on the Design for Diversity course in general:

The best thing about this course was when the guest speakers had some sort of disability. It was interesting to hear their views on the problems of accessibility.

The class gave me the new perspective I've gained that has affected my whole life in a very short time.

I realize how little professionals know about universal design. This course should be a required facet of the design sequence.

Faculty expected that work produced in the landscape architecture classes taught in the fall semester of 1993 would reflect the changing attitudes learned in the Design for Diversity course. They hoped that, in the eight weeks that the course overlapped with other studio activities, students would apply universal design to their fall semester projects. In classes where physical design drawings or construction drawings were the primary product, students were moderately successful. In classes producing planning documents or graphics, the connection to universal design was weaker. The information presented in the Design for Diversity class could be particularly well-incorporated into the junior level design project programming process.

Speakers for the Design for Diversity course visited other landscape architecture classes as guest experts. Students in those classes learned a great deal from these additional opportunities for interaction and discussion. Students and community residents with disabilities were not engaged as consultants for studio projects during the 1993–94 school year. Their involvement would have provided feedback throughout the design process and may be the crucial link between an intellectual appreciation of the importance of universal design and its application in practical settings.

UDEP has continued to be implemented beyond the fall 1993 course offering. The 1994 spring semester classes in landscape architecture were taught using the universal design approach. The results of those classes, coupled with the efforts of the fall semester, will provide a fuller indication of the awareness gained by the students in the Design for Diversity course. The Design for Diversity course was offered again during the second half of the fall 1994 semester.

The other ongoing portion of the project is the outreach effort by student interns. Students are currently preparing the *Co-op Guidebook for Universal Design*, a vehicle to disseminate the concepts of universal design to professional practitioners. The *Guidebook* will draw upon a highly successful project undertaken by students in the junior-level site construction class in the fall of 1993. The booklet will describe the basic objectives of universal design, outline an approach to interviewing clients to elicit unique needs, and offer suggestions for envisioning new design solutions.

Evaluation

At the time of the initial project proposal, the landscape architecture faculty was in unanimous support of the project and in agreement with the importance of incorporating universal design across the curriculum. Although that support never wavered, there was variation in the extent to which these concepts actually permeated the classroom and studio experience. While several faculty members highlighted these concepts throughout their courses and articulated them explicitly at every opportunity, others found it more difficult to modify their established patterns of teaching. The following list of courses indicates how faculty incorporated universal design into the fall 1993 curriculum.

LA 101—Introduction to Landscape Architecture. The concept of universal design was discussed and the video *Towards Universal Design* was shown. The class met its objective.

LA 116—Graphic Communication for Landscape Architects. Although the class does not specifically lend itself to universal design, sketch work opens the student's eyes to seeing the world around them differently. The goal of enhancing students' appreciation for the role of textures in universal design was not carried out. The class minimally met its goals.

LA 166—History of Landscape Architecture. The thorny issue of design adaptation of historic structures and gardens was apparently not addressed. The class did not meet its goals.

LA 216—Landscape Architecture Design I. An introduction to the design process (problem, analysis, and solution approach) is a part of the normal content of this class. The class met its goals.

LA 316—Landscape Architectural Design III. The class syllabus placed universal design in a central position. All projects drew on an awareness of universal design concepts that were incorporated with sustainable design and environmental considerations. The class met its goals.

LA 325—Planting Design. Although the macro-scale planting design approach used in this course does not specifically mesh with universal design solutions, two of the group projects emphasized universal design in their final reports. Most important-ly, the two projects, one for Zionsville, Indiana, and one for Shelbyville, Indiana, were real projects with government clients. The class met its goals.

LA 346—Site Systems II. This class included a major project in universal design. The instructor developed a project that included writing individual user profiles of the twenty-six workers at the client corporation. Twenty-four of the twenty-six had some kind of permanent or temporary disability, ranging from a sprained ankle to loss of limbs. Students interviewed the users with a standard set of questions and compiled the responses into a database that guided their design. The students handled the pro-gramming effort well, but the resulting design projects were uninspired. The class met its goals, but more potential could have been realized.

LA 416—Urban Design. Two historic urban renovation projects were undertak-en in Chicago, one of which was coordinated with teams of architects, sculptors, and other designers. While the class was successful at incorporating universal design into an urban setting, the scale of the design solutions was too large to permit specifics to be visible.

LA 516—Regional Design. The scale of the projects in this class was also too large to address some of the details, but the concepts of universal design were includ-ed in project discussions.

The success of the outreach to professional practitioners through co-op students cannot yet be assessed, as this effort is in its infancy.

Reflection

The activities encompassed by UDEP at Purdue during the 1993–94 school year have planted a seed that can be expected to bear increasing fruit in years to come. Students in landscape architecture, particularly those who participated in the Design for Diversity course, have undergone a momentous change in their attitude toward issues of universal design. Concepts that felt somewhat awkward and foreign when initially introduced became almost reflexive by the following semester, as the language of universal design became more fully integrated into everyday parlance of students and faculty.

Given the time constraints of the course and the expected diversity of the enroll-ment, there was little opportunity to move from the general level of consciousness-raising to the more specific level of design details. Although such activities might be best addressed within the context of each program's studio design courses, student feedback indicated some need to bring the explored concepts to a more practical level. Students did suggest the incorporation into the course of more practical design information and projects, thereby solidifying the link between theory and practice. The placement of the course in the second half of the fall semester was unfortunate, as students had little opportunity to put the principles learned into immediate practice.

It is likely that, as time passes and the faculty's comfort level with the concepts of universal design grows, the inclusion of these concepts in all aspects of teaching will increase. The faculty guidebook, which recommended changes or additions to each course, is a template for exposing students in increasing degrees to the concept of universal design. It may have been overly optimistic to expect radical changes to be made in all classes. A year later, however, some course syllabi still do not address the concept of universal design. While some students are well exposed to both the concept and the application of universal design, others are receiving little encouragement to integrate the objectives of universal design into their thinking.

In studio design courses, universal design principles appeared to be most readily incorporated at the stage of project concepts. Incorporating universal design into the final stages of design appeared to be more challenging and less successful, at least within courses taught in the fall semester of 1993. Universal design principles seemed to "sink in" more fully by the spring semester, and they were stressed quite consistently by both faculty and students in several spring core courses. Further faculty education may be necessary to ease the introduction of these concepts into the well-trodden grooves in which some courses are taught.

Pre-class and post-class feedback from students in the Design for Diversity class indicated a marked linguistic and attitudinal change. At the beginning of the class, some students demonstrated indifferent or unknowing attitudes toward individuals with disabilities, while others reported significant experiences with people having various types of abilities. By the end of the class, a change in attitude was apparent, with individuals with disabilities no longer viewed as special people with access problems but as part of the spectrum of users served by good design. Students ceased to regard universal design as necessary for "others" and made the conceptual leap to understanding its applicability to "all of us." Many spoke of the importance of avoiding an attitude toward individuals with disabilities as different or special and some mentioned a new respect for the determination those individuals show in overcoming significant cultural and physical challenges.

Most participants felt that the highlight of the course was the two-hour sensory awareness workshop. Comments after this workshop indicated that participants had experienced a conceptual breakthrough in the form of a new level of understanding of the importance and nuances of universal design. Participants felt that extending this workshop to include additional disabilities or to span an entire day might enhance the realism of the experience. The powerful impact of the hands-on experience suggests that this workshop might be a useful exercise to bring into a variety of settings, including professional offices and public agencies.

It is not enough to rely on an able-bodied professor to convey to students the needs of a wide range of people with differing abilities. The use of consultants in the classroom was unfortunately limited to the guest speakers in the Design for Diversity course. At this point, no other course has drawn upon the services of individuals with disabilities to provide feedback and suggestions during the development of design projects. In short, the human element of universal design was, for the most part, lacking. This omission may be part of the reason the students' work showed a lack of innovation. The involvement of such consultants, especially students with disabilities from the campus or the local community, will certainly add a significant dimension to student understanding of the nuances of individual needs. Students who have several years left within the landscape architecture program and who are regularly exposed to such experiences are likely to become fluent with universal design principles by the time they enter the professional world.

Although not all of the objectives were met, the program clearly opened the eyes, minds, and hearts of students and faculty alike in the Purdue community. The more far-reaching effects of the program will only become apparent with the passage of time. The Design for Diversity course was offered again in the fall 1994 semester and the landscape architecture curriculum will continue to be modified to better reflect current thinking in universal design. Even more significantly, the graduates and intern students of Purdue's landscape architecture program will affect the thinking of the profession of landscape architecture by providing a wider awareness of the need for universal design as *the* way to design.

Acknowledgements

We gratefully acknowledge the invaluable inputs of the following individuals who served as guest speakers or consultants: Dr. Tim Nugget, professor emeritus, University of Illinois; Chris Palames, Independent Living Resources; Jim Whittington, Lafayette Disabilities Coalition; Kathy Lyons, Personnel Services, Purdue University; Joe Meade, access specialist, USDA Forest Service; Steve Visser, Department of Visual and Performing Arts, Purdue University; Susan Goltsman, MIG, Inc.; Dr. Barbara Flannery and Ken Special, Department of Interior Design, University of Miami, Ohio. We also appreciate the assistance of the following members of the Purdue University landscape architecture faculty: Phillip E. DeTurk, Harrison L. Flint, Donald J. Molnar, Gregory M. Pierceall, Virginia L. Russell, Kenneth A. Schuette, Jr., and Rob Sovinski.

A Workbook Students Can Use Forever

Team members:

Ruth Beals
Instructor
Susan Behar
Interior Design Consultant

Proposal

Ringling proposed to develop a workbook on universal design issues so that any student could apply the concept in any design class, independent of faculty direction. The plan was to introduce and test the workbook in ID 365, Space Planning I, in the fall of 1993. This activity would be accompanied by a workshop for all faculty and students in the interior design department and the introduction of an advisory board of people with disabilities. By introducing people with disabilities as consultants, students would be exposed to how people with physical challenges feel about the limits of the built environment around them and to the implications of their design decisions. These discoveries would lead students to develop new guidelines for their project solutions. They would use the newly created worksheets in the classroom and then be able to use these worksheets independently for other projects, both real and hypothetical. The goal was to create a method that interior design educators could use to easily integrate universal design into their studio classes. The workbook's title would be RIDDLE, an acronym for Ringling Interior Designers Design for Life Enrichment, to remind its users of its beneficial goal.

Funding limitations reduced the scope of this proposal but not the emphasis. The revised proposal had two parts:

- To plan and conduct a workshop or seminar for both faculty and students on what universal design is and why it is important; and

- To develop a universal design worksheet for students to reinforce what they have learned and to serve as a guideline for solutions to their design projects.

Activity

A workshop for all interior design students and faculty was scheduled for September 1993. The goals were to have the attendees become aware of what universal design is, to have them experience their own prejudices and bias toward people with disabilities, to have them meet community members with disabilities who could sensitize them to universal design issues, and to introduce the RIDDLE worksheet and its application. Susan Behar would assist me, and community members would attend, primarily to talk with the students and faculty about having disabilities and how interiors affect them.

"The goal of the worksheets was to provide a tool that students and faculty could use to record accessibility issues, solutions, and products..."

We planned to recruit enough community members to have someone for each of several groups. The community members would be advocates of supporting independence for people with disabilities, or board members or employees of the Mayor's Council for People with Disabilities, the Easter Seal Society, the Center for Independent Living, Manasota Lighthouse for the Blind, Goodwill Industries, and the Sarasota Memorial Hospital Rehabilitation Unit.

The first activity of the workshop would be surveying the attendees on their knowledge of the needs of people with disabilities. Our hypothesis was that few students and faculty have had relationships with people who have disabilities and that many harbor prejudice and bias. By tabulating the responses immediately we could use the results to stimulate group discussion.

We planned for Susan Behar to introduce universal design, its philosophy, and applications in a slide presentation. This would lead to roundtable discussions on the five A's of good accessible design as set forth by Susan: Attitudes, Accessibility, Affordability, Adaptability, and Aesthetics. The final activity of the workshop would be to introduce the RIDDLE worksheet.

The goal of the worksheets was to provide a tool that students and faculty could use to record accessibility issues, solutions, and products, thereby producing a guideline to use during the design process and to have for future reference. Faculty could easily use this tool in their classes by having students identify the issues and their resolution during the project analysis or programming phase of design. They could then record additional ideas, solutions, and products used during the space planning and design documentation phases.

The acronym RIDDLE is used for several reasons. The word *riddle* implies fun—a puzzle or mystery to solve. The acronym is faster and easier to say than "universal design worksheet." The phrase within the acronym "design for life enrichment" reinforces the goal. Interior designers need to be reminded of the capacity we have to enrich people's lives. The built environment is ours to design and we must always seek to integrate the positive elements in life; to design not just for adequate health, safety, and welfare—but soar above the banal, and create respect, dignity, spiritual uplifting, social responsibility, and beauty.

The worksheet has three sections. The first section identifies the student, project, project type, scope of services, and end users. The second section covers universal design considerations and recommendations, and is subdivided into the physical building components (floors, walls, doors, etc.) and their finishes. The third section is for recording noteworthy solutions and important products used. Students fill in their findings for each section during the applicable phases of the class project.

Outcome

In early September, I requested funding from the Department of Interior Design to cover some of the workshop costs, but I was not persuasive enough and funding was not made available. Previously, the department had sponsored a speaker on accessibility and several students had told the department head that the presentation was boring. The possibility of this outcome had been identified in *Key Obstacles to Implementing Objectives of the Universal Design Education Project,* a handout at the UDEP colloquium.

My teaching assignment for fall semester was the third-year studio course, ID 365, Interior Design III, dedicated to an in-depth design project focusing on health care design. The design project was an Ob/Gyn clinic for two doctors, one of whom uses a cane and, when tired, a wheelchair. Because the doctor requires complete accessibility for herself, the class had to take this project beyond the requirements of codes and ADA to meet the client's needs. The course syllabus included reviewing the interior designer's contract for services, program writing, space planning/schematic design, developing presentations, and producing some working drawings. Universal design was explored through the RIDDLE worksheets.

The workshop had been planned to support the programming phase of this class. Three videos were used as a substitute for the workshop. Two were produced by the National Easter Seal Society: *Nobody is Burning Wheelchairs* and *Part of the Team— External Vision.*[1] They feature people with disabilities in the workplace. The third was about seeing-eye dogs. It described the training program for dogs and their owners and how the dogs offer their owners mobility and independence. Short discussions followed each viewing. Prejudice, bias, design constraints, dignity, and respect were the main topics of the discussions.

The programming phase also included research on the standard building codes, ADA, and accessibility. The students were required to develop a written guideline that summarized the applicable codes and ADA requirements and to make recommendations for universal design solutions. This guideline would be used during the design development phase.

The first two sections of the RIDDLE worksheet were completed from the programming information. Many students copied the sheets into their word processors, making them easier to fill out and giving them a very professional appearance.

Paul Grayson, our UDEP advisor, had been scheduled to speak at the workshop. Instead, we arranged for him to make a presentation to the second- and third-year students, the majority of our department's enrollment. We also sent invitations to twenty-

The RIDDLE Worksheet developed for UDEP and used in Interior Design III, fall 1993–94. This worksheet has been filled out by a student (nonbold text represents the student's entries).

RINGLING INTERIOR DESIGNERS DESIGN FOR LIFE ENRICHMENT (RIDDLE) UNIVERSAL DESIGN WORKSHEET

Student name: *Cindy Davis*
Project name: *Sarasota OB/GYN Clinic*
Project type: *Healthcare*

Areas involved: *Lobby, waiting, reception and office, accountant's office, office manager's office, staff lounge, meeting room, nurses' stations, laboratory, exam rooms, 2 doctors' offices, public and staff rest rooms*

Scope of services: *Programming, space planning, design/decorate, presentation, working drawings—floor plan, elevations, ceiling plan*

A. PEOPLE/USERS (RESIDENTS, STAFF, CLIENTS, PATRONS, GUESTS, ETC.)

Age: *12%* **under 18;** *70%* **under 40;** *15%* **under 70;** *2%* **over 70**

Gender: *90%* **female;** *10%* **male**

Special attributes: *Women clients are often in pain; and may be pregnant—requiring more space for them, more support from chairs to raise themselves, close access to rest rooms. They also may be apprehensive about their examination due to inexperience or to a fear of a health condition. Clients may also be physically challenged. Dr. Rusk is physically challenged and uses a cane, and will use a walker or a wheelchair when tired.*

B. UNIVERSAL DESIGN CONSIDERATIONS AND RECOMMENDATIONS

Entry: *Graphically discernible, level flooring, provides view to lobby/receptionist.*

Doors: *32" to 36" wide.*

Hardware: *Openers to be latches—no knobs. Easy to open—8 lb. pressure or less.*

Windows: *Able to be opened, attractive, sound absorptive. Visually softening treatments that allow privacy and glare prevention where needed.*

Hardware: *No knobs, should be able to open with "clenched fist." Treatment should be able to be operated from a 34"-48" height.*

Flooring: *Level or ramped, no thresholds higher than 1/2"; contrasting borders, textures, and/or colors to define where flooring ends or to indicate different areas—such as private or public, waiting or lobby.*

Finishes: *Non-skid, easy to maintain, no high gloss, select textures or patterns to provide interest and hide soilage, anti-microbial carpet o.k. for exams. Resilient tile or ceramic tile for rest rooms and lounge. Carpet should be low level loop.*

Walls: *Surface should be pleasant to touch and look at, consider height above ceiling for better acoustical privacy in Drs.' offices, exam rooms, nurses' stations and meet-*

ing room; add handrails in hallway and Dr. Rusk's office. Contrasting borders will provide definition to wall areas and chair rails will protect wall from damage. Add corner guards and lower wall protection where applicable.

Finishes: *Paint, wall coverings, paneling; colors should support activity and desired mood for the area.*

Ceiling: *Acoustical, cleanable, interesting to look at—especially in exam rooms.*

Finishes: *Painted dry wall, acoustical tile, decorative acoustical tile, incorporate trim or structural materials if applicable.*

Trim: *Use to identify areas, provide contrast. Use where different materials join.*

Finishes: *Painted or stained wood, metal door and window casing if necessary. Easy to clean.*

Rest Rooms: *Accessible, easy to clean, analyze each for the best location for the fixtures, etc. Go beyond code, ADA if possible. Provide storage for supplies used to establish proper sight lines for privacy. One must provide "family" usage.*

Lighting: *Minimize use of recessed or ceiling mounted fixtures in exam room. Provide no glare lighting throughout. Levels should be adjustable. Incorporate structural lighting. Controls to be at accessible heights and locations.*

Way Finding: *Illuminated signage where required and where applicable, follow ADA guidelines for signage. Color and/or textures used to define specific area—different door colors or flooring changes. Lay-out to support traffic patterns, minimize backtracking. Receptionist should be visible from entry. Private areas should be remote from public and/or clearly identified.*

Acoustics: *Privacy should be maintained—see walls, ceilings, and window notes.*

Seating: *Client seating—stable, with arms, pain waiting needs sofa and chair. Children's height for waiting play area. Staff—ergonomic. Lounge—lightweight and easy to move. Finishes should be easy to maintain, attractive, medium to light tone, and textured or patterned to hide soilage.*

Tables: *Adjustable height preferred. Pedestal support preferred.*

Counters: *Reception and pay counters must have a standing height and a seated heigth area. Heights must be customized for use and end-users—mostly women. Dr. Rusk's exam rooms, her office, and the lounge must allow use of wheelchair.*

Cabinetry: *Low enough in Dr. Rusk's exam room for her to access when in wheelchair.*

Fixtures: *19" h. in rest rooms.*

Equipment: *Placement must be accessible from wheelchair.*

Other: *Gooseneck faucets with paddle controls.*

Noteworthy solutions and products used: *Hafele door latches, Lutron rocker switches, American Standard toilets and sinks, Borders lead into rooms, flooring finish changes at entry (from foyer), and into r. r.'s and lounge. Custom work station for Dr. Rusk to accommodate wheelchair. Hand rail system in corridor. Entire office wheelchair accessible.*

one community members and designers. At the same time, a noted reporter from our local newspaper, the *Sarasota Herald Tribune,* was researching an article on accessible housing design. The article appeared in the Sunday edition one week before Grayson's presentation and mentioned the presentation date and location. As a result, several additional community members attended.

More videos were shown to the class to prepare for Grayson's visit. A film produced by Barrier Free Lifts, entitled *Helping You to Achieve Greater Mobility,* demonstrated people using a lift product that is integrated into a ceiling track in their homes.[1] This was a good choice because none of the students were aware of this product. The video *Toward Universal Design* was also shown. Class discussion followed both presentations.

Grayson's visit included lunch with several faculty and stimulated a discussion on the ethics of design. The luncheon was held in the department's critique room where work-in-progress on the Ob/Gyn clinic was displayed. His lecture on universal design, especially the accompanying slides of applications and products, inspired the entire audience. Attendance included a few faculty, the students, Susan Behar, and community guests—the facilities architect from the city hospital, two counselors from Florida's Department of Vocational Rehabilitation, and some practicing alumni. The only disappointment was the absence of people with disabilities.

The students completed their RIDDLE worksheets for the presentation of the schematic phase of the health-care project. Students were very conscientious about using what they had learned, following their RIDDLE worksheet guidelines, using the principles and elements of design, and following guidelines on the use of color that they had researched in the programming phase. The worksheets were turned in with the projects and a percentage of their grade was based on the accuracy and completeness of the information contained in those worksheets.

The final phase for the semester, producing working drawings, was an additional opportunity to use the RIDDLE worksheets. Many of the students had recorded vertical dimensions in the second section. These were now used to complete the required elevations of the restrooms, doctor's office, and exam rooms. Students who had not recorded the dimensions found themselves back in the library repeating earlier research and copying guidelines.

Reflection

Organizing this project, showing and discussing the videos, inviting a guest speaker, and using the RIDDLE worksheets did not take a lot of time or money.[1] Students learn a great deal from videos and speakers. They respond well to teaching aids that go beyond teachers' notes and the blackboard, especially those that explain how interior design effects people's movement through the built environment.

The RIDDLE worksheet saved time during the grading process because students' work could be evaluated against the guidelines they had developed. The RIDDLE worksheets can be adapted for use in other studio design projects as well as actual projects. If faculty encouraged their use, it would encourage students to retain and apply universal design concepts over time.

The one goal that was not satisfactorily met was having community members participate in sensitizing students. Luckily, many of the students know and have classes with students who have disabilities. Although this unstructured knowledge does not fulfill the classroom goal, at least the students are exposed to and able to interact with students different from themselves.

The methods used in this class to communicate universal design can easily be incorporated into any or all classroom projects by any faculty member in interior design and architecture departments. This project underscores the importance of including the awareness of people with disabilities as active end-users within classroom design projects. Asking students to design for all types of people is the best way to sensitive them to the entire community that designers serve.

Notes

1. Videos are easily obtained from the National Easter Seal Society ($18 each from local offices), other organizations, and manufacturers (Barrier Free Lifts, 1-800-582-8732, video at no charge).

Studio Education through Universal Design

Team members:

Edward Steinfeld
Professor
Jason Hagin
Teaching Assistant
Gary Day
Associate Professor
Theodore Lowne
Professor
Todd Marsh
Visiting Assistant Professor
Ole Mouritsen
Visiting Professor
Abir Mullick
Assistant Professor

Proposal

It is our contention that universal design is not a content or skill area of design education. Rather, it is a mode of thinking and an attitude that engages many content areas and skills. To perceive universal design as a technical specialty would only limit the realization of the idea. We sought to fully integrate universal design into our curriculum in a way that will improve the teaching of architecture in general. We believe this can best be accomplished by using universal design to engage students and faculty in a critical dialogue about the nature of architecture as a social construction. This is at the heart of the universal design idea.

More and more, society is not willing to let professional subcultures define "good design" on their own. The development of barrier-free design and its evolution into universal design demonstrates how cultural forces can redefine the object and social context of design, often in resistance to the established professional position. We used universal design to challenge traditional and emerging professional perspectives and examine the limits of expert knowledge.

An essential focus of our activities was the definition of good design. We took the position that good design is socially constructed and user-centered. Good design is discovered through a process of reflective dialogue with the intended users. By reflecting on the design project from the perspective of building users, the designer imagines what it would be like to use the design. This imaginative process is different than mere translation of user needs. It involves the personal interpretations of the designer. This process unleashes creative thinking and a search for forms that embody the designer's interpretations. Through argumentation, the designer investigates and resolves the appropriateness of the forms, technical issues, and other concerns. Engaging in universal design requires the designer's commitment to a dialogue with users, to bridge the social gap between the designer and the ultimate client—the end-user. But, such engagement cannot neglect the imaginative process. Without it, the designer would merely be a technician following instructions.

Most design students and faculty are temporarily able-bodied, young or middle-aged, white, and male. Issues related to disability and age are not well-represented in their consciousness. Women; members of racial, religious, and ethnic minorities; and gays and lesbians are also generally "outsiders." Practicing universal design implies overcoming these gaps in design consciousness. Universal design helps professional designers (including educators) learn how to engage questions of difference—an increasingly important aspect of contemporary design practice.

In addition to the broader goals of teaching universal design concepts and user diversity, we had several specific educational objectives:

- Avoid a "special" emphasis;

- Take a critical position;

- Emphasize an imaginative, user-centered approach;

- Bridge the gap of difference; and

- Engage in an aesthetic debate.

An essential idea behind our work was that we would not be concerned solely with how to teach universal design, but also how to teach design in general. Universal design concepts are extremely relevant to contemporary design education, not only as a response to disability and aging, but to broader cultural changes that are demanding a new approach to professional education.

Activity

Participants in the project included five faculty members teaching two senior-level undergraduate design courses, a second-year architectural design studio (four classes of twelve students each) and an interior design studio (fifteen students). A sixth faculty member served as a roving guest critic. Four of the instructors were architects. The other two were a product designer and a landscape architect. One of the architects was a part-time instructor with an established practice in Buffalo. The landscape architect was an exchange visitor from Denmark. One of the architects and the product designer were experts in the field of accessible design.

Faculty plan the next project.

Twelve consultants, all people with disabilities or older people and from a wide variety of backgrounds, were recruited to attend classes and provide critiques. Most consultants visited five times. Three or four consultants were assigned to each faculty member who coordinated their visits independently. Each studio class had about twelve to fifteen consultant visits, although more than one consultant often came to a single class.

The focus of the semester was the design of a complex of buildings for Artpark, a state park devoted to performing and visual arts in Lewiston, New York. The semester was structured as a sequence of four related projects. The first of these was a team project; the others were individual efforts.

In the first project, each team had three weeks to complete an analysis of sites for the complex within the Artpark property. Their analysis included an investigation and presentation of information on: natural and physical systems; legal-political issues; and social, historical, and cultural issues. For the second project, about three weeks in length, each student designed a cluster of five artist cottages, including working and living space and one communal kitchen and dining facility. The third project, lasting about five weeks, was the design of a hotel/inn with twenty sleeping rooms, a small conference center, a restaurant, outdoor recreation spaces, and support facilities. The last project, a product design, was completed in two weeks. Students chose a building product for the hotel or a travel-related consumer product. Some students designed products that would have broader use.

Group discussion at a site visit with students simulating disabilities.

Three special workshops complemented the design projects:

Workshop #1, "Thinking Like Others," asked students to simulate having one or more disabilities for twelve hours and, drawing from that experience, develop a fictional biography of a person with similar disabilities. The biographies were revised periodically during the semester to reinforce the workshop theme. Students were encouraged to project their imaginary users into their designs to explore a different perspective. The knowledge students gained from these characterizations also proved useful in critiques of other students' work.

Workshop #2, "Movement and Imagination," explored human movement as a source of technical knowledge about building use as aesthetic inspiration. Based on the students' experiences simulating disabilities, each student completed a series of transformations that lead from observation to built form.

Workshop #3, "Product Design," was a lecture and four-hour sketch problem on the universal design of a consumer product. Teams of students, representing imaginary clients with different types of disabilities, selected an everyday consumer product. The students analyzed the products' utility, user-fitness, and visual appeal and proposed product concepts that would meet the needs of all users.

Universal product: *Checkers game with pieces that are easy to handle.*

Universal product: *Railing with tactile information for wayfinding.*

Student simulating blindness.

In addition to the standard individual and group critiques, technical information was presented in two other formats—a packet of resource materials and a series of lectures and field trips. A resource packet was provided for each studio; it included the ADA Guidelines for Accessible Design, New York state code provisions, and a guidebook on making hotels accessible. The lecture series was held during class time but was not required. The topics were: fitting the building to the site, accessible ramps and bathrooms, accessible doors and circulation, and differences in aesthetic values between professionals and consumers. Field trips were organized to three local hotels with accessible rooms and one with a conference center.

As a culmination of UDEP, an exhibit and symposium on universal design were held at the beginning of the following semester. This one-day event celebrated the students' work and promoted public discussion of universal design.

Outcome

Workshop #1—Thinking Like Others. This workshop asked students to simulate having one or more disabilities for a twelve-hour period. However, there was not enough class time to ensure that each student completed the simulation as required. Because of the size of the class, we could not get enough equipment for everyone to do it at once. The class only met for four hours so it was up to the students to complete the additional hours. Informal questioning indicated that, while all students probably did a simulation on their own, few did it for the full twelve hours.

Empirical attitudinal studies[1] demonstrate that short disability simulations do not change attitudes. They may, in fact, reinforce negative perceptions about disability. In hindsight, it would be better to do the simulation briefly in class as part of a problem-solving activity, or not at all. The exercise needs to be conducted in small groups and scheduled with adequate time for learning adjustment and coping behaviors to begin understanding the limitations imposed by a disability.

Based on their simulation experience, students developed fictional biographies of people with similar disabilities. Unfortunately, the majority of the biographies presented misconceptions about persons with disabilities. They dwelt on traumatic and dramatic accidents and tragically debilitating illnesses. On the whole they presented made-for-TV-movie portraits.

For example, one student concluded his biography with the following statements: "Stan is fighting this [disease] as tenaciously as he can. He's got much to live for and maintains a hopeful attitude." Along similar lines, a student described the realization of disability with the words, "I was transformed from a kid who could walk, run, bike, and swim, to a paraplegic." This sort of hopeless-hopefulness and unyielding determination was echoed in nearly all the imaginary biographies. This is not to belittle the students' writing abilities, but rather to suggest that there were other facets to such biographical accounts that the students ignored.

"...it would be better to do the simulation briefly in class as part of a problem-solving activity or not at all."

One student described a football player accidentally paralyzed due to a spinal-cord injury received during a game. The student explained, "It is a disability that only affects him physically, because he is a pleasant person with a positive attitude that is not going to let his injury ruin or inhibit his life any more than it has already done." With few exceptions, the biographies presented this sort of unreal story. At one extreme, a student graphically described a woodsman who amputates his own leg after it becomes pinned under a felled tree. This student wrote, "Seven inches below his left knee there is nothing except the memory of what he used to be; woodcutter extraordinaire... Doctors say that with the advancements in medicine today Don should be able to lead a perfectly normal life." In many cases, the students presented "heroic" representations of disabled persons; "normal" characters tragically flawed, overcoming hardship with little grief in order to persevere.

The tone of some biographies could be interpreted as cynical or satirical, although the majority did not take such a stance. Rather than confront their image of a person with disabilities through introspection and imagination or by actually interviewing a person who has had to live with a disability, most students used a television recipe that produced "disability pastiche." Few students created an "imaginary friend" with real problems, emotions, and situations.

Biographies with insightful characterizations offered more substance that had design application. For example, one student described questions that probably came from meetings with a faculty member or consultant: "How far's the parking from the main building?" and "Is there enough room in the bathroom so that I can move around without feeling like I'm locked in a trunk?" On a different level, another student wrote of a person who is blind: "In an unfamiliar environment, my ears, sense of touch, and smell become a substitute for eyes. I listen and feel, then use those existing images in my mind to constitute the whole space." Such representations show a thoughtful vision of people, generally, and people with disabilities, specifically. Though imaginative, they transcend popular attitudes or past experiences, making the character somehow more real, more believable, and more readily accessible.

"...the development of biographies was a very good way to engage students in the imaginative projection of other people's needs."

The most popular biographic subject was the blind artist or craftsperson. In fact, almost all of the biographies were about disabled artists or craftspeople. This is interesting since mainstream representations of persons with disabilities, as well as current accessibility codes, generally focus on persons who use wheelchairs. The popularity of the blind artist as subject may be explained as the most obvious way for students to connect a "disability" with the program. Only a few biographies used a character who was part of the local community.

In spite of these criticisms, the development of biographies was a very good way to engage students in the imaginative projection of other people's needs. We learned that biographies require considerable review and discussion to avoid reinforcing stereotypes, misconceptions, and unrealistic portrayals of disability. The students constantly referred to their biographies in developing their designs. But on the evaluation questionnaire none of the students identified the biographies among the most informative resources.

In retrospect, it would have been more useful for students to interview persons with disabilities to learn real stories. A student could then compare what she learned from the interview with her beliefs and experiences and with the media's representation of people with disabilities. "Educated biographies" would be more informative in the design process and lend themselves to re-examination during the course of the project.

Workshop #2—Movement and Imagination. This workshop had three related parts: a simulation exercise, a movement exercise, and a "poetic expression" exercise.

The simulation exercise was very successful. Teams of students, simulating disabilities, used an adjustable full-scale model of a bathroom to gain firsthand experience of an inaccessible environment and how design changes can improve accessibility. It raised many technical questions and provoked considerable discussion on construction details and product selection.

For a number of my students the bathroom simulation had a big impact. In a way such simple changes in layout, design, and size brought about changes in thinking. (Day)

There is no substitute for the knowledge students gain from performing an activity in a simulated space. They get exposed to issues only understandable through experience in three-dimensional space. Full-scale simulation was a great idea. (Mullick)

In the movement exercise, a choreographer engaged students and faculty in exercises to demonstrate how movement can be designed in an aesthetic sense. It was also very well received by both faculty and students.

The choreographer was excellent in getting everyone to participate and enjoy themselves. She was also able to demonstrate how movements can be 'designed' and how all movements can be beautiful if we understand how to perceive the beauty in them. (Steinfeld)

Movement was difficult at times for the students to put into their design in a direct way. I think it became a way to discuss aesthetic ideas of movement sequence and experience that was different from the directness of the bathroom workshop. (Day)

In the third part of this workshop, linking the movement experience more directly to the design project, students developed a "poetic expression" of a movement related to use of the hotel (a poem, graphic, or sculpture). This exercise was not as successful. Although some students developed ideas they used later in the project, most students found the exercise too burdensome and peripheral. Two of the faculty did not put much pressure on their students to do this exercise.

Workshop #3—Product Design. This was a successful workshop in all respects. Some very interesting ideas for universal design were developed in a very short time. Most students brought a great deal of enthusiasm to the design exercise and the critique at the end. A few, who had created frivolous and facetious products, gave us the opportunity during the critique to convey the seriousness of our intent. The exercise was a good introduction to the final project.

The product design workshop was the best means of communicating the basic principles of universal design. The small scale of the products allowed students to touch, feel, handle, and make connection with them. This helped them to gain better insight into accessibility and universal design. (Mullick)

Exhibit and Symposium. For this one-day event each student designed an exhibit to present his or her own work. The exhibit was actually the first design project of the spring semester. The symposium included a lecture and discussion about the Americans with Disabilities Act and the lessons learned from the previous semester's activities. John Salmen, the UDEP advisor, and Brian Black, an advocate from the Eastern Paralyzed Veterans Association (EPVA), were the speakers. Several of the consultants also attended the symposium. The University News Bureau covered the event and wrote a story on it for the media.

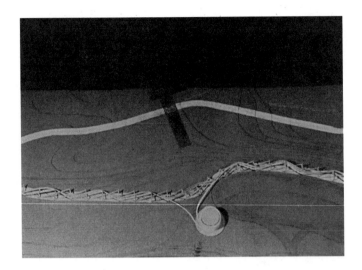

Project for hotel design—site model and room model—used movement as a generating idea.

Competition. EPVA sponsored a competition to honor the best work of the fall studio. While the exhibit was up, a jury that included faculty, John Salmen, Thomas Hodney, and an EPVA representative reviewed the work and assigned awards. Monetary awards were given in each of three categories: overall design excellence, hotel design, and product design. The awards were announced during the symposium and all award recipients were honored during the school's Annual Awards Day.

Reflection

Student Attitudes. From the start, most students showed strong interest in the topic of universal design. They put a lot of energy into their work and did not voice any negative opinions regarding the value of the topic as an educational focus. The group as a whole was challenged intellectually by the topic and sought many different ways to incorporate the universal design perspective into their projects. But not all students were able to grasp and appreciate the idea.

Some students were overwhelmed by the term *universal design* because they took it too literally. They felt universal design meant 'designing for everyone,' an impossibility. They were not sure if their design could live up to the expectations of such a term, and thus, they felt incapable and helpless.

Even though we tried to expose students to all the issues of universal design, most students focused on facilitating movement. They failed to address the broader aspects of universal design. (Mullick)

Some students clearly harbored negative opinions about the topic but, given that the professors had chosen it, they kept these opinions to themselves. As the project developed and we started to focus on the details of accessibility, these submerged negative attitudes did arise. This happened during the design of the hotel project. In our general critique of the cottage projects, faculty pointed out that students had not explored thoroughly enough the details of accessibility. We insisted that the hotel project address these details and develop them in depth.

Some students, and this is definitely a minority, reacted against a focus on prosaic details like bathroom design. They were interested in the broader issues of aesthetics, overall building form, site relationships, etc., that they considered to be more important. We pushed the students to revise and perfect the bathroom and room designs of the hotel units. This resulted in, initially, less emphasis on other issues. In one critique several students strongly challenged this emphasis. (Steinfeld)

The outburst led to an intense, hourlong dialogue in the studio critique between several students, two professors, and one consultant. It was illuminating in that the negative feelings previously unstated came to the foreground as a few students vented their frustration with this change of emphasis from previous studios and deviation from their expectations. While it is true that the focus on universal design diverted attention that would otherwise be given to design concerns such as structures, construction, circulation, and aesthetics, the universal design perspective can be viewed as a response to the general neglect of accessibility issues in the past. In other words, a change in emphasis is needed.

During that critique we had been particularly hard on the students for not addressing both the universal design issues and the other basic architectural concerns. This episode illustrates the problem with using universal design as the major theme of the studio. (Steinfeld)

Accepting universal design implies the activation of a 'universal consciousness.' Some students voiced criticism of a 'practical' design problem in academic pursuits, feeling that this was to be learned later in practice—not in school. (Hagin)

Often students feel that we faculty are 'doing things' to them or making them do things that interfere with their creativity. It's true with structural requirements, or appropriate construction technology, or site constraints. Universal design was sometimes viewed this way as well. There is always some resistance to the introduction of 'boundaries' or a new overlay in design. (Day)

A student prepares for final presentation, making his drawings easy to read by someone with limited vision.

Critical dialogue about the philosophy of universal design is useful for explaining, elaborating, and demonstrating the value of a universal design approach. Our teaching assistant felt that this dialogue was missing.

One faculty member suggested that the name 'universal design' was perhaps a utopian or, at least theoretically, ideal construction. The nature of such a theory and philosophy was not discussed. In addition, few alternative theories or philosophies were offered and no critique of utopian or idealistic theory or philosophy was presented.

I would argue that this sort of representation hinders beginning architecture students by forcing them to question the relevance, rather than the validity, of the design philosophy. As a result, I sensed that more time was spent in trying to convince students of the relevance of universal design, so that discussion about the validity of universal design was marginalized. (Hagin)

In light of this critique, perhaps contrary opinions should be incorporated, such as having faculty and students who do not necessarily "buy in" to the philosophy participate in a dialogue about the validity of universal design. The attitude of the faculty, both those in the second-year team and other critics who attended reviews, was very positive. Perhaps that is why reflective criticism was missing. All faculty embraced the concept of universal design as a pedagogic vehicle and supported individual differences in approach and emphasis.

Admittedly, in the early stages of this exploration I was suspicious of universal design and I think I noticed similar misgivings in my students. Our feelings probably had something to do with the newness of the idea and the name as well. From the impossible challenge to create universal design emerges a new awareness and a new and broader understanding of design. Universal design—for lack of a better term—is a place toward which we constantly strive, with the realization that we might never reach it. But the emphasis should not be placed on the final destination—it is elusive and might not even exist. The emphasis should be placed on the process, the struggle in which we as designers and as a society are constantly engaged. (Marsh)

Design Approaches. All students incorporated basic accessibility in their building designs. They all had generous room sizes and this made accessibility easy to achieve. Many of their projects were one story. In the cottage design project, a two-story approach was actually unnecessary but could lead to some interesting solutions.

Making a two-story cottage accessible without resorting to expensive elevators was clearly a formidable challenge. The large site also made a one-story hotel design possible. However, multi-story solutions provided some interesting architectural opportunities. In the hotel project, elevators were appropriate. There were many examples of multi-story projects and, in fact, a few very tall buildings that were successful designs.

Many students were preoccupied with the form and symbolic meaning of their building designs. They tended to search for unusual interpretations of the universal design idea. Only a few students used ergonomics and function as the major generator of aesthetic ideas although many incorporated pragmatic ergonomic features in their projects.

I think many students are unsatisfied with a 'functional' approach to building design. They are driven to engage issues related to site context, historic context, and social criticism. Functionalism to them does not present a rich enough intellectual ground for the making of architecture. Surprisingly, few of the students grasped the fact that a re-interpretation of functionalism can be a social critique. The objective is to empower people that use buildings by increasing instrumentality. (Steinfeld)

I think students get the feeling that functionalism is 'out' in some design circles—no longer the cutting edge—so that students feel they shouldn't be exploring this in an academic setting. They need to be taught that functionalism is still a valid base from which to expand the discourse in the field. (Hagin)

We did present lectures and criticism about functionalism. Either we were not successful in communicating it or it was not a satisfying approach from the students' perspective.

The curriculum could be designed to engage a more pragmatic approach to design. Our selection of Artpark with its rich historical context, dramatic topography, and arts culture may have diverted attention from pragmatics. (Steinfeld)

Hotel and cottage design in progress. The tall building provided dramatic views as well as full access by elevator.

The cottage design should not have taken place! The whole art focus of the project could have been minimized. Too many students considered their fictional person to have a career as an artist. The art as emphasis caused a lack of reality in a lot of the cottage designs and further influenced the hotel design. (Mouritsen)

Site model for cottages design. An orientation wall was used as a wayfinding tool as well as a major element for spatial definition.

We needed more emphasis on the meaning of universal design including concepts such as choice and inclusiveness. In my opinion, students would have been more intellectually engaged if they had more opportunity to explore these issues. (Mullick)

In spite of these criticisms, the students' creative perspectives on the idea of universal design led to some very interesting architecture. Many projects can be used as examples of how universal design involves more than pragmatic functional concerns. We cannot expect all students to embrace instrumentality as an ideological agenda. Faculty need to demonstrate other dimensions of universal design that will interest a broader constituency of students.

This type of project could be used to experiment with the sociology, philosophy, and aesthetics of design. We needed to develop a less structured problem statement that would have allowed some students to develop non-tangible, non-workable solutions. This would have offered new insights into the context and content of universal design, allowed students to find a focus for themselves, and provided an array of solutions capable of exposing unique aspects of the universal design perspective. (Mullick)

Hotel room model. The bathroom was designed for convenient wheelchair use and to allow the door to remain open most of the time. A greenhouse space moderates climate and reduces glare.

It might have been more constructive to offer 'other' perspectives (personal, ethnic, cultural, social, political, environmental, and even religious positions, brought to light in the spirit of the universal design philosophy), rather than marginalize these positions in presenting the philosophy as if it were inscribed in stone tablets. (Hagin)

Technical Knowledge. Each studio had a package of technical resource material available in the classroom space. Many students used this material without prompting, while others used it only when the instructor explicitly referred them to it. It was clear that some students never consulted any of the technical material. To some students, academic architecture is a purely intuitive activity. They are uncomfortable and unfamiliar with systematic research of a knowledge base. Even though the material was readily available, they were not inclined to use it in the form presented. These students rely on the master-apprentice model for obtaining knowledge. They do a design, present it to the instructor, get feedback from the instructor, and revise the design.

I think universal design could be used to demonstrate the importance of research as part of the design activity. In our conception of the studio, we did not emphasize this idea enough, and perhaps we should have incorporated an exercise early on in the semester that demonstrated to the students the value of independent research into a knowledge base using original source material. (Steinfeld)

More needs to be said about the current tendency of students to see design as a means of personal expression and emotional release. They tend not to view social issues as a design responsibility but see design as a means to critique social ills— not as a potential solution to those concerns. They are more comfortable in the world of critique and its purity, rather than entering into design, solution, and action with the possibility of not attaining perfection. (Day)

We organized lectures on accessibility when we realized students were not doing independent research. Students had many questions and a seminar format proved to be very useful for identifying technical issues and conveying basic design principles and criteria. About half of the students attended. The faculty agreed that we should have had more lectures over the course of the semester and included some on construction, landscape design, circulation, and other basic issues. In retrospect, required technical "seminars" on a weekly basis should be incorporated into a studio of this sort, with universal design being only one of the topics. This would mean reducing the number of other activities planned or increasing the credit hours for the course.

Rather than simply presenting the students with precedents for accessibility, there should be more time spent on the criticism of those precedents. Detailed discussions and dialogue on existing examples of accessibility can be a good way to encourage the development of innovative ideas. We did not do enough of this. (Steinfeld)

The technical knowledge on accessibility needed for a studio project at this level is not extensive. Accessibility could be provided simply by making all spaces generous in size, ensuring that doorways and corridors are wide, and eliminating stairs.

It is fairly easy to achieve accessibility if one provides generous spaces. Our project did not have any economic constraints. Some ground rules for cost-conscious design and an emphasis on doing the most with the least could have provided more challenge in meeting general accessibility goals. (Steinfeld)

With faculty encouragement, students expanded their investigations to consider overall circulation, wayfinding, emergency egress, and several other universal design issues. A few students designed ramps and extensive walkway systems over sloping ground. To ensure that the students investigated more of the details of accessible design, we required a detailed design of a hotel room and bathroom. Many detailed technical issues were also pursued in the product design project. Some very interesting concepts for universal design emerged.

Universal design is best understood through interaction. This is why small-scale objects that allow interaction are best. Universal design is also about details. It is difficult to judge the universality of products if they do not have detailed parts. (Mullick)

Use of Consultants. In general, the consultants were a valuable part of the overall program.

The consultants were perhaps the most pivotal [connection] in the whole process of learning. Some consultants were very good, some only average. (Day)

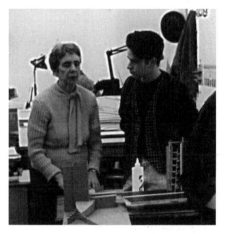

Because most students do not get the opportunity to interact with disabled persons on a daily basis, the consultants were an important way to develop insights into the unique needs of individuals. They were instrumental in making the students think about the needs of people who are unlike themselves... If universal design is about diversity, then it should be represented in the selection of consultants. They could have been artists, scientists, sociologists, and politicians—some who were disabled and others who were not. (Mullick)

A consultant with a visual impairment works with a student in the studio.

Despite the complexities of integrating a wide variety of physically challenged consultants into the studio environment, it is an invaluable introduction of reality into the design process. The more sophisticated the consultant, the more meaningful the interactive experience can be. (Lownie)

Although students listened to consultants when they offered opinions about functional issues, they often ignored or even ridiculed their aesthetic observations.

Most students seemed willing to give the consultants a voice in pragmatic decisions. Many of the projects resulting from this exploration were very successful at providing physical accessibility to products and buildings. They gave them less of a voice in aesthetic decisions. We saw few projects that attempted to be visually, aesthetically, and psychologically accessible to the consultants... In some way, students should be encouraged/required to give the consultants a voice in aesthetic decisions. This would generate valuable discourse on some important questions: Where do we draw the line between artistic freedom and social obligation? Is it possible to have both? How is it possible to have both? (Marsh)

Chapter 17: State University of New York at Buffalo

The consultants were very critical of the lack of seriousness in the work; they provided the most benefits in the studio classes working with individual students. They were less useful in response and participation in the critiques. (Mouritsen)

The consultants interacted with the students in various ways. Some were very inquisitive and informative, providing much useful criticism. Some were confrontational, uncovering negative attitudes and inaccuracies, challenging students to change their perspectives. These consultants were not afraid to provoke reaction and used strong argumentation in their championship of accessibility. A few consultants were very passive. They did not question the students in detail and responded weakly to what they were presented. On the whole, the younger and middle-aged people with disabilities were the most effective in the studio context. The older people did not have as strong a message nor did they pursue it with as much diligence. Some consultants made a strong effort to engage students in discussion. Others left it up to the students to engage them, which was not always successful.

Continuing effort is necessary to coordinate the consultants and to ensure that they will be present when scheduled. A few consultants were lax about appointments and others became confused about which studio they were to attend. The most effective way to reduce coordination problems is to establish a consistent schedule and location for the whole semester.

Final presentation:
Jurors review students' work. Consultants attended all reviews.

Timing of consultant visits is the key to successful interaction both for a student and consultant. The student must have sufficient work completed to be able to discuss their design ideas and allow for reasonable comprehension and feedback from the consultant. Possibly having the students participate in the scheduling would help. (Lownie)

I noticed the tendency for many students to avoid interaction with the consultants. In several instances, a consultant was in the studio and had finished talking with a student. The other students did not come forward to invite the consultant to review their project. In some cases, students left the room and were not available when the consultant was present. (Steinfeld)

We used consultants in three different venues: individual board critiques, single studio stage reviews, and final reviews with the two studios together. The faculty all agreed that the individual board reviews were the most appropriate and effective format for involving consultants. However, consultants like to see the final products and to be invited to the final reviews. We planned an exhibition for all the consultants to attend as well as other faculty and students. In studios with multiple projects, consultants can see the final results of the earlier project when they come back for the subsequent project. They are not as concerned with the formal ritual of presentations as faculty and students.

Problem Type and Sequence. The use of several related projects with multiple scales, ranging from a product to a complex building, sustained student interest and created a richer, more diverse learning situation. Students had greater opportunity for design success by having more than one problem to solve. However, the sequence of projects could be improved and the number of projects reduced.

Universal product: *This drinking fountain adjusts to people who stand or sit, who are tall or short.*

The hotel design was a well-chosen vehicle for the universal design study. It covered many functions, was complete, and was a public place where it's obviously necessary to consider all aspects of universal design. (Mouritsen)

In my opinion, the process we followed, starting with overall architectural projects and moving to more detailed issues and product design, should be reversed. The product design project engaged the students most easily in universal design. Product design generates enthusiasm and ideas most effectively. Moreover, consultants can relate to it more easily. Many ideas and approaches for product design can be carried over to building design. It is also a good way to introduce ergonomics as a basis for design. (Steinfeld)

Faculty were dissatisfied with the level of attention students gave to detailed technical issues.

Universal product: *This fire extinguisher can be easily operated without fine motor control. Its design easily communicates how it operates.*

Looking backwards it seems to be that instead of having the cottages project, we should have given more time to the hotel design and product design. We got two 'sketch-type' projects. Too few of the students came close enough to a level of detailing interior and exterior design, where design solutions with serious consequences for use and accessibility are generated. The architectural quality of a facade isn't very closely linked to universal design. The design of the bathroom of the guest rooms was an exception from this general statement. (Mouritsen)

In regard to the workshops, hindsight illuminated some need for reorganization and editing:

- To help ensure that the extra work does not divert from the major projects, each workshop should be limited to one afternoon or overnight assignment.

- By focusing Workshop #1 on development of the biography, there would be more time for discussion and several cycles of revisions. Each student should write a real biography of a person with a disability based on observations and interviews. This would avoid the soap opera phenomenon.

- The simulation of disability in Workshop #1 should be integrated with the full-scale model exercise in Workshop #2 or the product design in Workshop #3. This way it could become part of a problem-solving task under faculty supervision.

- The full-scale model should be used in more than one workshop and, if time permits, even more emphasis should be given to building technology.

- The movement exercise should be a separate activity and linked more directly to the ongoing project with a structured and explicit connection.

Evaluation

A group of seventy or more students, faculty, and consultants actively participated in the Universal Design Education Project (UDEP). The evaluative questionnaire, developed by the sponsor of UDEP for use at all project sites, was completed by fifty people. The respondents consisted of nine consultants, thirty-seven students (twenty-seven undergraduate students and ten graduate students), and four faculty members—more than two-thirds of the project participants.

The following analysis examines the answers to four questions on the questionnaire. The answer categories emerged from a content analysis of open-ended answers. Ideally, all answers to the four questions analyzed should be related. UDEP sought to reaffirm an understanding of the physical environment by way of the philosophy and practice of universal design. It also attempted to reconfirm and foster universal design and its associated attitudes. Any apparent inconsistency in answers with respect to these two goals is likely due to the somewhat personal nature of such an evaluation and should not be taken as a direct indication of a shortcoming in the project or the way in which the project was presented.

Question Two. This question asked participants to reflect on their present understanding of the physical environment. Many of the respondents indicated that their participation sparked a realization of the need for "adaptation and accommodation." This answer heading was the answer given by one consultant. Similar responses included value judgments and specific criticisms regarding the disabling qualities of existing physical environments and the need for some alteration.

Most of the undergraduate student answers reiterated this newly acquired understanding of the physical environment, but in more general terms. These students indicated a general overall awareness of the physical environment as well as a general awareness of access issues in the present physical environment. This is the case for the graduate students as well, though three students stressed the need for a social change in attitude, an overall disability consciousness.

Most respondents to Question Two indicated that their participation had positive value in their understanding of the physical environment. Many remarked that they became more aware of its limiting factors; they began to notice environmental barriers more often. Some took a critical stance on the state of the physical environment, which was evidently new for them. Most reflected on their new understanding of universal design as well as an overall universal design consciousness.

Question Three. This question asked participants to reflect on their present understanding of universal design. Many of the respondents answered by indicating a general awareness of universal design. Evidently, this design ideology and philosophy was relatively new for all but two undergraduate students, who remarked that their participation simply expanded their existing understanding of universal design.

Fourteen respondents out of fifty (28 percent) answered this question with an indication that the term *universal design* was perhaps a misnomer. These responses fall into the category best described by the statement, "It made me realize that universal design is not absolute." It included such statements as "made me realize how un-universal our world is" and "there is no such thing as universal design—only 'most inclusive' design." This is evidence of understanding the universal design ideology since it indicates that the students struggled with the concept and took a critical stance on the naming of that concept.

The majority of the respondents to Question Three indicated an increased awareness of universal design and its associated objectives. Three students (two graduate and one undergraduate) indicated that they had no conception of universal design, but this is perhaps an empty criticism. Those who remarked that universal design is not absolute seemed to understand the ideology but pleaded for a more appropriate name. The clear majority evidently came away with an increased understanding of the philosophy, practice, and overall objectives of universal design.

"universal design should become a routine matter for our new 'crop' of architects..."

Question Six. This question asked participants to describe the most valuable new thing gained from their participation in the project and to name the aspect of the project that contributed most to learning this new thing. Many responses to the first part of Question Six indicated a newly learned awareness of "the other" as well as a new perspective on the design process. Participants also seemed to value their social interaction in the academic setting. They came to realize their knowledge of universal design in this context. Many indicated a positive experience in working with others. Though some focused on their struggle with particular design issues, more remarked on their specific inclusion and awareness of "the other." Five students (three graduate and two undergraduate) made some indication of "responsibility" toward that other. Some pointed to a new respect for particular design issues. Some felt a responsibility toward universal design indicating a pathos for disability awareness and an increased consciousness of this perspective.

The majority of the respondents answered the second part of Question Six by indicating that the interactions in the academic setting contributed most to their learning that design must incorporate the needs of others. Thirty percent replied that interaction with consultants contributed most. Twenty-two percent indicated that their most valuable learning was the result of the studio environment, critiques, informal discussions, lectures, presentations and the like. Sixteen percent praised the simulation of disability, the empathetic experience, as the greatest contributor. The remaining thirty-two percent gave more subjective replies.

General Observations. The majority of participants in UDEP became aware of the physical environment, its barriers, and the way they and others interact with the physical environment. They became sensitized enough to universal design objectives and attitudes for them to take a position on what this type of design philosophy should be called. They realized a general awareness of "the other" and a moral position that design should incorporate their needs. Finally, they realized that their new perspective was greatly influenced by the active presence of the consultants, the experience of simulating a disability, and the studio project on the whole.

The analysis of the questionnaire responses demonstrates clearly that, in the words of one respondent, "universal design should become a routine matter for our new 'crop' of architects, as the aged, physically challenged, blind, well, [and] young are all integrated into a society where most are functional." Most of the participants in UDEP would probably agree with this statement and perhaps even argue that universal design is becoming more routine every day.

In conclusion, the general consensus of the faculty was that the focus on universal design was a good approach to teaching architecture. We were definitely successful in reaching our objectives. Through good faculty support, positive student attitudes, and eager consultants, the message of universal design was communicated.

The ultimate evaluation, the work produced by students, clearly reflects the student's integration of that message. Only three of one hundred and fifty projects were "specially" designed for people with disabilities. Through universal design we were able to engage the students in a critique of the contemporary environment and their own work. The students, in fact, challenged faculty to broaden our perspective on universal design. Some students developed projects that were critiques of universal design itself. The work exhibited a great deal of imagination in how universal design can be implemented. Students explored a full range of aesthetic ideas from the "funky" to the "high-tech." They demonstrated how universal design does not limit aesthetic exploration; if anything, it provokes and sustains a search for innovative ideas.

The faculty also learned a lot from this experience. To encourage the most positive student attitudes, we now know that we should present universal design so that it does not compete with learning other fundamental aspects of architecture and product design. We have learned how to improve the use of consultants and the delivery of technical information. And we have learned that our second-year students are able and eager to engage in a high level of intellectual debate about the intent and value of universal design. Such debate is a healthy way to introduce universal design in both theory and practice.

We believe, more strongly than ever, that universal design is good design. Design that seeks inclusion of others' needs and values, at the broadest level, is the most meaningful design. There are no universal solutions, only universal goals. The engagement of the search and a serious effort to reach those goals is what distinguishes "good" from "bad" in this context. To achieve universal design requires deliberate and considered attempts to understand the needs and values of others.

Acknowledgements

We would like to thank all of the participating consultants for their time, willingness, and enthusiasm. Without them, this project would not have been successful.

Notes

1. See Yuker, H.E. (1988). "The Effect of Contact on Attitudes toward Disabled Persons: Some Empirical Generalizations." In *Attitudes towards Persons with Disabilities,* edited by H.E. Yuker. New York: Springer.

Linking the Curriculum with Life Stages and Landscapes

Faculty coordinator:

Jean Stephans Kavanagh
Assistant Professor

Proposal

Landscape architecture has no prototype for modifying the curriculum of five-year degree programs to incorporate the value of universal design. Rather than presenting minimum standards for accessibility, this effort proposed to link the curriculum with life stages and landscapes by stressing functional, aesthetic, and technical aspects of the outdoor spatial experience for people of all abilities.

Universal design should be introduced into the curriculum not as a new area of technology, but as a basic element of ordinary learning and practice for each studio-based course. By introducing universal design as a fundamental attribute of good design, students can readily integrate it into problem-solving strategies and aesthetic objectives when they begin to formulate their design thinking. Universal design values, if reinforced in later coursework, serve as a vehicle for expanding the relationships between function, aesthetic understanding, and traditional design forms.

Integrating universal design across the curriculum proved to be too ambitious with the available funding, so the strategy was modified. In the first semester of the professional design sequence, universal design was introduced into the introductory studio, the third professional graphics course, and the landforms course (the first course in the construction sequence). In the second semester, universal design was further emphasized in the design studio as a fundamental aspect of site investigation and master planning. It was emphasized in the second construction course as a significant factor in the selection of materials and detail construction decisions. In the fourth semester, universal design was stressed in the site design studio as a natural function of designing for diversity and for the life stages of people. These curriculum changes provided exceptionally thorough emphasis on universal design in the initial semesters, followed by redirection and reinforcement of universal design principles in the fourth semester of the studio design sequence.

Activity

The projects were assigned in the following sequence:

Semester 1: Modelling landscape spaces for all participants; Tactile rendering of landscape plans; Drawing file of nontraditional people; and Symposium.

Semester 2: Path of travel analysis.

Semester 4: Design a Family; Universal Design in the Rube Goldberg Experience; and Stringin'em ALL Along.

We reorganized the introductory landscape design studio to incorporate the value of designing for all people. We also developed a few special exercises that made universal access an integral part of the scope of the problem in three semesters of work.

Modelling Landscape Spaces for All Participants. The syllabus and seven-project sequence for the introductory studio rely on a three-dimensional, model-based format to establish universal participation as a fundamental premise for design. The model sequence emphasizes spatial and visual alternatives in the experience of landscape space. Students were asked to design and build landscape models for theoretical settings using three specific landscape media in three different contextual settings (supportive on all sides, supportive on a single side, and conflicting on all sides). Furthermore, students were restricted to a simplified morphology prescribing a single form generation for each model in the sequence. Principles of enclosure, movement, legibility, and experience were introduced and project models were critiqued as components of universal design. This studio establishes at the earliest stage of design education that all structures, features, and experiences must be inclusionary, nonrestrictive, and integrating. Associated courses in the first semester of the design sequence support and elaborate on the principles introduced in this studio.

Tactile Rendering of Landscape Plans. In this exercise, students explored how plans could be made more accessible to people with low vision. Students were given the principles for Braille map-making and were asked to transform one of their projects that required a model and plan submission into a tactile plan which could be readily understandable by a person with low vision. We were fortunate that a local individual with extremely low vision was eager to participate in the classroom critiques and theoretical development for this project. Format size was assigned but material selection, graphic style, and interpretation of designed features were determined by student innovations.

Drawing File of Nontraditional People. Students are often unable to visualize how to draw people who are not young, vigorous, and in peak condition. When they rely on drawing files to animate their drawings, they are no better off because most entourage figures lack diversity as well. Since designers rely heavily on graphic visualization techniques for design exploration and communication, having available images of people who are old, young, caring for children, pregnant, injured, using a cane, or signing increases the likelihood that universal design principles will be employed in the design of outdoor spaces. For the assignment, students located photographs of people with diverse characteristics. Most periodicals and texts still feature "beautiful" people and lack visual representation of the rest of us. The research introduced students to specialized texts that they normally would not run across and gave them an opportunity to explore books on disabilities and aging through an engaging technique.

Symposium. In addition to introducing universal design to Texas Tech students through classroom assignments, the landscape architecture department sponsored a special symposium on making outdoor and recreational environments accessible. Co-sponsorship came from the College of Agricultural Sciences and Natural Resources and the West Texas section of the American Society of Landscape Architects. Susan Goltsman, our UDEP advisor, was a keynote speaker along with Ruth Doyle, a U.S. Forest Service Accessibility Specialist.

Path of Travel Analysis. This exercise familiarized students with the difference between ADA compliance and universal design. Students were asked to conduct an ADA site evaluation. Then they reconsidered the site from a non-regulatory perspective—as a recreational experience for the student, accompanied by a family member or friend with a disability—and compared the results of the two approaches. At least two sites were compared, including, where possible, a site the student was designing. This exercise was assigned in the first design studio and reissued in subsequent design studios to build on the student's prior insights and understandings.

Design a Family. In this exercise students described families who would serve as prototypical users for the entire semester of design studio. Site-specific planning and design activity is fundamentally dependent upon the modification of natural environments for the utility and enjoyment of a specific group of people. When no specific client group is defined, students and designers often imagine a prototypical person or group of people who will be using their landscapes. Students' ability to critique their own work is dependent on knowing the characteristics of these imaginary users. Problems in designed landscapes can be traced to the designer's inadequate understanding or biased critique of the ways in which real people interact with their landscape. To avoid the pitfalls of bias in having a nonspecific, imaginary user, students were asked to define a group or "family" with specific characteristics who will be the users or visitors to each of the landscape problems given during the semester. The family had to include people with a range of ages, genders, and physical abilities. The family descriptions helped the instructor critique the students' work.

Universal Design in the Rube Goldberg Experience. Landscape architects are frequently called upon to develop site designs offering innovative and entertaining pedestrian experiences. This assignment asked students to stretch their imaginations in the manner of Rube Goldberg, the early twentieth-century American cartoonist, who specialized in illustrating ludicrously complex machines to accomplish simple, basic tasks. Students designed and built Rube Goldberg machines as metaphors for self-propelled movement through landscape space that exhibits all of the principles of universal design. The "pedestrians" were represented by ping pong balls and the "site" was one cubic yard of space. Students were reminded that the ping pong person was generic so had a sixty percent chance of having some disability. Movement had to be powered by mechanical or gravitational sources. The students' inventions were evaluated for: amusement value to the ping pong person, variety of moving experiences, utilization of the entire volume, degree of care afforded the person/user, adherence to the project definition, and workmanship.

Stringin'em ALL Along. This project reinforced the learning in the previous project by encouraging students to employ expressive and definitive elements in outdoor space. A few trees, some shrubs, and simple changes in the ground plane surface can very clearly define space in the landscape. This space carries a wealth of associations that entice, enhance, encourage, discourage, complicate, forbid, or enhance human interactions and enjoyment of that landscape. Students were asked to design a complete pedestrian experience, composed entirely of string, in a series of outdoor spaces that would be used by everyone. The string was to be *the* element by which

pedestrians are guided through the site, without creating an obstacle course or playground. The design was intended to heighten the visitor's experience, enjoyment, and understanding of landscape while exploiting the expressive qualities of string. Disabilities were not only accommodated, they were to be celebrated. The projects were judged on, among other things: their intrigue value; the quality, variety, universality, and safety of pedestrian experiences; and transitions between spaces as crafted experiences. Students selected one project from the models built by the class to build on the actual site in the central campus area. Students judged the universal design success of the landscape design by carrying out a disability simulation exercise within the string construction.

Rube Goldberg Landscape Experience model completed in Studio IV by fourth year student, Jesus Ramirez.

Outcome

The introductory studio met with resistance from the first-year students who were unfamiliar with the ADA, not to mention universal design. The continuity of faculty and the repeated emphasis on people of every ability in assignments throughout the introductory curriculum were extremely important to validating universal design in the eyes of the students. Once initial objections were addressed, the studio participants produced designs that successfully explored the nature of universal design in the landscape.

The most troublesome of the assignments described above was the Path of Travel Analysis because it relied heavily on attitudes presented and supported by the instructor. Although the assignment sought independent thinking and evaluation, the students needed constant encouragement and reinforcement to overcome ingrained expectations about users of designed landscapes. The assignment's concurrent evaluation of a site from the viewpoint of a visitor with a disability proved to be a valuable component. One student commented: "ADA alone wouldn't make the landscape suitable for my elderly person to visit," and "It really helped to imagine a visit with my visitor and her two babies. I'd never have identified problems without that part of the assignment."

The string landscape proved to be a very exciting project. However, its strength was primarily as a visual element in the landscape. The simulation exercise identified only a few problems in terms of access. In the future greater emphasis will be placed upon the experiential qualities during the design phases.

Evaluation

Since the projects required students to make a shift in viewpoint rather than absorb new technologies, the degree of learning was difficult to evaluate. Attitudes were clearly different after the sequence but students did not recognize that they had made radical changes in either their approach or their values. Later projects, especially those in the fourth semester, were viewed by students as regular projects, not specifically as universal design projects. We view this as a significant measure of success.

Comparing students' submissions in these studios with those of studios in prior years reveals significant shifts in providing for people of diverse abilities. In particular, emphasizing universal design reduced the reliance on stairs for level changes and excessive grades.

Reflection

Our project has progressed with a minimum of funding. As a result, our efforts have not included any stipends for the continuous paid involvement of consultants. However, we have found that volunteer consultants with disabilities are often eager to participate in a design studio experience on an occasional basis. Our most enthusiastic volunteer was a person with low vision whose influence is evidenced in our emphasis on communication during the design process as well as on universal design in the designed landscape. We have also been pleasantly surprised to realize that this occasional intervention by volunteers with disabilities has proven to be a very effective method of introducing universal design in the landscape architecture curriculum.

Familiarity with people who have disabilities and with disabling conditions is best realized by inviting a wide range of people to participate in the classroom. Early introduction seems to work extremely well. However, as our students engage in summer internships in professional design offices, much of the universal design emphasis is undermined by employers who are not supportive of universal design or, in many cases, are not convinced that people with disabilities should receive "special design consideration."

Acknowledgements

This work at Texas Tech University resulted from the efforts of Professor Kavanagh working in collaboration with colleague and department head Thomas A. Musiak. Professor Musiak's introduction of universal design concepts and methods and materials in the construction sequence underscored issues introduced in the design core.

19 University of Michigan – Ann Arbor, Michigan and Eastern Michigan University – Ypsilanti, Michigan

Collaboration between Interior Design, Industrial Design, and Architecture

A Day's Journey Through Life©: A Design Education Game

Principal investigator:

Leon A. Pastalan
Professor,
University of Michigan

Team members:

Louise Jones
Associate Professor,
Eastern Michigan University
Ronald A. Sekulski
Assistant Professor,
University of Michigan

Proposal

People who are disabled, frail, or elderly (D/F/E), most of whom want to maintain independent lifestyles, make up an increasingly large segment of the population. In 1900, there were 3 million Americans 65 years of age or older (1 in 25 Americans), comprising 4 percent of the population. By 1990, 1 in 8 people were 65 or older (12.6 percent or 30.5 million people). By the year 2030, 1 in 5 Americans (22 percent or 67 million) will be 65 or older (U.S. Bureau of the Census, 1990). As the median age increases, the United States will become a nation with more elderly people (predominantly female) who require many of the services and supportive environments that are currently earmarked for people with disabilities. Of the population 65 years of age and older, 46 percent have a health impairment resulting in ambulatory limitations—often confining them to home.

These figures suggest that the design professions need to be more cognizant of universal design criteria. Not only is the D/F/E population expanding, but there is increasing recognition of the pervasiveness of temporary disabilities. All Americans, if they live long enough, will experience a disability (e.g., a problem with walking, seeing, or hearing) at some point in their lives. Universal design—designing all products, buildings, and interiors to be usable by all people to the greatest extent possible (Lusher)—offers a solution to the design challenges presented by the D/F/E population.

Unfortunately, there is little information on the D/F/E population available in an accessible format for students to integrate into the design process. Moreover, there is little documentation of how D/F/E persons, their families, and their friends have attempted to modify products or the physical environment to meet their individual requirements. Knowledge of their needs and adaptations would be invaluable to design students and practitioners seeking to incorporate universal design criteria into their design work.

The goal of our project was to introduce design students to an experiential, interactive, design research method and to demonstrate that the game/simulation *A Day's Journey Through Life©* (GS) offers students significant insight into the environmental and performance needs of a diverse population, thereby changing their perception of accessibility and universal design issues.

To fully understand the complexity of everyday life for D/F/E people, the form of inquiry must address a level of specificity and richness of experience that is not captured through self-administered questionnaires or structured interviews. In seeking this knowledge, however, traditional data collection techniques are problematic because of the demands of time related to interviews, the contamination of data related to participant observation, and the low response rate associated with survey questionnaire requests.

Students studying the relationship between environment and behavior need data that has not been contaminated by interpretation of others. Relying on design research that has been collected, compiled, and interpreted by others removes the student from direct interaction with the subjects. Survey data are devoid of the direct insight into human conditions that are not only diverse but also constantly changing. The spirit or essence of some critical issues may only be perceived by interacting with the individual within the context of the immediate environs. Exposure of students to some of the changes associated with the lifespan can best be accomplished through one-on-one direct communication with those who are attempting to maintain independent lifestyles.

To expand the breadth of students' empirical experience, a game/simulation titled *A Day's Journey Through Life*© was developed as a design research technique.[1] As a data collection instrument, the game/simulation can provide access to formerly inaccessible information and stimulate interaction and discussion, which may yield new insights and new attitudes regarding universal design issues.

Formal game theory attempts to correlate certain human behavior with game-like characteristics. In the 1960s at John Hopkins University, sociologist James Coleman initiated the development of games for use in educational settings. Most educational games attempt to portray both a realistic model of a particular environment as well as specific subject matter content. At the University of Michigan, Richard D. Duke, Allan Feldt, Layman Allen, Fred Goodman, and others continued that development and investigated multiple uses for games. Duke (1991) describes gaming as a hybrid communication form that has the ability to accurately convey sophisticated information with a greater perception of the interrelationships involved than is possible through simple language forms. At the Western Behavioral Institute, Gary Shirts, Hall Sprague, John Raser, and Waymon J. Crow extended the investigation to include the use of simulation in educational settings. Simulations are closely linked to games; the distinctions are more a matter of technical differences than of theory or purpose. A simulation may be described as an operational model that illustrates functional and structural relationships of the central features of a system (Duke, 1991).

Games serve as metaphors of reality that permit the participant to develop a common language for discussing the problems at hand. Games may serve as a simulation model of some part of reality, or they may represent an abstract world. A game can provide a skeletal model of a system in order to structure communication in a productive way. The primary features of the system are presented to motivate players to discuss the problems at hand. Gaming improves communication about a complex environment to enable new alternatives to be envisioned and tested.

Games are frequently described as a safe environment for learning. This, combined with their ability to hold the participants' attention and to quickly convey the central characteristics of a complex environment, makes them excellent as innovative design research instruments. They are designed to free participants from everyday constraints, to encourage innovation, and to assist in the communication of complex and emergent ideas about possible alternate paths (Duke, 1991).

Activity

The UDEP grant supported activities in two design studios, industrial design at the University of Michigan (working with Ron Sekulski) and interior design at Eastern Michigan University (working with Louise Jones). Both faculty members and Lee Pastalan, who served as advisor for both groups, met frequently to coordinate activities.

At Eastern Michigan University, senior interior design students were invited by a nonprofit agency to develop a design proposal for the adaptive reuse of the Ann Arbor Inn. Industrial design students at the University of Michigan were invited to identify and develop products that could be used in this environment.

The Allenel Hotel was originally built on the site of the Ann Arbor Inn in the 1840s. Although the original building was razed in 1963, a hotel was in operation on the site until 1990 when the owner declared bankruptcy and the furnishings, fixtures, and equipment were sold. The vacant eleven-story, 145,000-square-foot building was zoned for residential, commercial, and retail use. The program for adaptive reuse was to incorporate office space; an indoor, year-round park; retail spaces; classrooms and offices for the local community college's outreach program; senior co-op apartments; management offices; resident activity rooms; an indoor pool and physical fitness center; and a restaurant for both residents and the general public.

Model of Ann Arbor Inn. (Courtesy of Kadushin Associates Architects and Planners)

Students from both universities were assigned to teams to play the game, ensuring that each team would have both industrial and interior design representation. Each student team was assigned to a consultant, an individual selected from the local D/F/E population, with whom they would play the game. Consultants were identified by the instructors using personal contacts, personnel at the local

Center for Independent Living, and individuals with disabilities who had participated in The ADA Implementation Network Training sessions through the Disability and Business Technical Assistance Centers. There were two consultants representing each of the user groups: hearing impaired; vision impaired; mobility impaired (both permanent and temporary); frail elderly (musculoskeletal problems); manipulation, dexterity, grip problems; and those who fell in the anthropometric extremes (less than the 5th percentile or greater than the 95th percentile). Some consultants had multiple problems. For example, one consultant was a 48-year-old man with Parkinson's disease whose wife has Lou Gehrig's disease; another was a 22-year-old man who lost his eyesight and one leg in a small plane crash; a third consultant was a 40-year-old woman with multiple sclerosis.

A Day's Journey Through Life© is part of a longstanding gaming/simulation tradition that structures communication in a context of multilogue as compared to dialogue. Words in sequence are less powerful than the combined interactive effects of words, objects, and actions in a situational context. The combination can more readily convey totality and therefore speed understanding and the generation of information about complex environmental design problems. Multilogue has been shown to be effective at sensitizing the design student to disability and lifespan concerns and to the uniqueness of each individual's experiences (Sekulski, Jones, and Pastalan, 1994). Use of interactive programming (i.e., data collection in conjunction with specific performance criteria) will enable design students to consider the particular functional needs that come with age, varying abilities, and disabilities in order to design products and facilities that are accessible by all people to the greatest extent possible.

The components of A Day's Journey Through Life.©

The game board and sequence of play were developed to move participants through the activities of daily life (for example, grooming, dressing, cooking, cleaning) in a setting familiar to the consultant. During the game, the consultant is considered the VIP (Very Important Person) because she is teaching the students about life as a member of that user group. During a two- to three-hour time period that includes orientation, game play, and debriefing, a student team engages the VIP and a caregiver (if applicable) in a multilogue to identify the aspects of the micro- and macro-environment that inhibit autonomy and independence.

The game is played in the VIP's residence to encourage identification of specific problem areas in the home environment. The familiarity of the home setting encourages a more relaxed ambiance where the VIP is willing to share insights and intimate experiences, disclosures that might be inhibited by clinical or unfamiliar surroundings. During the game play, the VIP, a caregiver (if applicable), the facilitator, and a recorder are seated around a table large enough to accommodate the gameboard and playing pieces. The facilitator's role is to engage the VIP in the play of the game and ask probing questions to encourage full disclosure of the complexity of the activities of daily living (ADLs). The recorder, sometimes assisted by audio or videotape recordings, stays in the background, using the recorder's notebook to capture the information revealed.

To initiate the game, the facilitator, using a series of twenty ADL icon cards, requests the VIP to determine whether each ADL is difficult or easy to execute. This round of play introduces the range of ADLs that will be discussed and initiates consideration of the limitations and challenges associated with the VIP's specific abilities and living environment. The facilitator and VIP move quickly through the cards without pausing to discuss problems or issues.

In the second round of play, the VIP identifies the time of day when a particular ADL is most likely to be performed or, if performed several times a day, when it is most troublesome. The activity cards are placed on the game playing field in one of four time quadrants (morning, afternoon, evening, or night) according to the VIP's responses. The next round of play brings more depth to the inquiry by prompting the VIP to relive *A Day's Journey Through Life©*. Starting with the morning quadrant and progressing through the time periods, the VIP chooses an ADL activity card and responds to the question printed on the card (i.e., What do you do when you first wake up?). This elicits both the problems encountered on a day-to-day basis and the coping strategies routinely implemented to address them. The final round of play identifies any remaining issues by inviting the VIP to describe the most troublesome activity experienced on a daily basis and the product she finds most difficult to use.

Outcome

Early in the semester, students brainstormed the problems that users of different ages and abilities might have with the environment. Due to students' youth, firsthand experience with stroke rehabilitation or cataracts was limited, although some could discuss problems their parents or grandparents were having. Very few students acknowledged having friends or relatives who had disabling conditions. However, temporary mobility problems caused by athletic injuries or Michigan winters provided some insight on the problems that might be encountered and possible coping mechanisms.

Many students expressed apprehension about meeting the consultants in their homes, but in most instances the consultants were a wealth of insights and imaginative coping strategies. As one student explained, "We began to see universal design as a way to assist users of products or environments to function efficiently and inde-

A Day's Journey Through Life© gameboard set up for round two, showing the four time quadrants and ADL activity cards.

pendently. By incorporating these parameters and asking these questions during the design research phase, the likely outcome is a product or environment that can be used by a broad spectrum of users."

A consultant with industrial and interior design students in round three of playing the game.

After playing the game with the consultants, students recognized the need for both a broader perspective and for more specific criteria for each impairment. They extended their research to the library to identify the underlying characteristics of the impairments (e.g., conditions that lead to use of a wheelchair), the prevalence of the conditions (e.g., 31 million Americans have mobility problems), the magnitude of the problems (e.g., not all wheelchairs are created equal), and the relevant codes and legislation (e.g., barrier-free building codes, ADAAG, and the Fair Housing Amendments Act). This information was essential in understanding the full scope of the problems rather than focusing exclusively on the narrow perspective narrated by one consultant.

Industrial design students met with other professors, research scientists, and experts in the field. One student noted, "We were very surprised to find that extensive statistical and human factors data simply doesn't exist for many of these groups (e.g., 'frail elderly').... We benefited greatly by hearing the sometimes contradictory directions their answers gave us."

Interior design students' research included interviews with elderly people and members of the user groups; interviews with directors of senior housing and activity

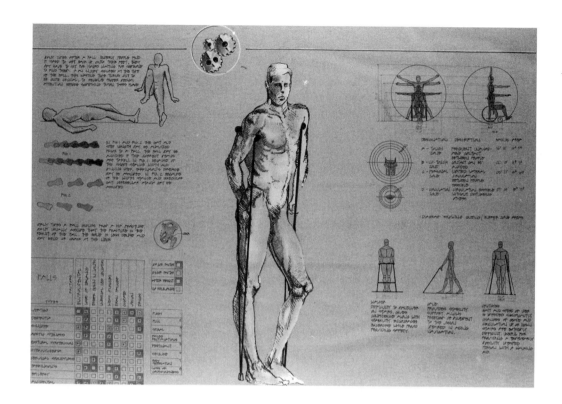

Industrial design students' research presentation board.

centers; participant observation at senior centers; visits to the local Center for Independent Living; attendance at a full-day workshop on the ADA by Cynthia Leibrock (author of *Beautiful Barrier-Free*); and interviews with agencies interested in the Ann Arbor Inn renovation.

At the conclusion of the design research phase, students faced the challenge of organizing and presenting the scientific, statistical, and anecdotal data. Industrial design student teams prepared large-scale presentation boards that used both text and drawings to present the information. Interior design student teams prepared concise "Design Reference Sheets" for each user group for fellow students to use during design conceptualization and development. This handout described the disability factually, identified the most common design concerns, and included an annotated bibliography of source material.

Through research and the interactive programming experiences (participant observations, interviews, and game play), design students came to know, understand, and empathize with the particular user group being investigated. Students served as advocates for their user groups for the duration of the semester. This included working with classmates to resolve design concerns and critiquing design proposals for their appropriateness for the particular user group.

*Interior design students'
design reference sheet for
hearing impairment.*

DESIGN REFERENCE SHEET
HEARING IMPAIRMENT

DEFINITION

There are many degrees of hearing impairment experienced by the 1 in 10 Americans with a hearing loss. The medical and social problems experienced by people with a partial hearing loss are quite different from those experienced by people who have a total hearing loss. The two groups should not be grouped together indiscriminately.

Deafness: A total or severe impairment of hearing. Individuals may use sign language and/or speech reading (i.e., lip reading) to compensate for their hearing loss. Pre-lingual deafness occurs before auditory language skills are developed. Individuals often use sign language as the first language with English (or another spoken language) as a second language. Post lingual deafness occurs after auditory language skills are developed. Individuals typically have more advanced speaking skills and a better understanding of spoken language.

Hard of hearing: A partial impairment of hearing, often the result of illness, injury, or aging. Individuals typically use a spoken language to communicate. Individuals may benefit from surgery and/or hearing aides and may read lips to facilitate communication.

INTERIOR DESIGN GUIDELINES

*Specify and/or provide for use of assistive devises such as TDD attachments for the telephone, closed caption television decoders, vibrating alarm clocks, and blinking light alarms/timers.

*Keep "visual noise" to a minimum to provide a neutral ground for signing.

*Provide generous, non-glare lighting to facilitate speech reading or sign.

*Specify sound absorbing materials and finishes to minimize reflected noise and reduce background noise for those with a partial hearing impairment.

*Specify appropriate electrical wiring and controls to permit lights to flicker when phone or doorbell rings.

*Use visual icons for multiple cueing whenever possible. People who use sign as their first language may have difficulty understanding written language.

*Specify supplementary visual alert systems for fire alarms.

*Provide alternate communication systems in locations where emergency phones are used.

*Design furniture arrangements that do not profile people in front of window glazing to assist those who read lips or sign.

REFERENCES

Suss, Elaine. (1993). <u>When the Hearing Gets Hard</u>. New York: Plenum Publishing. A hearing impaired journalist discusses the problems experiences by people with hearing impairments in a "hearing world".

Schein, Jerome. (1989). <u>At Home Among Strangers</u>. Washington, DC: Galluadet University Press. Informative text written by an educator at one of the foremost institutions of higher learning to help others understand the "deaf community".

Rezen, Susan & Hausman, Carl. (1985). <u>Coping with a Hearing Loss</u>. New York: Dembner Books. The book provides a sensitive discussion of the physical and psychological effects of hearing loss and suggests methods of coping with the related problems.

Turkington, C. & Sussman, A. (1992). <u>Encyclopedia of Deafness and Hearing Disorders</u>. New York: Facts on File. Text defines words and terms, discusses causes and characteristics of hearing impairments, and identifies assistive devices and support organizations.

Ritter, Audrey (1985). <u>A Deafness Collection: Selected and Annotated</u>. Rochester Institute of Technology & The National Technical Institute for the Deaf. Bibliography of related readings.

Van Itallie, Phillip. <u>How to Live with a Hearing Handicap</u>. New York: Paul Ericksson Inc. Author uses his own experiences as a person who is hard of hearing to help others with similar problems understand and adjust to the problems experienced in everyday life.

Chapter 19: University of Michigan and Eastern Michigan University

Consultants and UDEP advisor participating in joint mid-term critique for interior design and industrial design students.

Working in their respective studios, students moved from design research to conceptualization. Industrial design students drew from the areas of difficulty most commonly cited by consultants to identify product opportunities. They selected four opportunities for design innovation: parking meters; eating utensils; wayfinding systems; and portable postural support systems.

Interior design students began concept development for both the public spaces and the private apartments in the renovation project.[2] To encourage cooperative learning, the students worked in teams to develop proposals for the public spaces. They were required to recognize the needs of users of all ages and abilities by employing universal design guidelines in their proposals for the public spaces. Students used the concept of adaptable housing for the apartment units to improve the quality of life for all residents. Each student developed a base plan for an apartment using universal design criteria (e.g., wider doorways and adjustable height cabinetry). Modifications were then developed for different user groups (e.g., visual alarms for those with hearing impairments or removable base cabinets for those who use a wheelchair). When done well, universal design implementation is invisible—that is, it is simply perceived as good design. Therefore, students were asked to document their proposals for implementing universal design and adaptable housing considerations using both traditional design drawings (including sketches, floor plans, and elevations) and annotated overlays.

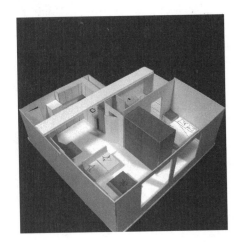

Interior design student's model for an apartment based on universal design considerations and modifications for particular user groups.

At the mid-term critiques, students from both programs presented their work to peers, faculty, consultants, and the UDEP advisor, Polly Welch. Students gained a better understanding of each discipline's design process during the lively discussions that celebrated successful iterations and identified opportunities for improvements to ensure that the needs of all users would be fully addressed.

The second half of the semester was spent in design development with frequent peer and faculty critiques within the respective studios. Although students from both schools might have benefited from more frequent interaction, conflicting schedules made this logistically infeasible. An end-of-term presentation to the general public provided an opportunity for students to showcase their work. Faculty reserved an assembly hall and sent invitations to university administrators, colleagues, consultants, city administrators involved in the decision-making for the renovation project, and the press. The evening opened with one-on-one discussions of product solutions and apartment plans using a poster session format. The informal discussions and refreshments that followed the interior design student teams' presentation of the proposals for the public spaces provided an appropriate finale for the semester.

Evaluation

Students were overwhelmingly positive concerning their learning experiences during the semester-long UDEP project. Responses to the open-ended questions on the end-of-term evaluation forms indicated that students found the studio experiences to be challenging but rewarding. Many seemed to have adopted a universal design perspective. When asked how universal design might impact them professionally, one responded succinctly, "I will design for it!" Many found that their understanding of the relationship between user needs and the physical environment changed, "[I've] become more aware of what actually limits one's freedom of choice." When asked what was the single most important thing learned that semester, one student replied, "to design for everyone, not just the 'average' individual."

For a more formal evaluation, a pilot assessment project was initiated to assess the change in knowledge and attitude experienced by students participating in the UDEP project. UDEP students at both schools completed a brief questionnaire[3] at the beginning of the semester to determine their attitudes and knowledge of ADA guidelines, universal design, and the environmental problems associated with disability and lifespan issues. Students were retested at the end of the semester to assess changes in knowledge or attitude. A second group of design students who were enrolled in a human factors class, completed the pre-/post-tests as a comparison group. Format for the class included lectures, films, speakers, and empathic experiences such as using a wheelchair and navigating the environment while blindfolded. A third group of design students who were enrolled in a studio class, completed the pretest, saw a video related to the universal design, and were retested. A fourth group of design students served as the control group. They were enrolled in a studio class and completed the pre/post-tests but had no specific introduction to ADA legislation or universal design principles. Scores for the five groups were compared[4] to assess the effectiveness of the UDEP project in acquiring knowledge and in promoting attitudinal change. Highlights from the analysis are summarized below.[5]

Students present their proposals at an end-of-term event for the general public.

The a priori expectation was that scores for industrial and interior design students who participated in the UDEP project could be combined. This proved to be infeasible when major differences were discovered in the pretest analysis. Although 100 percent of the interior design students indicated they were familiar with the ADA, only 13 percent of the industrial design students did so. This familiarity probably reflects the mandate that interior design work comply with building codes, ADA guidelines, and barrier-free legislation; there is no equivalent requirement for industrial design. However, chi square analysis indicated a statistically significant difference in post-test scores for industrial design students who participated in the UDEP project (87 percent) when compared with scores for the control group (31 percent), indicating a significant change in knowledge of ADA associated with participation in the UDEP project.

There were similar differences in industrial design students' and interior design students' pretest scores for correctly defining universal design (13 percent and 35 percent, respectively). Chi square analysis indicated statistically significant differences in post-test scores between interior and industrial design UDEP students and the control group, suggesting a significant change in knowledge of universal design associated with participation in the UDEP project. Post-test scores increased to 86 percent for industrial design students and 94 percent for interior design students, compared with a consistent 31 percent for the control group.

Pre-test scores for the industrial design UDEP students indicated that 50 percent believed ADA would impact them professionally after graduation and 56 percent believed universal design would do so. Post-test scores increased to 75 percent for ADA and 94 percent for universal design, suggesting a change in attitude. Although pre-test data indicated that 94 percent of the interior design UDEP students believed the ADA would impact them professionally after graduation, only 25 percent believed universal design would do so. Post-test scores increased to 100 percent for both questions, suggesting a significant change of attitude.

Reflection

Gaming. *A Day's Journey Through Life*© helped students obtain a more in-depth understanding of the task and performance needs of special populations and an appreciation for universal design considerations. The insights developed while playing the game with the consultants led to new conceptual directions through which to envision supportive environments. Students acquired an increased awareness of the value of integrating design features that expand the breadth of application and use.

Cross-Disciplinary Understanding. Interaction between the interior and industrial design students enabled them to compare the design process used in each profession, heightening their awareness of similar as well as distinctive aspects. Industrial design students gained a fuller understanding of the scope of the interior designer's role in protecting the health, safety, and welfare of the public through enhancement of the quality of life of the users. Interior design students came to understand the extent of human performance research initiated by industrial designers in order to develop design criteria that shape product configurations.

Interaction of User, Product, and Place. Both groups of students gained a fuller understanding of the complex interactions that occur between the user and the

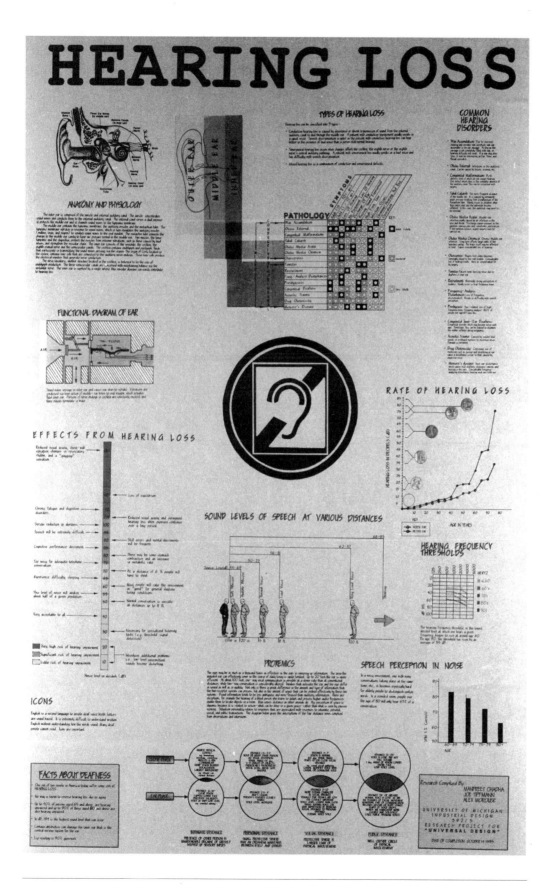

*Industrial design students'
research presentation
board.*

Chapter 19: University of Michigan and
Eastern Michigan University

Industrial design student presents his portable seating proposal.

environment. Their comprehension of the mutual interdependence of the micro and macro elements of objects and environments was enhanced by examining the interplay among product, place, and user. By advancing their understanding of the environmental context in which products are used, industrial design students became more sensitive to many aspects of accessibility, comfort, and ease of use. Interior design students benefited from the collaboration by developing an increased awareness of how the design of objects that constitute the micro-environment influences the behavior of the user and, ultimately, the design of the macro-environment.

Based on their identification of product needs through the game, and their research related to kinesthetics, anthropometrics, and ergonomics, industrial design students developed a portable chair that could be adjusted to fit the comfort requirements of a particular user. Interior design students, knowing that residents would be storing these chairs, moving them through the building, and using them in public places, utilized this information in developing their design proposals.

A vivid illustration of the intersection between industrial and interior design students' concerns centered around wayfinding. Students initiated research on the process of wayfinding. The literature review indicated that people's primary means of directional information is visual. However, people who have a severe visual impairment rely upon their other senses—touch, hearing, and smell. The most commonly used cues include sound, light/dark contrast, temperature changes, and, most importantly, changes in surface texture (Finkel, 1993). Insights gained from the game play identified a change in floor surfacing (e.g., color contrast, tactile and resiliency receptivity, and sound reflectivity) as one of the most useful cues in wayfinding.

Students discovered that architectural cueing informed directional decisions. A person with sight may use a window in a hallway as a marker to find the door to the restroom; a person with visual impairment may also use the window as a marker by sensing a change in temperature, air pressure, or light levels. Students learned that people with vision impairments are acutely aware of the architectural design details that impede or assist them in wayfinding. The typical problems with wayfinding are exacerbated when there is an absence of architectural cueing. People with sight also experience frustration when the design of the building does not clearly communicate wayfinding information, but it is more difficult for a person with a visual impairment to recover after missing a cue (Finkel, 1993). Students realized that the integration of interior architectural features and surface finishes that offer redundant cueing would benefit both those who are visually impaired and those with good vision—a universal design solution.

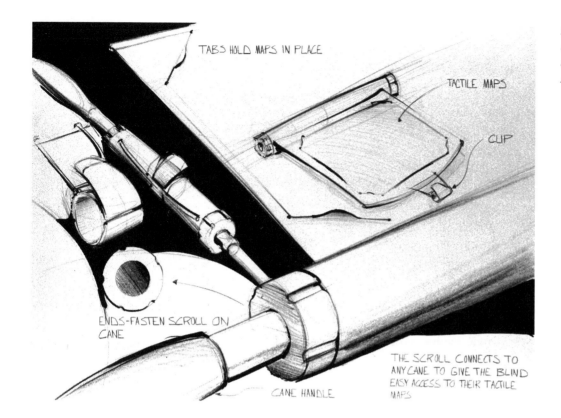

Industrial design students' design proposal for a guidance system for the Ann Arbor Inn renovation.

Students from both disciplines were able to use this design research information to define performance criteria for the interior and product design solutions. An industrial design product team developed a guidance system that integrated environmental cues such as texture changes, sound reflectivity, and resiliency receptivity. The interior design students specified interior surface finishes with a rich diversity of texture (e.g., smooth/rough wall finishes, soft/hard floor treatments) and specified a variation in lighting levels to provide redundant cueing for wayfinding.

Dispelling Myths. "I have met the enemy and he is us" (Pogo). Because people are often uncomfortable with anything different or unknown, and because disabilities remind them of their own frailty, some people disassociate themselves from those who have obvious physical differences. *A Day's Journey Through Life©* provided an opportunity for students to interact with people of different ages and abilities. Myths and phobias were dispelled as students realized that not only do they experience similar performance problems with environmental barriers, but they also share common dreams, expectations, and aspirations with people who are different from themselves.

The students discovered that designers created many of the physical barriers that inhibit independent living. As students, however, they were being given an opportunity to develop the knowledge and skills to create products and places that can facilitate access, interaction, and task accomplishment with ease, comfort, and safety. In the words of one student, "I enhanced my knowledge of design this semester, but of greater importance, I learned more about people and myself than in any other course I have ever taken!"

A New Paradigm. Universal design represents a major direction of current design theory: accessible, adaptable, and transgenerational design practices. When projects are designed using universal design precepts, the results can be aesthetically pleasing and cost effective as well as accessible to all. Instead of responding only to the minimum requirements of laws which mandate a few special features for individuals with disabilities, 'good design' can meet the needs of many different user groups.

Design practitioners, however, need assistance in responding to the mandate that design should serve the broadest possible population, including people of different ages and ability levels. Many traditionally schooled educators and practitioners are poorly prepared to implement universal design concepts. Preconceptions and myths must be challenged with new perspectives and knowledge. Data collection instruments that involve the user in the design process are needed. Design criteria must be developed to define performance requirements for both products and the physical environment.

The UDEP project introduced a design research method that involves the D/F/E individual and the design student in a multilogue to identify the problems experienced in accomplishing the activities of daily living. The replication of this project can expand the repertoire of research methods available to design educators and practitioners, facilitate adoption of universal design guidelines, and facilitate a shift in paradigm from exclusive to inclusive design.

Closing Thoughts. Collaboration between schools and disciplines is never as easy as a singular effort. The singular effort, however, is seldom as rewarding as collaborative work. The increased understanding that accompanies collaborative work and the comprehensiveness of the design solutions make the effort worthwhile. Involvement of "real-life" participants and incorporation of out-of-classroom experiences require more extensive preparation than simulated experiences; but the depth of understanding and commitment to problem resolution are enhanced by interactions with the ultimate users in the contextual setting.

The benefits of structuring multidisciplinary student research teams and playing *A Day's Journey Through Life*© with the consultants in their homes were demonstrated by the students' increased sensitivity to user needs and by the integration of universal design considerations into their projects. Students successfully translated the insights developed during the game into design decisions that reflected a commitment to enhancing the accessibility and use of both products and environments. Students are more comfortable interacting with people of different ages and ability levels and have internalized pertinent design recommendations, regulations, and codes. Their projects reflect a heightened sensitivity to the design needs of people of different ages and abilities and a proficiency in the development of design criteria reflective of the needs of a diverse population.

The administrations and fellow faculty at both universities were supportive of the UDEP project and are interested in sustaining students' commitment to the integration of universal design considerations. Lessons learned (e.g., remuneration for consultants to encourage full participation and additional opportunities for joint student activities to enhance understanding and respect) would make replication of the collaboration easier than the initial experience. The rewards justify the expenditure of time and energy required to ensure a positive experience for both students and faculty.

Acknowledgements

Participation by the consultants was essential to the success of this project and is gratefully acknowledged: Ann Marie Barnes, Paul Cartman, Jeanne Clerc, Vivian Connor, Danielle Denston, Barb and Doug Doty, Owen Eshenroder, Gloria Grametbauer, Mildred McArdell, Annette Peel, Cathy Rathwell, Mariam Sampson, Andrea Solsburg, and John Viery.

References

Duke, R. (1991). *People at Play*. UNESCO. New York: United Nations.

Lusher, R. (1991). *Universal Design: Access to Daily Living*. CADRE. Brooklyn, N.Y.: Pratt Institute.

Finkel (1993). *Wayfinding by People with Visual Impairments in the Built Environment*. Unpublished master's thesis. Winnipeg, Manitoba: University of Manitoba.

Sekulski, R., L. Jones, and L. Pastalan (1994). *A Day's Journey Through Life©: An Assessment Game*. Paper presented at the Measuring Handicapping Environments Conference sponsored by The Adaptive Environments Laboratory. Buffalo, N.Y.: State University of New York.

U.S. Bureau of the Census (1992). *1990 Census of Population and Housing Summary Social, Economic and Housing Characteristics of the United States*. Washington, D.C.: U.S. Government Printing Office.

Chapter 19: University of Michigan and Eastern Michigan University

Notes

1. *A Day's Journey Through Life©: A Design Education Game* is derived from a generic game developed by Environmental Design for Aging Research Group (EDARG) associates Leon A. Pastalan, Louise Jones, Benyamin Schwarz, Ronald A. Sekulski, and Laura Struble.

2. The senior interior design studio was team taught by Eastern Michigan University design faculty. Dr. Deb DeLaski-Smith supervised selection and specification of materials, surface finishes, and furnishings; Dr. Louise Jones supervised design exploration and development including incorporation of universal design considerations as well as compliance with barrier free building codes and ADAAG; Abe Kadushin supervised time management plans and adaptive reuse considerations, including construction, HVAC, electrical, and plumbing; Dr. Virginia North supervised programming and concept development, lighting design, and design presentation.

3. William McKeachie, an expert in educational curriculum development and testing with the Center for Research on Learning and Teaching at the University of Michigan, provided support in the development of the test instruments.

4. The Center for Statistical Consultation and research at the University of Michigan provided support and guidance in the design of the evaluation project and in the analysis of the data.

5. Contact the authors for a complete reporting of the statistical analysis.

Educating Reflective Practitioners through Universal Design

Team members:

Ruth Brent
Professor
Benyamin Schwarz
Assistant Professor
Gary Hennigh
Associate Professor

Proposal

Educating design students to make sustained arguments, ethical commitments, and independent judgments based on internalized values is an overriding goal in teaching universal design at the University of Missouri. Using William Perry's theory on how students think, faculty proposed to challenge students to move beyond dualist thinking, which considers right or wrong, and relativistic thinking, which considers the context, to advanced reflective thinking. Kitchener and King (1990) describe the reflective thinker as "someone who is aware that a problematic situation exists and is able to bring critical judgment to bear on the problem." Along with Kitchener and King, James Davis (1993) advocates a teaching approach and "educational milieu" that help students move to the next stage of cognitive development. This can be done by introducing developmentally appropriate activities that stimulate students to evaluate where they are and consider the next alternative.

University of Missouri faculty originally proposed to implement a program-wide enrichment through an awareness week, a design charrette, student reference kits, teaching packages, and public events. In addition, they planned to coordinate eight conferences in Missouri to provide hands-on experience to students, 4-H leaders, teachers, design professionals, and facility managers. Some of these activities were scaled back because of funding availability.

Activity

During the past academic year, the University of Missouri facilitated a broad range of activities involving students, faculty, outside guests, and community leaders. Universal design was integrated into the program through studio teaching, senior thesis projects, lecture classes, faculty research, visits from universal design experts, and involvement of community organizations. These multiple efforts in universal design education were intended to bring all design students in the Department of Environmental Design to the reflective judgment level in learning.

Outcome

Studio Projects. The primary focus for teaching universal design was in a design studio for an assisted living project. It was supported by faculty research on assisted living for older adults.[1] This design studio combined the fundamental values of universal design with the realities of aging. The design program was to create an envi-

Two students critique one another's work.

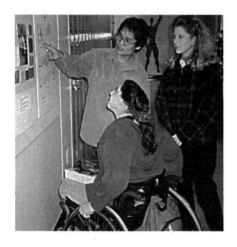

A graduate student empha-sizes access during a review.

Dan Kem evaluates a student's design work.

ronment for older adults with disabilities who wanted to retain their independence while receiving the services they needed. A wide range of individual assistance would be available to residents in a homelike setting that ensured privacy and supported maximum independence. Students were asked to design a small-scale, community-based facility, addressing issues at the level of the dwelling unit, the common space shared by the residents, and the site plan.

All design faculty, a national expert on universal design, and persons with disabilities served as critics for the studio. Final projects were reviewed by the executive director and board members of a retirement community, faculty, three practicing designers, and four members of the college's 50th Anniversary Graduating Class.

In other studios, outside guests and field trips helped enrich the students' understanding of universal design. On two separate projects, students visited the homes of fellow students and a professional librarian—all of whom use wheelchairs. Students studied how these individuals resolved problems in their environments.

Senior Thesis Projects. At the senior level, students in the environmental design program conduct an independent, capstone studio project of their choice. They write a thesis proposal and work intensively with a faculty thesis advisor. One third of the graduating seniors chose to pursue a project on universal design. Projects included:

- Intergenerational Daycare, design of a facility for child and adult day care;

- Dementia Special Care Unit, design for four levels of care;

- Camp for Children with Disabilities, renovation of children's camp; and

- ADA Assessment of Businesses in Downtown Columbia, Missouri (a quantitative and qualitative analysis of commercial locations).

Lecture Courses. The junior-level lecture course, Resources and Materials, and the senior-level course, Design and Behavior, emphasized the promotional theme of ADA/Universal Design Week, "Beyond ADA to Universal Design." The week included the showing of universal design films, a blindfolded walk across campus, and student participation in the Access

Office Wheel-a-thon. Field trips offered students multiple opportunities to learn about barriers in buildings, to discuss alternatives for correcting them, and to consider their personal judgments and values. In the Resources and Materials course, a faculty article on design foundations and assertions was the basis for a discussion on values in universal design.[2]

Faculty Involvement. While some faculty are more knowledgeable about ADA and universal design than others, all faculty participated in teaching universal design. Three faculty are environmental gerontology researchers, one faculty member attended the UDEP conference, and three others heard Elaine Ostroff, director of UDEP, speak at the Interior Design Educators Council annual meeting. Having a critical mass of faculty was significant in transmitting this subject matter to all design students. Knowledge of universal design gained from lectures was integrated at more advanced levels of learning in the studio, where students were internalizing a set of values in creating new places for people. Faculty's ongoing research in this area further demonstrates to students an intellectual advocacy of universal design principles.[3]

National Expert. Regular classroom instruction was enhanced by the visit of a nationally recognized expert on universal design, UDEP advisor John Salmen. He gave the keynote address, "Beyond ADA to Universal Design," at Universal Design Week; participated in a design critique; consulted with a student on her senior thesis project; and met with faculty and sponsors. Faculty in three courses featured the lecture as part of their classes. Guests from the community brought the total audience to more than two hundred people. The presentation was videotaped and covered by *Mid-Missouri Business Magazine.*

UDEP advisor John Salmen presenting at Universal Design Week.

While on campus, Salmen participated in a meeting with program faculty and Extension field faculty at which each person described his or her teaching and research interests. He discussed instructional strategies, recommended film and written materials, and helped brainstorm future funding opportunities. He also met with the dean of the College of Human Environmental Sciences, the associate dean for research, and the assistant dean for student services.

Student Involvement. A student with a disability had an opportunity to do some teaching by bringing to the attention of faculty that the announcement for the public lecture did not include the clause: "If special accommodations are necessary, please contact…" Adding a new "W" to the age-old checklist of Who, What, Where, When, and Why would help assure that all persons are welcomed. Integrating the "welcoming" variable is an important step in realizing universal design, similar to the notion that universal design should not be taught as a specific class per se, but should be part of the gestalt of design education.

"The challenge of teaching universal design is matched by the deficit of research on the subject."

Advisory Board Member Participation. One of the department's advisory board members offered another instructional resource. Chuck Graham, who leads a Midwest training project on the Americans with Disabilities Act supported by the National Institute on Disability and Rehabilitation Research, participated in teaching by regularly speaking to classes and student groups, and serving on design critique panels.

Partnering with Community Agencies. A number of community organizations sponsored the keynote address and actively supported the program's effort to incorporate universal design in the classroom: American Society of Interior Designers, MU Student Chapter; American Institute of Architects, Mid-Missouri Chapter; Access Office for Students with Disabilities; Department of Environmental Design; Great Plains Disability and Business Technical Assistance Center; Human Resource Services, MU; Services for Independent Living; University Extension[4]; Campus Planning Committee for Facilities and Grounds, MU; and Campus Facilities, MU.

Representatives from the above agencies attended the keynote address and participated in a work session after the lecture to discuss future cooperation. At this work session, various types of partnerships were discussed such as employment and volunteer opportunities and faculty leadership on the campus planning committee. It was suggested that community participation be expanded to include the Chamber of Commerce to reinforce the goal of more businesses being made accessible. The idea that organizations might fund student charrette prize money emerged in a brainstorming session.

Reflection

Clearly, this project forced the department to focus and expose faculty and students to the issues of universal design. It also helped raise attention and awareness at the college and campus levels.

While this educational project succeeded in advocating universal design, the challenge of educating reflective design practitioners who are capable of making sustained arguments and ethical commitments continues. Universal design education in the university setting must concentrate on approaches based on "technical rationality" as well as "reflection in action." Thinking at advanced levels of the psychomotor, cognitive, and affective domains[5] also gives designers the freedom to reflect, invent, and differentiate as a reflective practitioner (Schon, 1983).

Focusing education on awareness of problems is at the lowest level of learning. Simply recognizing the "right way to meet ADA guidelines" is not sufficient.

Learning to identify the doors that need widening, the restroom fixtures that need repositioning, or places to add Braille signage is just not enough. To teach our students problem solving, we give them guidelines to help them make decisions. This assumes they will select from available means a solution best suited to establish ends. An emphasis on problem solving, however, can ignore problem setting. As Schon argues, "Problem setting is a process in which, interactively, we name the things to which we will attend and frame the context in which we will attend to them." Students have to be introduced to processes by which to define decisions before they can advance to levels of learning where they can independently make judgments based on their internalized values for human rights.

The educational milieu for reflective learning must be attentive to student perceptions and needs in their physical environment as well as the philosophical environment. Students were enthusiastic about participating in empathic experiences such as the blindfold walk across campus, use of wheelchairs, and use of a kit of materials donated by an advisory board member from a national furniture manufacturing company. The physical environment where universal design is being taught, however, does not necessarily mirror the educational milieu. Perhaps, symbolically, during ADA/Universal Design Week, renovations for ADA compliance were completed on the restrooms in the studio building. Providing physical facilities that are supportive to students with disabilities was a visible message to all students that the program affirms universal design.

The challenge of teaching universal design is matched by the deficit of research on the subject. There is a need for collaboration between practitioners and reflective researchers to study issues of universal design and its implementation. Researchers need insight into practice and practitioners need to reveal the ways of thinking that they bring to their practice. Reflective research allows practitioners to gain insight as they look for effective ways to improve the physical environment for all people.

Acknowledgements

This project was made possible because of a team effort in promoting universal design. Sincere thanks are due to: Maggy Danley, interim associate state specialist, University of Missouri Extension; Wanda Eubank, information/education specialist, USDA Soil Conservation Service; Chuck Graham, Missouri coordinator, Great Plains Disability and Business Technical Assistance Center; Dan Kem, executive director of Lenoir Retirement Community; faculty of the Department of Environmental Design at the University of Missouri—Pat Hilderbrand, Richard Helmick, Ronald Phillips, and John Pruitt; and our students—Corbin Bair, Chun Lu, Heather DeMian, Angela Burger, Chun-Fa Su, and Rachel Coffey.

Chapter 20: University of Missouri

References

Davis, James R. (1993). *Better Teaching, More Learning.* Phoenix, Ariz.: American Council on Education. The Oryx Press.

Gronlund, Norman E. (1981). *Measurement and Evaluation in Teaching.* New York: Macmillan.

Kitchener, Karen and Patricia King (1990). "The Reflective Judgment Model: Transforming Assumptions About Knowing." In *Fostering Critical Reflection in Adulthood,* edited by Jack Mezirow.

Perry, William (1970). *Forms of Intellectual and Ethical Development in the College Years: A Scheme.* New York: Holt, Rinehart, and Winston.

Schon, Donald A. (1983). *The Reflective Practitioner: How Professionals Think in Action.* New York: Basic Books.

Notes

1. Eldercare in the United States and in several other countries around the world is in transition, shifting away from the medical model of long-term care toward models that combine medical care with supportive housing and social services. Descriptions and definitions of this "new" model vary. Provision of the same kind of services may be called assisted living, board and care, personal care homes, residential care facilities, rest homes, and others. However, one of the key variables shared among the philosophies of operation of these new facilities is the environmental design of the settings. These designs emphasize homelike living units and attempt to address effectively the wants as well as the needs of frail elderly. The physical environment represents an important component of the quality of life for older people. Its primary goal in this context is to maximize a person's independence, lifestyle choices, opportunities for social interaction, privacy, and safety and security.

2. "Hands-On Approach to the Americans with Disabilities Act." *Journal of Interior Design* 19, no. 1 (1993): 47–50.

3. A paper on access to design education by persons with learning disabilities, "Nurturing Design Students with Learning Disabilities," by Ruth Brent, Benyamin Schwarz, and Richard Helmick, is pending publication.

4. Linkage with University Extension assured the greatest mileage from resources because they serve as a clearinghouse for resources to be catalogued and available for check-out.

5. Norman Gronlund (1976) divides teaching into the psychomotor, cognitive, and affective domains. The psychomotor domain ranges from perceiving and imitating to a more advanced level of being able to perform independently and automatically. The cognitive domain ranges from a basic level of recognizing to a more advanced level of making a judgment. The affective domain ranges from the lower awareness level to the more sophisticated level of internalizing a set of values.

A Summer Workshop to Raise Awareness

Team members:

Alexander Ratensky
Program Director
Steven Cooke
Assistant Professor
Theodore Trent Green
Assistant Professor
James Moore
Associate Professor
Daniel Powers
Associate Professor
Susan Behar
Interior Design Consultant

Proposal

As director of the architecture program, I proposed to formally and permanently integrate universal design issues into the program's curriculum. The program is somewhat unique among architecture schools because it is exclusively a graduate program and has made a point of integrating ethical issues into every aspect of its curriculum. The faculty is committed to user needs, not gift-of-the-gods object design. This is an opportunity to change the direction of architectural education, which, for the last two decades at least, has gone in the direction of the architecture of ideas, and of objects, with less and less focus on the user. Information on lifespan design is available, as the sponsor's bibliography attests. Implementation strategies are required to refocus architecture on its users.

We proposed a ten-week summer-session design workshop as the primary component of our project, involving six to eight students and all available faculty in the department. Running in parallel with this workshop was to be a less structured discussion seminar for which students would be compensated. The discussion sessions were intended as the primary place where materials for subsequent teaching efforts would be developed.

Nothing in this proposal is, in itself, revolutionary. Its strength is its inclusiveness. The project will not be the special province of one faculty member, but rather will raise universal design as an issue for the whole faculty and the whole curriculum. Although faculty and students are familiar with issues of disability and have been involved in completing the ADA assessment for the university, the program curriculum was missing a systematic approach to teaching universal design and lifespan issues.

Activity

Our course was described as follows:

Universal/Lifespan Design Workshop
Summer 1993, Monday and Wednesday, 4–6:45 p.m.
Faculty: Ratensky, Cooke, Powers, Green, Moore, Susan Behar

Chapter 21: University of South Florida

This hands-on design workshop for 6–8 students and several full-time faculty and an adjunct practitioner will explore the meaning and practice of universal/lifespan design.

Universal/lifespan design addresses the differing abilities, physical and mental, of people of different age groups, as well as those with environmental, accidental, or congenital challenges.

"Universal design means simply designing all products, buildings, and exterior spaces to be usable by all people to the greatest extent possible. It is advanced here as a sensible and economical way to reconcile the artistic integrity of a design with human needs in the environment. Solutions which result in no additional cost and no noticeable change in appearance can come about from knowledge about people, simple planning, and careful selection of conventional products."
—Mace, Hardie, and Place. "Accessible Environments: Toward Universal Design." In Design Intervention, *edited by Preiser, Vischer, and White.*

For our design project we have in mind a housing type sometimes referred to as "co-housing," located adjacent to USF's Tampa campus. Issues of privacy and mutual dependence will be explored. During the workshop, programmatic and cost-effectiveness issues associated with universal design will also be explored. We intend to pursue the eventual actual construction of a prototype residence.

Our methods will include ongoing videotaping of the workshop, and occasional videotape review and discussion sessions to extract key issues or breakthroughs. The faculty will develop curriculum ideas and components that can be integrated with regular course materials. Students will be expected to participate in the discussions that will develop these teaching materials for the regular curriculum, and will each be paid a $500 honorarium to compensate them for the additional time.

As a student in the course you will be participating, along with your faculty, in a nationwide project to improve design school curricula in these areas. Here's a chance to gain elective or technical elective credits, earn a modest sum, influence the architectural curriculum, and gain knowledge that will increase your value to future employers.

**UNIVERSAL LIFESPAN DESIGN STUDIO * COOPERATIVE HOUSING PROJECT   SUMMER 1993**

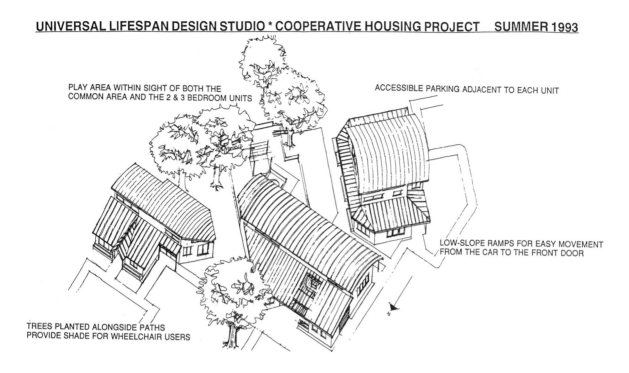

PLAY AREA WITHIN SIGHT OF BOTH THE
COMMON AREA AND THE 2 & 3 BEDROOM UNITS

ACCESSIBLE PARKING ADJACENT TO EACH UNIT

LOW-SLOPE RAMPS FOR EASY MOVEMENT
FROM THE CAR TO THE FRONT DOOR

TREES PLANTED ALONGSIDE PATHS
PROVIDE SHADE FOR WHEELCHAIR USERS

The strategy of paying students to participate in the course was to give them collegial status with faculty in the critical discussion of course materials. Because of student commitments to other classes in the summer session, the discussions were postponed from summer to fall.

In the fall we undertook another class. As an outcome of our summer experiences, Professor Daniel Powers made universal/lifespan design an integral part of third-semester design. His exercises included a weekend at home with a wheelchair for every student and an exercise simulating visual impairment. He set a three-stage design problem: the design of a residence for a newly married couple, an expansion to include children, and a further expansion to include aging grandparents, one of whom uses a wheelchair. These exercises are seen as a first component of universal design teaching that will span three studios and be reinforced in lecture classes, including Professional Practice and Environmental Technology.

Outcome

The deferred seminar discussions described above occurred in October. Each student contributed approximately forty hours of effort to accomplish the following: represent two of the projects from the summer and relevant code requirements in illustrations that are accessible to the nondesigner; complete a library of equipment information and samples of materials and products that support the underlying principles of universal design; develop a directory to agencies, people, and other resources in the Tampa Bay region who are engaged in assisting persons with disabilities; and provide *pro bono* design assistance to the Access Sub-Committee of the [Tampa] Mayor's Alliance for Person's with Disabilities. Such real-world exercises were very stimulating to the students, and we are certain that we will be able to find similar opportunities at least once each year.

Reflection

In our ten-week summer workshop we made many blunders. Indeed, we discovered new ways to teach universal design badly. What is remarkable is the extent to which the teaching succeeded despite our blunders, and the remarkable persistence of interest in the subject matter on the part of the students. We have concluded that it is the compelling nature of the subject matter and the consultants we used that sustained students' interest and learning.

Our first error was in setting design criteria that were too general. Our original program was for twelve units of affordable rental housing to be built adjacent to the University of South Florida. Because architecture faculty predominated in our group, it became evident that the issues for universal design—effort, placement, simple motion, and choice—were not getting addressed. Once we realized this and started to design the units, progress was pretty rapid.

Nevertheless, we were unprepared for the resistance we encountered from students. Most of us have infrequent contact with persons with serious disabilities in this culture, and the tendency of students to condescend, either verbally or by providing limited opportunity in their designs, was surprising. It took almost the full ten weeks for them to internalize the issues and raise their levels of sensitivity. As late as week eight, one of our students referred to "something that even a 'normal' person could do" in conversation with a consultant who uses a wheelchair. Fortunately, the consultant was not offended, and the event became the breakthrough for that particular student.

These experiences, reinforced by feedback from the students, have led us to conclude that the summer session should have been much less a design studio and much more a lecture/seminar/field trip format. Familiarization with individuals, role-playing experiments to simulate various disabilities, and field observation are all important. The design component was essential, but we would not again make it the principal armature of such a course. The whole issue of code interpretation was of much greater importance than we realized. We will be developing materials to make code requirements visual and readily understandable to students and the public.

UNIVERSAL LIFESPAN DESIGN STUDIO * COOPERATIVE HOUSING PROJECT   SUMMER 1993
THE FRONT ENTRY

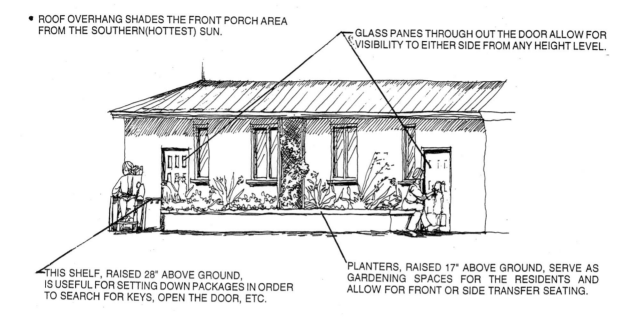

- ROOF OVERHANG SHADES THE FRONT PORCH AREA FROM THE SOUTHERN(HOTTEST) SUN.

GLASS PANES THROUGH OUT THE DOOR ALLOW FOR VISIBILITY TO EITHER SIDE FROM ANY HEIGHT LEVEL.

THIS SHELF, RAISED 28" ABOVE GROUND, IS USEFUL FOR SETTING DOWN PACKAGES IN ORDER TO SEARCH FOR KEYS, OPEN THE DOOR, ETC.

PLANTERS, RAISED 17" ABOVE GROUND, SERVE AS GARDENING SPACES FOR THE RESIDENTS AND ALLOW FOR FRONT OR SIDE TRANSFER SEATING.

In week two of the summer session we were given two wheelchairs. These proved to be the single most effective aspect of the course. Everyone in the class used the wheelchairs at one time or another to move around the program premises. All discovered how differently things look from a seated perspective. At our final class wrap-up, the students volunteered that there was "a lot of stuff" in the studios intruding into the aisles that would impede a wheelchair user. This had been the faculty's observation too, but it was gratifying to have the students articulate it.

The second most useful teaching strategy was the consultants. Articulate and self-aware persons with disabilities make wonderful studio critics. Our consultants were very clear on the unnecessary limitations imposed by the built environment. Our favorite consultant saw every unit our students designed as a dwelling for himself. He lives with his parents, and made clear the limits of privacy and dependence that he and they are willing to tolerate. Subsequent class discussion allowed us to generalize the input from this man. Our consultants came from the community. One had contacted us some years ago about co-sponsoring an ADA seminar and was the lead to the others. They were excited that the architecture program was involved in UDEP and "their" issues.

The most helpful tool for discussions with consultants was unit models at 1"=1' scale. This is dollhouse scale and therefore easy to furnish. Our models were made of corrugated cardboard, and were easy to make, tear apart, and rearrange. These became a primary tool for the critique.

UNIVERSAL LIFESPAN DESIGN STUDIO * COOPERATIVE HOUSING PROJECT   SUMMER 1993
THE COMMUNITY AREA

AMPLE ROOM FOR
OPENING AND
CLOSING THE
DOOR

LEVER HANDLES

COVERED ENTRY

OPEN SPACE FOR PERSONS
IN WHEELCHAIRS TO GATHER

PLANTERS ARE RAISED 17" ABOVE GROUND AND
PROVIDE SEATING AREAS FOR GATHERINGS

UNIVERSAL LIFESPAN DESIGN STUDIO * COOPERATIVE HOUSING PROJECT   SUMMER 1993
THE LIVING AREA

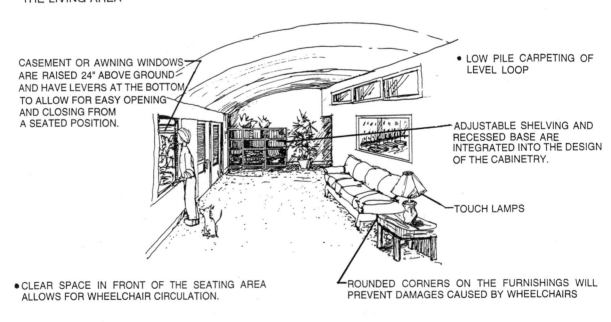

CASEMENT OR AWNING WINDOWS
ARE RAISED 24" ABOVE GROUND
AND HAVE LEVERS AT THE BOTTOM
TO ALLOW FOR EASY OPENING
AND CLOSING FROM
A SEATED POSITION.

• LOW PILE CARPETING OF
LEVEL LOOP

ADJUSTABLE SHELVING AND
RECESSED BASE ARE
INTEGRATED INTO THE DESIGN
OF THE CABINETRY.

TOUCH LAMPS

• CLEAR SPACE IN FRONT OF THE SEATING AREA
ALLOWS FOR WHEELCHAIR CIRCULATION.

ROUNDED CORNERS ON THE FURNISHINGS WILL
PREVENT DAMAGES CAUSED BY WHEELCHAIRS

What have we learned? At this stage, faculty believe that universal design needs to become an integral, repeated, component of our design studios. At least two of the six students who completed the course disagree and want a separate elective course. This formed part of our later discussions.

Enrolling Students with Disabilities in a Design Class

Team members:

Charlotte Roberts
Assistant Professor
Brian Powell
Assistant Professor

Proposal

This team proposed to develop a course in the School of Architecture that would expose students to the concept of universal design through personal experiences with people different from themselves. While the ADA is necessary to ensure protection of people's civil rights, these educators, among others, question the value of design criteria in stimulating a creative approach to inclusive design. Does holding a student accountable for implementing minimum guidelines for accessibility provide them with an understanding of the people for whom they design? Roberts and Powell's goal was to move beyond the application of architectural guidelines for accessibility to provide opportunities for awareness so that students can design from personal sensitivity and empathic connection to the issues.

They proposed two levels of implementation. On the departmental level, they sought to enhance the resource materials available to faculty and students of the three programs. On the instructional level, they planned a course with the objective of increasing student awareness and sensitivity to the diverse needs of the population through direct contact with persons with disabilities.

To accomplish this object, the project proposed to enroll students with disabilities as participants in the course along with design students. Raymond Lifchez's video, documenting design studio activities that involve persons with disabilities as outside consultants, emphasizes the importance of direct contact as a means of increasing student awareness. Collaboration between design students and nondesign students provides individuals in both groups with reciprocal opportunities. Design students contribute their expertise about the built environment and learn about people who have disabilities. Students with disabilities provide a view of life from their various perspectives and learn how they can become actively engaged in shaping their world through participation in the design process (Lifchez, 1979).

The course strived to provide a foundation in universal design through three components: awareness, knowledge, and application. The awareness component would be introduced through experiential activities exposing the students to attitudinal and communication barriers as well as barriers in the built environment. The knowledge component, through lectures and handouts, would provide an overview of human factors, functional limitations, accessibility guidelines, and design process. The application of universal design concepts would be achieved by having student teams design projects with each member contributing according to his or her ability.

USL/Universal Design logo designed by industrial design student Doug Lobb.

Activity

A faculty workshop was held at the beginning of fall semester to open a dialogue on universal design education and to engage the rest of the faculty in bringing universal design into their classrooms and studios.

The course in universal design was held during fall semester as a three-hour elective. The course was targeted to upper-level design students from the architecture, interior design, and industrial design programs and students with various disabilities who were not design majors. Enrollment of students with disabilities was encouraged by offering them credit on an equal basis with design students. The format of the class was participatory and was structured to be nonthreatening to students without a design background.

Enrolling nondesign students raised challenging questions: Where do we find a sufficient number of students with disabilities and how do we convince them to enroll? How do we teach design to a nondesign student? How will they fit in and not feel intimidated by the abilities of the upper-level design students?

We worked with two organizations on campus in recruiting nondesign students for enrollment in the course. The Beacon Club, a student organization, is dedicated to

awareness of disability issues. The Office for Services for Students with Disabilities, which assists students with all facets of campus life, including counseling, academic advising, and accommodations, was also helpful.

Class enrollment included design students and nondesign students with disabilities.

The instructors distributed a recruitment flyer to explain the objectives of the course. Students were asked to submit personal data and a brief explanation of what they expected to contribute to the course in the way of skills, abilities, and experiences. Enrollment was selective because of space limitations and the importance of a workable ratio between design students and nondesign students.

Student participants included nine design majors and six nondesign majors. The design majors included one student in architecture, one in industrial design, and seven in interior design. Of the nondesign majors, three used wheelchairs; one had quadriplegic limitations and spoke with a mechanical larynx; one student was deaf; one had a visual impairment; and one was blind. The extended 'family' included two signing interpreters and a dog guide.

A primary concern of the faculty was to provide a safe and accessible environment for ease of movement and communication. The first obstacle was finding a place for the class to meet. The studio spaces in our building are equipped with 36-inch-high desks, which are unsuitable for persons using wheelchairs. The studio spaces are shared by the three programs, making it difficult to create the protected environment necessary for a more intimate exchange. A ground-level stage furnished with large tables and stools became our classroom. An adjacent auditorium was available for lectures, slide and video projection, and presentation of projects.

The textbook selected for the course was *Design Primer: Universal Design*, (Anders, 1992). It provided an introduction to universal design and information on various human factors to be considered when designing products and environments. In selecting handouts for the course, the intention was to provide basic information that would stimulate participation in class discussions and exercises. Over the course of the semester, guest lecturers were invited to provide specific information. The instructors elected not to use accessibility guidelines for instructional purposes, but instead encouraged students to find available reference materials on their own and to gather further information through direct contact with people and the environment.

The success of the course depended on the students' confidence in communicating and interacting with one another. At the beginning of the semester several interactive exercises encouraged open communication between the two groups of students and put everyone on an equal footing. Short writing exercises and guided discussions were introduced at various times throughout the semester and students were encouraged to reflect on and share their experiences. Different seating arrangements were tried: dividing students into small groups or placing them face-to-face to facilitate exchange. By rotating team members for each project or activity, everyone had an opportunity to work with everyone else.

Outcome

On the first day of class, the students were asked to introduce themselves, telling about their interests and academic background, why they enrolled in the course, and what they expected to contribute and to learn. At the next class meeting, to put everyone on a first name basis right away, students introduced a classmate that they had just met and told the group a little about that person.

Signing Exercise. As a first assignment, students were asked to give a brief greeting to the class using the signing alphabet or any other nonverbal means of communication. A handout illustrated the American Sign Language alphabet. An interior design student, Colleen, created a pie-shaped puzzle that spelled "universal design" in signing symbols when put together correctly. Each student was given a slice of the pie and had to place it correctly to help complete the message. A successful ice breaker, the exercise challenged everyone to communicate in a way that was unfamiliar to them.

Awareness Discussion. Two handouts—*Unhandicapping Our Language* (Longmore, 1988) and *Fact Sheet 3: Communicating with People with Disabilities* (Adaptive Environments Center, 1992)—were the springboard for discussing students' assumptions about abilities and limitations. Nondesign students were asked to respond to the handout recommendations in light of their personal experience. Danielle, a student who is blind, was asked how she felt about the recommendation, "touch a person's arm lightly when you speak." She responded that it was not necessary to touch her when speaking, but that she finds it rude when people leave a conversation without announcing their departure. The guidelines were very useful in explaining to students that Danielle's dog guide, Fagan, while in harness, was not to be touched, spoken to, or in any way distracted from its duty to Danielle.

Other students talked about barriers they encounter in day-to-day life, both in the built environment and in people's attitudes. Design students asked questions and related their own experiences involving people with disabilities, many describing their feelings of not knowing what to say or how to act. This exchange of feelings and needs put the students more at ease and gave them the confidence to approach each other.

Visual Documentation Project. In this interactive assignment, students documented an encounter with the environment. They used methods similar to those outlined by Lifchez for interviewing and gathering information about the lives of persons who have disabilities. The purpose of documenting an encounter with the site, according to Lifchez, is to provide information beyond what the personal interview can convey. Pictures or video can be used to capture what takes place for discussion after the actual event (Lifchez, 1979).

Teams of students selected sites on or near campus and proposed activities and the means of visual documentation they would use. Students continued to learn more about one another in planning the proposals. Doug, teamed up with Danielle, boldly stated, "I don't want this to come out wrong, but I've always been intrigued by blindness, with what it is like to be blind." Her response was a very revealing discourse on being blind.

Students selected a playground at a nearby park, the main entrance ramp at the university library, an elevator in a classroom building, and the suite of offices that provide services to students with disabilities. One team proposed to use black-and-white still photography supplemented by descriptions in Braille text. The other three teams proposed to videotape their encounters. Doug offered to teach all members of his team to use the

Danielle, a student who is blind, learns to videotape.

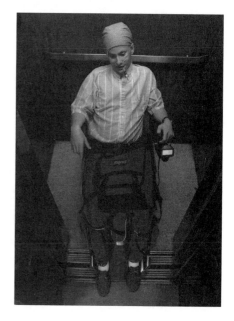

Octave encounters an inaccessible elevator.

video camera, including Danielle. Her segment of videotaping proved to be outstanding because of her ability to track voices.

The documentation activity was scheduled for one class period, but, due to technical difficulty with the equipment, two class periods were required. This problem enabled students to observe each other in the process of their documentation. Students became profoundly aware of the time and effort it takes a wheelchair user to get around campus. At the library, the slate surface of the ramp was wet and classmates witnessed Leroy's struggle to maneuver his wheelchair up to the entrance. Cheri, an interior design student commented, "I don't see why he didn't just give up." Students observed how others, not in the class, averted their eyes and passed Leroy without offering assistance. Because Leroy had become a friend, the students were personally affected by this event.

Design students, Kolla and Heather, who documented the inaccessibility of a small elevator in black-and-white photographs, captured a small child trying to reach the call buttons and a very large man crowding into the elevator with other people. Octave, one of the team members, demonstrated the process of disassembling the footrests on his oversized motorized wheelchair so that he could fit into the elevator to attend class on an upper floor.

For the park documentation, the students filmed Keith trying to maneuver his wheelchair around obstacles in the newly designed playground and park landscaping. This illustrated how a facility intended for fun and family gathering denied participation to someone using a wheelchair.

Kolla experiences a tactile site model while blindfolded.

In documenting the Office for Services for Students with Disabilities, the team proposed to illustrate communication difficulties that occur in the regular course of business. The office provides part-time employment for students with disabilities. Glennis, a member of the class who is deaf, works as receptionist. Posted signs give instructions to people seeking assistance, but people tend to ignore the signs and get impatient in their attempts to communicate with her. The team staged a reenactment of a typical encounter. While at this site, Misty, who has a visual impairment, demonstrated the process of translating written text into Braille.

Experiential Activity. In preparation for exercises in site analysis and planning, students were introduced to a scale model of the project site while blindfolded. This activity provided an empathic experience by having students assume a visual disability. An architecture student, Kerwin, constructed the model using various materials to provide tactile cues. A scale element was provided so that students could estimate the size of the site. Heather was surprised: "Being a very visual person, it was challenging to interact with the site by touch alone. The size of the model looked completely different than it felt." The model proved to be very useful throughout the semester because Danielle used it to participate in activities that are normally visually oriented.

Site Analysis. This assignment asked students to prepare an analysis of a given site. On a site plan, each team had to graphically represent factors such as natural elements, sun angles, prevailing winds, and relationship to adjacent properties as well as functional criteria such as drainage, noise, traffic, and possibilities for access to the site from adjacent streets.

Both the site analysis and planning exercises were executed in a simple cut-and-paste technique. Shapes cut from colored paper and other materials symbolized aesthetic, climatic, and landscape elements. In the spirit of inclusion, information was transferred to Danielle's site model to reflect the analysis executed by her team.

Site Planning. As a prelude to this exercise, students were asked to reflect on and describe in writing an ideal neighborhood, either fictitious or real. By sharing these "stories," students were able to identify the common values considered important to the concepts of neighborhood and community.

The site planning exercise involved designing a neighborhood that was universally accessible. The design problem was to enhance the spirit of community and promote interaction among the residents. Two-dimensional collage was the medium used to represent vehicular and pedestrian access, parking, an unspecified number of home sites, and amenities such as green spaces, outdoor gathering spaces, and areas for recreational activities.

Field Trip. After the planning exercise the class took a field trip to a national park facility. Students used an accessibility checklist from the textbook to conduct a survey of the new park exhibit building, which was not yet open to the public. They compiled a list of recommendations for adjustments and improvements such as providing more readable signage, Braille leaflets, and interpreters who could communicate in sign language. They also identified potential hazards such as inadequate handrails and landings at the entrance ramp.

Storyline and Scenario Mapping. These exercises, modeled after techniques outlined by Lifchez (1979), were a means of collecting information and providing a broader picture regarding the needs of the user in a specified activity. In the "storyline" exercise, students were to reflect on the phrase "having dinner with the

Kerwin and Danielle present the scenario mapping of "Sunday Dinner at Home."

family on a Sunday afternoon in April" and write a short story giving details of how this event might look.

With scenario mapping, the students translated their storylines into collages depicting the Sunday dinner event. Furniture and objects were represented by shapes that resembled the actual items. Scale figures represented the people involved in the activity. Students symbolically represented qualities with measurable properties, such as light, heat, and sound, as well as properties of a more subjective nature, such as intimacy, warmth, and hospitality, by placing shape or color where the quality is experienced. An idea that could not be expressed through shape or color could be written on the construction itself. Students worked individually on this exercise with the exception of Danielle, who was assisted by Kerwin in making her collage.

Designing the Living Environment. The design project involved programming a home for a fictitious family, selecting a home site from the site planning exercise, and designing the actual home. Each team began by creating a story about a day in the life of the family. Programs were developed, based on these stories. The students collaborated on the design of an accessible floor plan to meet the needs of individual family members as stated in the program. Study models were used to help nondesign students understand three-dimensional space. In presenting the design, the goal was not a finely crafted product, typical of a regular design studio, but rather, simple constructions of cardboard, paper, and glue that allowed for hands-on participation by everyone involved.

Collaborative projects engaged students at their individual levels of ability.

Whenever team projects were assigned during the semester, each team member identified an area of primary responsibility for the project according to his or her own ability. For example, tasks for the design project involved drawing floor plans, building models, writing descriptions of the project and the program, and verbally presenting the projects. Each student selected a primary task while contributing in the other areas as well. The students collectively built a large-scale site model of the entire community for the placement of individual houses. Presentations of the design project were made on the final day of class with everyone participating.

Evaluation

Students were graded for their level of participation in the course and degree of interaction with other students. Projects and exercises were evaluated for content and demonstration of knowledge and understanding. The final exam was a take-home questionnaire asking students to assess what they had learned from the projects and activities and from interaction with their classmates.

The primary purpose of the course was to change students' attitudes by developing their awareness of and sensitivity to people who have differing needs. To evaluate changes in attitude from the beginning of the course to the end, the instructors conducted videotaped entrance and exit interviews with individual students. Class activities were also photographed and videotaped, providing supporting information on the changes in attitude that occurred. Post-course observations of students who had participated further documented the impact of the course.

The instructors recorded events and commentary in journals as another means of observing attitudes and evaluating the success of the exercises. From those records came comments indicating that awareness and sensitivity were being enhanced by this experience. After participating in a site analysis exercise, Glennis commented, "At home I noticed how the sun lights my backyard in the morning and how my neighbor's yard is a bad view." Early in the semester, Leroy observed, "I was concerned about learning to design, but so far we are learning about people. (long pause) I guess you have to know about people before you can design for them."

The course had some unexpected outcomes. Building on the idea of pairing students with disabilities with able-bodied students, Leroy proposed a campus evacuation plan that would designate able-bodied sponsors at the beginning of each semester to assist their disabled classmates in case of an emergency. His plan has been approved by the university administration. He claims that his participation in the course has enabled him to get more involved with life and with helping others.

Design students who participated in the course were observed informally by faculty during the following semester. Two of the students were seniors in interior design and were involved in semester-long thesis projects. Kim's thesis, a children's museum, included exhibits designed to teach children about cultural diversity. One exhibit provided children with the experience of various disabilities, such as limited vision and using a wheelchair. Tracie's thesis involved the design of prototypical apartment units that were universally accessible. She developed a set of criteria for the design of cabinets, appliances, and fixtures as part of a modular wall-hung system. The sensitivity expressed in both thesis projects indicates that these students were greatly influenced by their participation in the course on universal design.

"Anything that I design will be universally accessible, not because of laws or codes, but because I want it that way. Universal design is part of my code of ethics now."

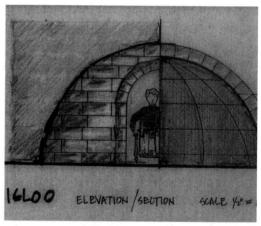

A drawing from a thesis on a children's museum (top) and a drawing of a washer and dryer from a thesis on universally designed housing (bottom).

"Direct contact with students with disabilities was an invaluable means for providing design students with sensitivity and awareness of diverse human needs."

The faculty reviewed videotaped entrance and exit interviews for indicators such as language use: how students refer to one another, what their assumptions are, and what they perceive as their ability to contribute. The initial interviews contained a strong "we"/"they" distinction when design students referred to nondesign students and vise versa. In the exit interviews this occurred less frequently. Many students spoke of gaining confidence through the course to interact with and reach out to other people. Kim commented, "My perception of people with disabilities has greatly changed. For some reason, I always believed that they were in pain. After spending some time with people with disabilities, I realized that yes, they do experience some pain, but that is not what their whole lives are about." In her exit interview, Tracie commented, "Anything that I design will be universally accessible, not because of laws or codes, but because I want it that way. Universal design is part of my code of ethics now."

Reflection

Within the first few weeks of the semester, the students developed a strong sense of community and the ability to communicate openly. They had enrolled in the course intentionally: for what they had to contribute as well as for what they could learn. The level of enthusiasm was very high and the students' insights inspiring.

We approached teaching this course with openness, allowing for necessary adjustments in time and specific activities based on the individual levels of ability and how students functioned together in teams. There was not enough time for all that was originally planned and some of the planned activities proved so successful that we allowed more time for them to fully develop. Many days students lingered for an hour or more after class to work on projects or to continue a discussion.

The awareness component proved to be the most significant part of the course. From the beginning, the discussions, exercises, and activities stimulated the students to be open in their communication with each other. The videotaped entry interviews, originally intended as an evaluation tool, were combined with footage from the visual documentation projects to produce a short video that illustrates students encountering physical and attitudinal barriers. In the exit interviews, students were asked which activities were most valuable to their learning. The experiential activities, especially the visual documentation exercise, were cited most frequently.

The knowledge component changed the most from the original proposal. It was quickly apparent that it would be redundant to teach students with disabilities about accessibility. We had a particularly knowledgeable group of people who were very familiar with their rights and with the issue of accessibility. Knowledge and awareness were reinforced through observation, interaction, and immersion in the design process, in addition to reading available resource materials.

Direct contact with students with disabilities was an invaluable means for providing design students with sensitivity and awareness of diverse human needs. Evidence of this enhanced sensitivity was visible in the more empathic and creative design solutions students produced in the following semester. The students with disabilities also gained through their association with people who were openly interested in learning about their special needs. They were moved by the spirit of inclusion and some even discovered new abilities. Overall, the course provided a meaningful educational experience for all participants.

We will continue to offer this course in universal design. Since it is not feasible to accommodate all students in the three programs and still maintain a workable ratio of design to nondesign students, the course will remain an elective. In addition, a course in human factors is recommended so that all design majors learn about physically diverse populations, accessibility guidelines, and universal design concepts. We hope that students from this course will carry their awareness and sensitivity of lifespan issues into the traditional design studio to inspire other students.

References

Adaptive Environments Center (1992). "Fact Sheet 3: Communicating with People with Disabilities" in the Americans with Disabilities Act Fact Sheet Series. Boston: Adaptive Environments Center.

Anders, Robert and Daniel Fechtner (1992). *Universal Design Primer*. Brooklyn, N.Y.: Pratt Institute Department of Industrial Design.

Lifchez, Raymond and Barbara Winslow (1979). *Designs for Independent Living*. Berkeley, Calif.: University of California Press.

Longmore, Paul and Piastro, Diane B. (1988). "Unhandicapping Our Language." Available from Cryptography, P.O. Box 454, Long Beach, CA 90809-0454.

Synthesizing Lifespan Issues within the Studio: Seeing, Experiencing, and Designing

Team members:

Nancy Canestaro
Associate Professor
Thomas Houser
Assistant Professor

Proposal

Interior design courses that address universal design issues usually focus on regulatory compliance or the needs of a particular group, such as the elderly or wheelchair users (Canestaro and Houser, 1993). It is imperative that we help students develop a sensitivity to universal design issues, provide them with experiences to elucidate growing old or having a disability, and give them comprehensive lectures and studio exercises that address issues across the lifespan. The challenge for faculty is to ensure that students synthesize these experiences into the very core of their psyches rather than simply learn to list spatial programmatic requirements or to recite codes.

Our project proposed to develop three interrelated instructional components—an introductory videotape, a game and simulation teaching manual, and computer-based instructional modules. The intent of these components was to sensitize interior design students to the physical and emotional ramifications of universal design by having them experience what it is like to be old or to have a disability. It was also our intent to go beyond, yet include, regulatory considerations. Subsequent studio problems would give students the opportunity to design with these issues in mind. Our final objective was to test what the students learned about universal design by evaluating studio exercises and projects.

We drew from the campus environment and the university community for settings and consultants. Our premise was that design students would identify and empathize with the problems encountered by students with disabilities more quickly than they would with similar circumstances faced by a less familiar population.

Following production, the components would be used sequentially throughout the interior design curriculum:

- All students would view the videotape during the introductory interior design course.

- Students would begin using selected computer-based learning modules during their second year and continue using modules developed for specific project types.

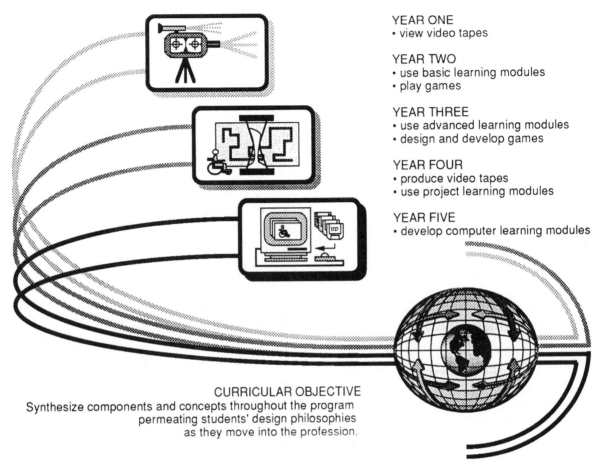

YEAR ONE
• view video tapes

YEAR TWO
• use basic learning modules
• play games

YEAR THREE
• use advanced learning modules
• design and develop games

YEAR FOUR
• produce video tapes
• use project learning modules

YEAR FIVE
• develop computer learning modules

CURRICULAR OBJECTIVE
Synthesize components and concepts throughout the program
permeating students' design philosophies
as they move into the profession.

Instructional components within the curriculum

The video was produced by seniors for use by first-year and transfer students. The games were developed by juniors to benefit sophomores. The computer-based learning modules were begun by fifth-year students for applications throughout the program. The pedagogical intent was for students to benefit from producing as well as using the three components.

- Third-year students would research universal design for particular settings and would design games to explain the issues to less advanced students.

- Subsequent studio projects would include a universal design analysis component, similar to a codes check.

As part of UDEP, we planned to test the validity of having students produce these components as a teaching technique. We did not intend to test the effectiveness of the proposed component sequence within the undergraduate interior design curriculum. The amount of time a class needs to produce these materials varies considerably depending on other classroom activities and the desired level of professionalism. Production video takes longer to shoot and edit than home movies and interactive learning modules require more time than simple HyperCard stacks.

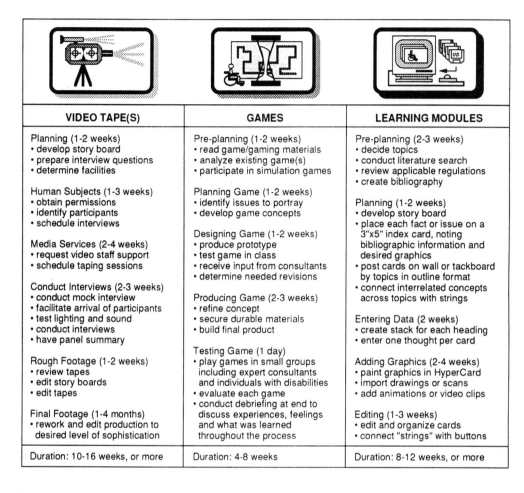

Development of instructional components.

These charts indicate the procedures followed for the production of the videotape, games, and computer-based learning modules.

VIDEO TAPE(S)	GAMES	LEARNING MODULES

Planning (1-2 weeks)
• develop story board
• prepare interview questions
• determine facilities
 	
Human Subjects (1-3 weeks)
• obtain permissions
• identify participants
• schedule interviews
 	
Media Services (2-4 weeks)
• request video staff support
• schedule taping sessions
 	
Conduct Interviews (2-3 weeks)
• conduct mock interview
• facilitate arrival of participants
• test lighting and sound
• conduct interviews
• have panel summary
 	
Rough Footage (1-2 weeks)
• review tapes
• edit story boards
• edit tapes
 	
Final Footage (1-4 months)
• rework and edit production to
  desired level of sophistication
	Pre-planning (1-2 weeks)
	• read game/gaming materials
	• analyze existing game(s)
	• participate in simulation games
	
	Planning Game (1-2 weeks)
	• identify issues to portray
	• develop game concepts
	
	Designing Game (1-2 weeks)
	• produce prototype
	• test game in class
	• receive input from consultants
	• determine needed revisions
	
	Producing Game (2-3 weeks)
	• refine concept
	• secure durable materials
	• build final product
	
	Testing Game (1 day)
	• play games in small groups
	  including expert consultants
	  and individuals with disabilities
	• evaluate each game
	• conduct debriefing at end to
	  discuss experiences, feelings
	  and what was learned
	  throughout the process
		Pre-planning (2-3 weeks)
		• decide topics
		• conduct literature search
		• review applicable regulations
		• create bibliography
		
		Planning (1-2 weeks)
		• develop story board
		• place each fact or issue on a
		  3"x5" index card, noting
		  bibliographic information and
		  desired graphics
		• post cards on wall or tackboard
		  by topics in outline format
		• connect interrelated concepts
		  across topics with strings
		
		Entering Data (2 weeks)
		• create stack for each heading
		• enter one thought per card
		
		Adding Graphics (2-4 weeks)
		• paint graphics in HyperCard
		• import drawings or scans
		• add animations or video clips
		
		Editing (1-3 weeks)
		• edit and organize cards
		• connect "strings" with buttons

Duration: 10-16 weeks, or more	Duration: 4-8 weeks	Duration: 8-12 weeks, or more

Activity

Depending on their academic level, students were assigned one of the following tasks to broaden their awareness of universal design issues:

- Interview or videotape individuals with disabilities;

- Develop universal design games; or

- Synthesize data into computer-based instructional modules.

Students who were not involved in production tasks benefited from the information and provided a valuable test of the components by viewing the video or playing the games. The computer learning modules were not tested with students at this time.

Chapter 23: University of Tennessee

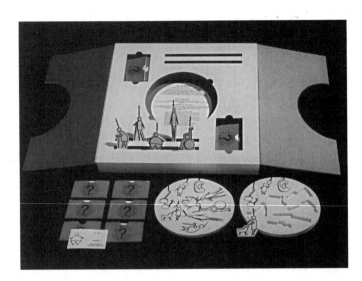

All participants applied their newly acquired knowledge by completing studio exercises with special emphasis on universal design. In each case, they were expected to meet the course objectives and demonstrate profound sensitivity to lifespan issues. At the completion of the class they presented their work to juries of administrators, educators, and individuals with disabilities and/or design practitioners.

Outcome

Introductory Videotape. An introductory videotape was developed by seniors for students in lower-division studios to help them understand how university citizens with different types of disabilities experience the campus environment. The exercise was a small component in an advanced interiors studio. We chose a video component for several reasons: this generation of design students relates well to media projects; tapes could be edited to create a concise experience for viewers; and excerpts from the tapes could be incorporated into computer-based learning modules in the future.

Representative universal design game.

"Universatile" was produced by Jenn Howard, Jan Murray, and Amy Smith to teach universal design issues across the lifespan.

To produce the video, students worked in teams and met with members of the university community. A student who uses a wheelchair, a student with a hearing impairment, and a student with a sight impairment participated in the videotaping. The director of handicapped student services for the university contacted these consultants for their assistance in the videotaping and participated in the sessions herself. Each session began with an introduction of the guests, who made general observations about the environmental challenges they face. Then the students moved through buildings on campus, developing "personal diaries" of their guests maneuvering through the university environment with its plethora of obstacles, both physical and social. At the end of each session there was a debriefing to summarize observations.

The objective of producing the videotape was to create material for introducing first-year students to universal design. The means, however, became an end. We discovered during the first taping session that the interior design students who assisted with the taping developed a new appreciation for the challenges faced by their peers with physical limitations. Students who had been using buildings on campus for four years began noticing obstacles and barriers that they had not seen before. A number of important lessons were learned. For example, a student who uses a wheelchair pointed out that he was unable to use most of a room designed for student organization meetings even though the room met accessibility codes.

Games. The use of simulation techniques to evaluate behavior and space usage is well documented (Appleyard et al., 1982; King et al., 1982; Greenblat, 1981; Hasell, 1980; Sanoff, 1977). Simulations vary from highly controlled experimental studies of behavior in architectural environments or even computer studies (Winkel and Sasanoff, 1976; Stahl, 1982) to quasi-experimental explorations of affective responses to certain conditions (Goodman and Horn, 1975; Canestaro, 1987). At the highly controlled end, some argue that the situation becomes so abstracted that the layers of reality are obliterated. This can be overcome by verifying findings with people who have experienced the condition under study. At the other end of the spectrum, it is argued that "touchy-feely" simulations do not produce enough usable information. This, too, can be overcome by concluding the simulation with a highly controlled debriefing that examines how to use new perceptions of a situation in real settings. Assessments and perceptions of environments are often studied indirectly through environments that are convenient and simulated (Bosselmann and Craik, 1990).

We prepared a course packet for third-year students to use in the design and production of the games. We also intended to use it as a framework for studio exercises. The packet included articles and data related to universal design, information about games and simulations, and course expectations. We also prepared a gaming and simulation teaching manual for use by faculty.

Teams of two or three students applied the materials from the packet to the design and production of games that explained or demonstrated universal design issues. They chose game subject material by researching the roles and characteristics of people with different disabilities, including those portrayed in the video diaries. They also reviewed the pertinent codes, regulations, and guidelines to building, life safety, and accessibility issues. We encouraged students to design the games to simulate the effects of the built environment on people with disabilities, as well as to test factual information. The resulting games were played by lower-division students to expose them to universal design issues, especially individuals' needs across the lifespan.

Playing the universal design games. *As a culminating experience in the game design and production process, the juniors presented and tested their games by playing them with their classmates, sophomore-level interior design students, university administrators, faculty, and the consultants with disabilities who participated in the videotape project.*

After playing the games, we held a debriefing to evaluate the games and to summarize observations and feelings about universal design issues. The students who designed the games appeared more sensitive to the problems experienced by their peers with disabilities than they were at the outset of the project. Course evaluations and subsequent studio design projects are further evidence of students' increased sensitivity since the beginning of the semester. At the end of the process, the consultants from the video project evaluated the games. They assessed how sensitive the games were in presenting the issues, how interesting the games were to play, and whether the games were successful as learning tools. These games were presented and exhibited at the 1994 Interior Design Educators Council Conference in San Antonio during the keynote session on universal design.

Computer-Based Learning Modules. The effectiveness and weakness inherent in computer-based learning modules are well documented in the literature (Case, 1990, for example). Modules designed to provide relative freedom of navigation through the learning sessions capitalize on research findings relevant to student satisfaction and effectiveness (Lanza and Roselli, 1991).

While the video diaries spoke to the emotional and practical sides of universal design and accessibility issues, the computer-based learning modules addressed regulatory concerns. This approach—melding subjective feelings expressed in the video diaries with objective requirements of guidelines and laws—appeared to help students understand the positive human concerns behind regulatory guidelines. For example, when students saw a person using a wheelchair struggle with a heavy door, they understood the necessity of specifying a maximum opening pressure for doors.

Modules for basic instruction of universal design issues and regulatory concerns were produced during the 1993–94 academic year by fifth-year students in a design synthesis course. Twelve HyperCard stacks containing over four hundred cards were developed to report findings from intensive literature searches on the topics listed below. These stacks will be available for use in future design studios to introduce universal design issues or to supplement course readings. The subject areas of the twelve stacks were:

- Introduction to and benefits from an approach to universal design;

- Disability statistics;

- General information about and categories of disabilities;

- Disadvantages experienced by those with disabilities;

- Information on aging;

- Information on dementia and Alzheimer's disease;

- Introduction to the Americans with Disabilities Act;

- General definitions concerning barriers and barrier-free design;

- Accessibility guidelines;

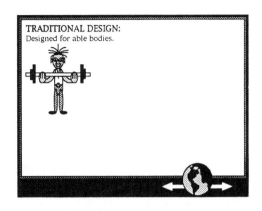

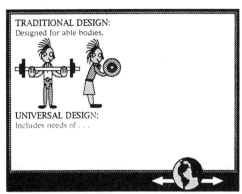

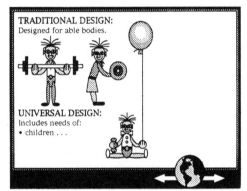

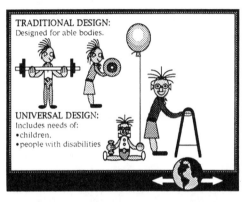

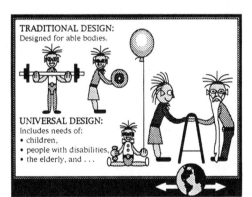

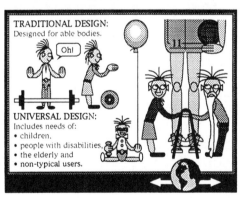

Excerpts from computer-based learning modules.
Concepts have been animated through a series of cards in HyperCard or slides in PowerPoint. Both text and graphics evolve through a series of images to convey one concept. Users can use the arrows in the righthand corner to move forward or backwards in the stack. Pressing the globe icon allows the user to go to a master (home) card that serves as a directory for all of the stacks.

- ADA requirements and guidelines relative to new construction and existing buildings;

- Environmental effects on physical and emotional well-being; and

- Wayfinding and coding of the environment.

Three basic software packages were used: HyperCard (Claris, 1990–92) for the development of informational databases and tutorials; PowerPoint (Microsoft, 1992) for the production of slides, and Director (MacroMind, 1992) for editing the videos. HyperCard was selected because it is widely disseminated throughout academia. PowerPoint was used for the ease of slide development and editing and the transferability of data between programs. Director was chosen for the ability to create standalone applications so that faculty at other programs would not need the original software to access the materials.

There are several advantages to storing information in HyperCard. The program can work somewhat like a database. Information is stored on cards, much like computerized index cards, and the cards are then stored in stacks, much like file folders. Users simply move through the stacks as they would thumb through files. Editing is relatively easy and additional learning modules can be developed for specific project types by simply rearranging cards from the appropriate stacks. New material can be inserted at any point without having to rework the existing stacks. As new project challenges are faced by students, appropriate building, life safety, and accessibility codes can be presented through customized computer-based modules.

Students learn to manipulate HyperCard quickly. By using options in the pull-down "Go" menu they can return to the home card (directory) to open another stack of cards, giving them another topic. Through the same menu they can go forward or backward in the stack. They also can see a record of all the cards they have viewed. The "Find" command lets students search for key words and the program moves to the appropriate card or cards automatically. Similar command options for moving through documents to retrieve information are available on PowerPoint and Director.

Studio Projects. We evaluated the success of these universal design teaching techniques by analyzing the visual evidence in studio design solutions from upper division courses. During the fall semester, students in a third-year interior design studio evaluated and partially redesigned an assisted-living facility that was under construction. They drew on their experiences from producing the universal design games, from interviews and observations made at the facility, and from the views expressed by consultants on the videotape. In the spring semester, this same studio of students designed weekend retreats for individual clients with specific physical disabilities. The fourth-year interior design students designed large-scale conference centers, based in part on previous knowledge of universal design issues and on their experiences from producing the video. They evaluated their proposed spaces in light of universal design issues and concerns with techniques such as proxemic zone analysis.

Students presented their work to university citizens with disabilities, professional designers, administrators, and faculty. Paul Grayson, our UDEP advisor, critiqued the juniors' studio design projects during his visit in the spring term. The review process

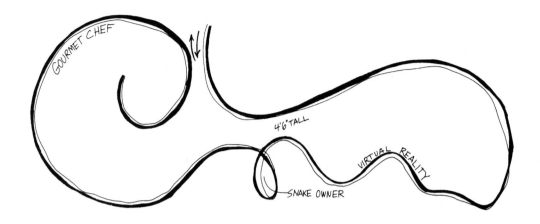

Weekend retreat project, gesture and plan. *Paula Will designed a refuge for a 4'-6" tall person with interests in gourmet cooking, virtual reality and pet snakes. She made a one-line gesture drawing that reflected the client's interests and personality, and then adapted it to become the base circulation pattern within the retreat. The project represented a melding of aesthetic, functional, lifespan, and production issues in a course focusing on construction contract documents.*

confirmed that the students had learned a great deal about universal design. It also underscored the need for vigilance in their quest to meet predictable needs of as many users as possible.

Through each of these components—the introductory videotape, games, computer-based learning modules, and studio projects—students gained an early understanding of some of the problems faced by people who have different abilities. They learned about some of the barriers and problems that many of their peers face everyday through producing and playing the games or taping and viewing the video. They also learned required building, life safety, fire, and accessibility standards, codes, and regulations.

Reflection

The emotions and frustrations experienced by students with disabilities, as portrayed in the video diaries, clearly affected the interior design students. Having consultants of the same age and experience as the design students underscored the relevance of universal design throughout the lifespan. Addressing design issues for people their own age charged the term *universal design* with new meaning: they are not just designing for the elderly, but for their peers, and for themselves someday.

Dialogue between consultants on the videotape captured the issue that meeting regulatory requirements often is not enough—accessible space is not always usable. While attempting to use spaces that meet applicable codes, a student using a wheelchair pointed out the functional deficits: "Okay, I can get to this [conference] table, but what if I don't want to sit here, but there?... I can reach these [library] shelves, but I have friends who couldn't.... There's nowhere on campus where two or more

Executive conference center project.

Registration, lobby, and lobby lounge. Virginia Montgomery designed a 200,000 square foot conference center in a fourth-year studio. This plan detail reflects the attention paid to the needs of people who use wheelchairs.

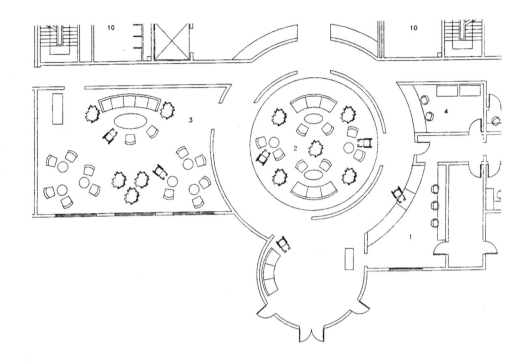

Executive conference center project, proxemic zones study. *Virginia Montgomery created a proxemic zone layer in her computer-based drawings to evaluate the ease with which wheelchair users could both access a space and interact with other users. The circles on this drawing represent the generally recognized boundaries of personal, social, and public interpersonal space.*

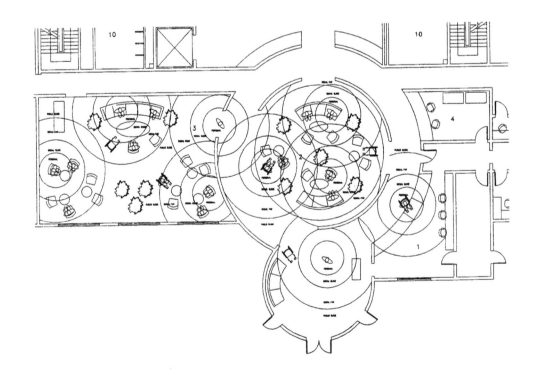

of us—and we do tend to travel in packs—can eat together without causing disturbances." A student with a hearing disability surprised the interior design students by pointing out how the activities of others affect him: "You might not notice the sound from a door hinge when you come to class late, but my hearing aid picks it up like squeaky chalk. It [conveys] all sounds, and doesn't know what to filter out."

A predictable result of the universal design games was that students had to learn detailed facets of universal design to formulate their games. Students playing each other's games were motivated to learn additional information to perform well before their peers. This desire to do well in each other's games reinforced learning and helped integrate information into the students' approaches to problem seeking and problem solving—results we seek as educators when we give exams.

UDEP advisor Paul Grayson critiques week-end retreat projects. *The posted projects represent work through the design development phase. Students subsequently completed working drawings that allowed for spatial adaptations to accommodate changes throughout their clients' lifespans.*

Fifth-year students preparing the computer-based instructional modules noted that they had been exposed to the same materials in previous courses but had experienced difficulty remembering the data. These students stated that HyperCard stacks could be tremendous aids for organizing and synthesizing information across courses.

Evaluation

We documented the process from the beginning, including writing objectives for each of the three components and methods of evaluation. In addition to the evaluative questionnaires developed by the sponsors of UDEP, we evaluated the effectiveness of the videotape, computer modules, and simulation by having students who experienced the process assess how much they learned. The consultants evaluated the universal design games for the amount of learning they thought the games achieved.

A marker for the successful completion of this process was inherently elusive, as our ultimate goal was to influence how students think, feel, and proceed while designing interiors. If the strategies implemented through this project were successful, the students would demonstrate heightened sensitivities to universal design issues. Presumably, their evolving personal design philosophies would include these issues and be visible in their approaches to designing interiors. Although the degree to which awareness of universal design and lifespan issues was increased by this project is difficult to assess, both faculty members have observed that students are incorporating universal design concepts into their projects without the resistance they usually express towards code issues.

Chapter 23: University of Tennessee

Perhaps the best evidence of success comes from impromptu comments made by students during studio sessions:

My client is getting older. Maybe I need to change this since she may use a wheelchair later.

But what if a taller person buys this house? I should put in supports so wall cabinets can be added. These [base] cabinets can be raised. These [others] could be left lower for a mixing center.

This recessed area fits the site better. A ramp can be worked in over here.... How will I know that another owner or contractor will know the extra floor joists are provided?

I've stacked these [walk-in] closets so an elevator could be added. I guess a fire pole is out of the question?

I ramped it just in case....

Other groups and individuals could benefit from this instructional development project. University administrators could benefit from viewing the video and going through the learning modules to sensitize them to the human dimensions of the regulatory issues raised by the ADA. Faculty in interior design could benefit from viewing the video, experiencing the games, reviewing the computer-based learning modules, and participating on design juries. Faculty outside the discipline of interior design could benefit as well. Administrators of our College have discussed how offshoots from the computer-based learning modules could be used in the retail, hotel-restaurant administration, and daycare classes to present an overview of universal design issues to majors in other fields. Students with disabilities at the university expressed appreciation at having the opportunity to speak out to young designers as well as to university decision-makers on the problems they encounter as they try to achieve their potential in this academic community.

Our participation in this process will continue well beyond the completion of this project. If nothing else, this project has reinforced our commitment to universal design as a mandate for our personal teaching and designing. We plan to continue using all the strategies developed here. All three strategies garner self-perpetuating products. Student output produces materials that can be used to edit earlier products. Work from each year reinforces the past and helps build a stronger base for the future.

Acknowledgements

Participation by the following individuals was essential to the success of this project and is gratefully acknowledged: Consultants Ricky Smith, Kathy Spruiell, and Bryan Vogt; Dr. Jan Howard, director of handicapped student services, UTK; William R. Terry, director of the Center for Telecommunications and Video, UTK; James Bell, video techni-cian; Randall Cooper and Marsh Frere, Byrd and Cooper Architects, Knoxville; Damon Falconnier, Accessible Design Architects, Knoxville; Architect Leroy Gerard of Knoxville; John Overly, architect-in-charge of barrier-free and ADA compliance, Martin Marietta, Oak Ridge, Tennessee; and Administrator William Thomas, Social Worker Jane Finn, and Director of Nursing Barbara Cooper of Shannondale Health Care Center, Knoxville.

References

Anders, R. and D. Fechtner (1992). "Universal Design." In *A Report on the Industrial Design Curriculum Development Program*. New York: Pratt Institute.

Bosselmann, P. and K.H. Craik (1990). "Perceptual Simulations of Environments." In *Methods in Environmental and Behavior Research*, edited by R.B. Bechtel, R.W. Marans, and W. Michelson, 162–190. Malabar, Fla.: Robert E. Kreiger Publishing Co.

Canestaro, N.C. (1987). "Open Office Programming: Assessment of 'The Work Station Game' as a Planning Tool. Unpublished dissertation from the University of Michigan, Ann Arbor, Mich.

Canestaro, N.C., ed. (1993–4). *Innovative Teaching Ideas*. Interior Design Educators Council.

Canestaro, N.C. and T.L. Houser. [Analysis of project descriptions and requirements in Canestaro, ed., *Innovative Teaching Ideas*.] Unpublished raw data.

Case, D. (1990). "Using HyperText to Create Design Programming Databases." *Journal of Interior Design Education and Research* 19, no. 1, 37–52.

Claris Corp. (1990–2). *HyperCard*® (Version 2.1) [Computer program]. Santa Clara, Calif.: Apple Computer, Inc.

Goodman, F.L. and A.T. Horn (1975). *The End of the Line: A Simulation Game*. Ann Arbor, Mich.: The Institute of Gerontology, University of Michigan/Wayne State University.

Greenblat, C.S. (1981). "Gaming-Simulation as a Tool for Social Research." In *Principles and Practices of Gaming-Simulation*, edited by C.S. Greenblat and R.D. Duke, 189–201. Beverly Hills, Calif.: Sage.

Hassell, M.J. (1980). "Urban Gaming Simulations and Evaluation." In *The Guide to Simulations/Games for Education and Training,* edited by R. Horn and A. Cleaves, 4th ed., 286–303. Beverly Hills, Calif.: Sage.

King, J., R.W. Marans, and L.A. Solomon (1982). *Pre-construction Evaluation: A Report on the Full Scale Mock-up and Evaluation of Hospital Rooms.* Ann Arbor, Mich.: Architectural Research Laboratory, University of Michigan.

Lanza, A., and T. Roselli (1991). "Effects of the Hypertextual Approach Versus the Structured Approach on Students' Achievement." *Journal of Computer-Based Instruction* 18, no. 2: 48–50.

MacroMind, Inc. (1992). *Director* (Version 3.1.1) [Computer program]. San Francisco: MacroMedia, Inc.

Microsoft Corp. (1992). *PowerPoint* (Version 3.0) [Computer program]. Redmond, Wash.: Microsoft Corp.

Sanoff, H. (1977). *Methods of Architectural Programming.* Stroudsbourg, Pa.: Dowden, Hutchinson and Ross, Inc.

Stahl, F. (1982). "Computer Simulation Modeling for Informed Decision-Making." In *EDRA 13: Knowledge for Design,* edited by P. Bart, A. Chen, and G. Francescato, 105–11. College Park, Md.: Environmental Design Research Association.

Winkel, G. and R. Sasanoff (1976). "An Approach to an Objective Analysis of Behavior in Architectural Space." In *Environmental Psychology: People and Their Physical Settings,* edited by H.M. Proshansky, W.H. Ittelson, and L.G. Rivlin, 2nd ed., 351–62. New York: Holt, Reinhold and Winston.

Across the Lifespan and the Curriculum

Team members:

Julia Beamish
Associate Professor
Anna Marshall-Baker
Assistant Professor
Eric Wiedegreen
Assistant Professor

Proposal

Meeting the needs of people has always been the cornerstone of the programs in Housing, Interior Design, and Resource Management (HIDM) at Virginia Tech. External support for universal design education has helped faculty highlight the value of designing for people of all ages and abilities in their teaching.

The Interior Design Program at Virginia Tech is within the HIDM Department in the College of Human Resources. The Interior Design Program is FIDER accredited and graduates approximately thirty-five students per year. For many years, students in Interior Design and Residential Property Management have been required, in their last year, to take Barrier-Free Design, a two-credit lecture course. The course concentrates on code requirements for accessibility. It also requires students to interview people with special needs, to assess buildings, and to consult with clients on unusable spaces.

Our proposal was to educate the faculty in the department through an orientation session and design process. Projects would be introduced in courses throughout the four-year degree program so that universal design would be an integral component of students' interior design work. In spite of receiving less funding, faculty who participated in submitting the proposal agreed to implement universal design in their classes during the fall and spring semesters.

Activity

As faculty discussed how to integrate universal design, we identified where related topics are already being presented in a variety of courses across program areas. Universal design is discussed as a component of the course on residential space planning and housing. Code requirements are identified in the design drawing class and applied in the senior contract design course and in health care design. Residential equipment and management courses highlight user-equipment interaction and discuss effective task completion, particularly among users with special needs.

More importantly, we realized that many of the faculty were familiar with the concept of universal design and had been proponents of its value for some time. The focus of the project became the task of educating students about universal design and lifespan issues.

For freshmen and sophomores, Anna Marshall-Baker and Eric Wiedegreen incorporated universal design into the sequence of Design Appreciation, Two-Dimensional Design, Three-Dimensional Design, and Presentation Techniques courses. Also at the sophomore level, Julia Beamish added universal design criteria to several projects in the House Planning course so that students would understand how user need criteria affect space requirements.

Barrier-Free Design, taught by Julia Beamish, continued to be the primary course for presenting universal design issues, supplementing the information presented on barrier-free design. The course addressed codes, legal requirements, and special design considerations for people with disabilities and for aging populations. Students participated in experiential exercises, discussed housing issues with students who use wheelchairs, conducted commercial and residential accessibility surveys, and worked in groups to design a residence for a woman who had lost an arm in an accident. Information on design and management concerns was presented to both interior design and property management students.

During the fall semester, the graduate seminar presented other opportunities to discuss universal design. Julia Beamish presented the universal design concept to students and asked them to keep a journal of their thoughts and observations on the topic. Students participated in focus groups to reflect on universal design in the department and wrote a brief summary of their reactions.

The department celebrated universal design with a visit by Dorothy Fowles, UDEP advisor. Her presentation drew over one hundred students and faculty to a lecture and slide show on universal design and its application to interior design. She met with HIDM faculty and graduate students to discuss universal design education efforts and further changes in the curriculum to continue incorporating this concept into the programs.

Outcome

2D and 3D Design Courses. We approached these courses with the belief that we could affect students' thinking about universal design most effectively at the introductory level. Total revision of courses was impractical so we emphasized universal design issues on a project-by-project basis within the first-year 2D Design and the second-year 3D Design classes. Our primary effort was to sensitize students to a broad spectrum of lifespan topics, including visual impairment, immobility, size differences, and age-related issues.

To heighten awareness of texture, students in 2D Design were asked to create a

collage of materials using only texture as a guide. The students were blindfolded while they chose materials and created the arrangement. In the subsequent exercises students graphically reproduced the actual texture arrangement in point and line and only as value, exploring the relationship between what is seen and what is felt.

Texture project in the 2D Design class (left and middle). Students in the 3D Design class used the wheelchair as inspiration for a design problem (right).

In the 3D Design class texture was introduced as the major design element in a project that required one geometric solid to metamorphose into another solid. The students judged their models while blindfolded. A blind sculptor who was invited as a juror described the heightened sensitivity of her other senses. Students discovered both the sensory and informational components of texture.

To explore the value of the wheelchair to people with mobility limitations, the students in the 3D Design class were asked to use the wheelchair as an object of inspiration for a design problem. Wheelchairs were brought to the classroom so students could sketch them, sit in them, ride in them, race them, and take a trip. The resulting projects portrayed the wheelchair as a liberating rather than a confining force.

Students in the 2D Design class created measurement tapes for individuals of different ages and body types (children, basketball players, older people) as an exercise in recognizing that people without disabilities have diverse needs because of their body size. Representative samples of the tapes were used by the 3D Design class in their final project, creating an architectural space within a twenty-foot cubic space, customized to the needs of the individuals documented on the tapes. The models and drawings reflected the different needs of individuals for qualities such as sight-lines, reaching, and sitting heights.

As a follow-up to the measurement tape project, students in the sophomore-level Presentation Techniques class were asked to tailor a space to the specific needs of two very different individuals, while maintaining a sense of spatial unity and parity of

Model of a space for two people of different sizes.

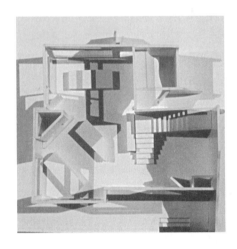

Model of a residence that accommodates visitors who use wheelchairs.

ownership for the clients. A continuation of the problem asked students to select appropriate furnishings and materials and to render several views of the space.

In a color project for the 2D Design class, students were introduced to age-related visual problems by looking at their multiple colored schemes with empathic devices.

Using strips of yellow cellophane as visual filters that approximate the heightened yellow-orange and diminished blue-green perception of advanced age, students evaluated their schemes for their appropriateness to aging eyesight.

House Planning Course. The concept of universal design has always been the basis of the House Planning course. User needs and functionalism are important in understanding how houses should work for people. This year the focus was more on the uniqueness of individuals.

Some basic spatial criteria based on the needs and measurements of the "typical" healthy, adult male (or female) were presented and students were encouraged to see that these standards would not work for everyone. Students measured themselves and children of different ages to see the spatial requirements of different people. These measurements became reference points for subsequent assignments involving children. Students also worked on retirement housing and residential designs that would accommodate visitors using wheelchairs.

Design assignments in the House Planning course have a limit on square footage. Usually it is generous, but it does require students to make choices about space allocation. Adding a "universal design" requirement affected the students' designs. Their projects had many fewer floor level changes than in previous years. Students sought to define open spaces with flooring changes, ceiling height changes, half walls, and other architectural features. They also allowed more space in baths, halls, and at doorways. The requirements frustrated them as they tried to work out the design of other spaces that had, as a consequence, become less spacious. Teaching this course with a consultant would be very helpful to the students as they struggle with the trade-offs.

Barrier-Free Design Course. Barrier-Free Design is a two-credit senior-level course for both interior design and residential property management students. The scope and complexity of design assignments were limited by the lecture format and the mix of students, many of whom have no design background. Juniors and seniors have fragmentary knowledge of barrier-free design through other classes but have not had systematic exposure to universal design. This course gives students with different majors an opportunity to interact and work on team assignments and presentations. Students in their junior year were very positive about the applicability of universal design information to their internship.

The residential property management students were particularly interested in the laws about barrier-free design and how to comply. Before assessing apartment complexes with a UFAS checklist they met with students using wheelchairs to hear about apartment design problems. One of the reviewers of students' work commented on their focus on wheelchair accessibility and their lack of attention to people with visual impairments, a large segment of the disabled student population. The reason for this may be attributable to the focus of the checklist, their experience with students in wheelchairs, or a lingering impression that disability means "wheelchair." In the future, inviting a wider range of consultants will encourage the students to assess apartments from a broader perspective.

Although the design students were concerned with legal issues, aesthetic solutions were clearly important to them. Examples of appealing, suitable, and well-designed products and up-to-date product information need to be available in the resource room. The design students worked in teams to design a residence for a real client—a woman who had lost one arm. Besides many typical residential design concerns, the students had to think about space requirements and products that met her needs. They researched products and met with her to discuss options. The client was most impressed with their effort and attention to detail. Ken Smith, a representative from the National Kitchen and Bath Association, critiqued the student work and commented on the detail and attention given to the client's needs. This project effectively challenged students to think about individual needs at the same time they were planning spaces that are universal.

Graduate Seminar. The graduate seminar gave students a chance to participate in the department's thinking about universal design. A number of graduate students are interested in research topics related to the concept. Most graduate students seemed somewhat familiar with the concept; the interior design majors were especially familiar with accessibility requirements. Most were able to tie the concept of universal design into their respective disciplines and engage in insightful observations and discussion.

Evaluation

Students completed written evaluations after their participation in the freshman and sophomore sequences. Prior to their coursework, most had limited understanding of the concept of universal design and of the full meaning of the term *disability*. In the evaluative questionnaire, the two projects that students identified as most helpful in developing an understanding of universal design were designing the architectural space for two disparate clients (43 percent) and using the wheelchairs (35 percent). Responses from the remaining 22 percent indicated that there was value in all of the projects in 3D Design, in designing public spaces in Presentation Techniques, and in using the yellow filters in 2D Design. More than half the students (52 percent) commented on their new awareness of accessibility in their day-to-day environments.

In Barrier-Free Design, students wrote reaction papers to various activities and interviews in which they participated. They found that experiencing the environment using a wheelchair or blindfolded helped them look at their environment more critically. Meeting students who use wheelchairs was very successful in illuminating the problems they experience in getting around campus and in their daily activities.

Meeting with the two handicapped students was very informative... it was beneficial to see the actual housing practices of the community and to hear the stories of those students that it effects. The most important point made, I think, was that each unit has to be individualized for the person using it. This was good information because it educated us not to typecast the "disabled" into one category with certain needs and specifications for comfortable living.

Reflection

Participation in UDEP has been an interesting and rewarding experience for the faculty. It has been a topic that has allowed us to work across our traditional subject lines. It has given us the opportunity to explore what we teach and to think about how it could be done differently. We have not completed the process of course and curriculum revisions, but we tried out new ideas with this purpose in mind.

One important change we made is introducing universal design and lifespan issues at the very beginning of students' coursework in interior design. We feel strongly that lifespan issues can be integrated into any basic design program or course of study. All of the techniques we used in this project were interjected into existing class assignments and problems. It took very little time to introduce the new subject matter and the major emphasis of the course remained focused on basic design instruction. We exposed students to a wide range of issues and sensitized them to the needs of people different from themselves, experiences that we hope they will carry into their design careers.

Our concept of presenting universal design to students gradually in a series of projects throughout the curriculum requires some rethinking about our program and the way in which other subject matter is taught. Many courses are segmented, topical courses. Integrating one topic throughout all courses may lead to other topics that need to be integrated. Some faculty argue for keeping courses separate so that they are identifiable by students and employers. A course on barrier-free design has been a fairly unique offering for design and property management students and gives them a distinct advantage with employers.

Our department head has been very supportive of UDEP. She publicized the project with a department newsletter article and by including information in a college report. Department faculty outside the interior design area have been very supportive of the concept of universal design. It was especially rewarding during a focus group session with faculty (only one from interior design) to witness their familiarity and understanding of the concept and to realize that these issues are being presented in other classes.

Other offshoots of the project include: three independent-study students; two papers being written by graduate students on universal design for submission to conferences and journals; and papers and presentations by Anna Marshall-Baker and Eric Wiedegreen for conferences and journal submissions related to their concepts of universal design and lifespan issues in the curriculum.

Overall, the students and faculty have benefited immensely from our program's participation in this project. It has opened our eyes to the many variations in people's needs and encouraged us to grow as we struggle to create designs that will meet specialized needs as well as the needs of all.

Virginia Polytechnic Institute and State University – Blacksburg, Virginia

Department of Landscape Architecture

Teaching Universal Design with Multimedia Tutorials

Team members:

Dean R. Bork
  Associate Professor
Rick Parrish
  Graduate Student
Dan Mahon
  Graduate Student

Proposal

There is no completely naturalistic way of resolving the question about what model of learner we want to enshrine at the center of our practice of education. For there are many ways to learn and many ways of encouraging different forms of learning with different ends in view. At the heart of the decision process there must be a value judgment about how the mind should be cultivated and to what end.
(Jerome Bruner, 1985)

I believe in an educational environment where a plurality of values are expressed. I also believe that students of design are obligated to examine the values that underpin their professional conduct and work. This does not mean all value sets are equally valid, only that each deserves to be heard and critically examined.
(Dean Bork, 1994)

The term *universal design* is credited to architect Ron Mace. According to Mace, universal design is a term used to label good design for all people. Mace says universal design requires an awareness of the abilities of people we design for and the incorporation of that knowledge into "design that is responsive" (*Toward Universal Design*, 1993).

UDEP is about promoting equity in design for people with disabilities. The project has an inherent supposition that designers have an ethical obligation to serve the needs of all who may use the products or environments that they create.

The design disciplines have enjoyed long-standing debate about their responsibilities to clients and users. If design educators choose to accept the supposition inherent in UDEP, then they may benefit from at least retaining a questioning attitude. While architect Mace's references to "good design" and "the range of abilities of users" sound noble, they will not provide the practitioner or student of design much of a foothold.

In public places, diversity among users and the specificity of individual needs will tend toward conflicting expectations. An example is the USDA Forest Service's "levels of access." Some recreationists see rating the level of challenge in recreational settings (in a manner similar to what is customary on ski slopes) as substantially expanding opportunities for people with disabilities. Others feel that creating various levels of challenge is a means of skirting hard-won disability rights legislation. It stands to reason that jocks, adventurers, couch potatoes, and convalescents will interpret recreational environments differently. Given the greatly varied and frequently conflicting needs of individuals, to whom should the designer of public places respond?

The ethical premises of universal design have, to our knowledge, received little study. Similarly, a substantial theory of practice has not been proposed. This leaves the design educator in the position of representing to students a nascent body of information that is largely political in its formulation and intent. Does a person with a disability have a greater inherent right to that nearest parking space than a person accompanied by a toddler and two infants? From practical and ethical standpoints we may see some room for debate, especially given certain circumstances. The law, however, leaves no question. There is sufficient political consensus to have rendered a definitive answer. To what extent is it our role and responsibility as design educators to impress the disability rights agenda upon our students?

Our project team treats the notion of socially equitable public environments as a self-evident truth flowing from the Bill of Rights and its ideological foundations. However, the interpretation of these rights into the built environment is far from a cut-and-dry issue. It is probable that we can design to serve the needs of a broader segment of the population and it is appropriate that our students undertake this challenge with us. For this reason, we have chosen to address students' values regarding people different from themselves, add to their conceptual knowledge in this area, and see that their work remains true to the position they espouse.

Clive Dilnot observed that design, in general, has nominal value in our culture because it seldom finds its way into public discourse (Dilnot, 1982). In ordinary social settings, it is common to hear casual conversation turn towards doctors, lawyers, and accountants, but rarely does it touch on architects, landscape architects, or planners. If what Dilnot observes is true, we may construct a parallel explanation for universal design receiving so little emphasis in the work of designers. Simply put, the subject of universal design is not a part of ordinary discourse within the community of designers and therefore is not integrated into the common value set. Through UDEP we propose to alter this condition within the Department of Landscape Architecture at Virginia Tech.

In discovery-based design education, moments of need occur as students conduct a form of dialogue with the various issues that come to bear in their decision making (Schon, 1983; Schon et al., 1992). Our project attempts to influence students' attention toward and response to universal design concerns by making instruction and information available precisely at the teachable moment. The project involves the development and testing of a collection of multimedia tutorials as a means of providing instruction and information to students on demand.

There are three levels of context that influence the development and evaluation of this project: 1) the educational forces in the university, 2) the general pedagogy of the department, and 3) the body of work previously undertaken by members of the project team.

Enrollment in Virginia's public universities is expected to increase by sixty thousand students over the next decade. Financial forecasters suggest that no additional general fund resources will become available to support the education of these students. One of the key strategies being promoted to meet this challenge is an increased reliance on educational technologies. Through this project, one such technology (multimedia) is examined as a tool for incorporating contemporary social and ethical issues into the design curriculum.

The general pedagogy of the Department of Landscape Architecture tends to lend credence to a computer-assisted and self-paced learning approach. A key goal of the landscape architecture faculty is to engender in students a designerly habit of mind and a sense of responsibility toward the development of a professional position grounded in philosophy, theory, and concept. Within the department, education is viewed as something students pursue, not as something they receive. This requires that students reside in an environment that is generative and rich in resources. Following the structuralist tradition, students at any academic level are viewed as capable of addressing any topic of inquiry (Bruner, 1977). This underscores the need to have resources available to students on a self-paced and user-controlled basis (Dewey, 1963; McNally, 1977).

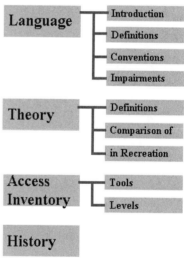

For the past several years, members of the project team and students from the department have been involved with the USDA Forest Service in assessing, designing, and constructing accessible recreation facilities. Many students gained exposure to universal design through these and related activities before UDEP began. Because of the resources available to the project team, accessible recreation became a topical area of focus for the prototype tutorials. Since students had multiple avenues for investigating the design-related needs of people with disabilities, it was not necessary to design the tutorials as a sole source of information on the subject. In this context, however, it was difficult to evaluate the influence of the prototype in isolation from related activities.

Prototype Menu Structure

Branching structure of the tutorial modules.

Menus offer freedom of navigation between tutorials and the database. Choices are presented in text and graphic form.

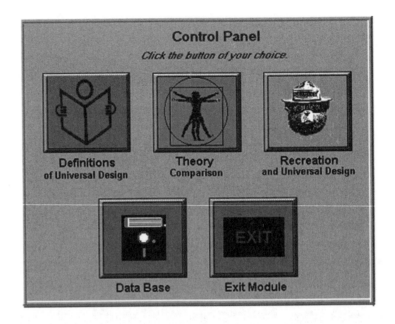

Activity

The tutorials produced for the prototype focused on awareness of universal design theory and principles. The tutorials are arranged under a nested menu system. There are four selections on the main menu. Under three of these are second level menus. Ten selections are available in total.

The tutorials are interactive, allowing the user to control the flow of information. Various user interfaces and graphic conventions are employed across the tutorials for the purpose of exploration. The ability to jump between tutorials is always available to the user. In some cases, the interface allows the user to jump out of a tutorial and later resume at the same position. In other cases, only a choice between tutorials is available. In all cases, the user navigates through the program by the use of menu buttons. However, some of the tutorials require slightly different forms of interaction such as dragging and dropping objects.

An important aspect of computer-based instruction is user feedback. In the tutorials, any user may gain access to any module at any time. Although user responses are not scored, the tutorials provide audio and text feedback whenever the user makes a decision.

The tutorials are structured to work with a connecting database searchable by subject keywords. From any tutorial, the user may "jump out" to the database to search for related information and then return. To facilitate connections between information, the team tested document linking via "hot words" in the text. Clicking

on a highlighted word immediately takes the user on a search for more information related to that topic or term. The database was not in place for evaluation of this prototype but should be available to students during the coming academic year.

Outcome

The modules were basically developed between July 1 and August 15. There are some major chunks still missing, but we have a useful prototype, which is what we promised. The biggest problem in getting the system running was coordinating hardware. The sound board didn't like the brand x chip set, the hard disk was full, and the machine needed memory management software. Altogether, we wasted three or four weeks getting that stuff going. The sign has been posted in the computer room with instructions for using the system for at least three weeks, maybe four. (Journal, 10/28/93, Principal Investigator)

During a program meeting at the beginning of the semester, students were told that the system would be available in the computing lab. The actual installation, which was to take place in August, was delayed. As the journal excerpt indicates, numerous hours were invested early in the fall term preparing a computer to deliver the tutorials. The problems were resolved around October 1 and a sign was posted in the lab providing instructions for students interested in exploring the tutorials. The system was checked periodically to see that it was functioning properly. Only minimal maintenance was required and the amount of "down time" was negligible.

Each tutorial module begins with an overview of content.

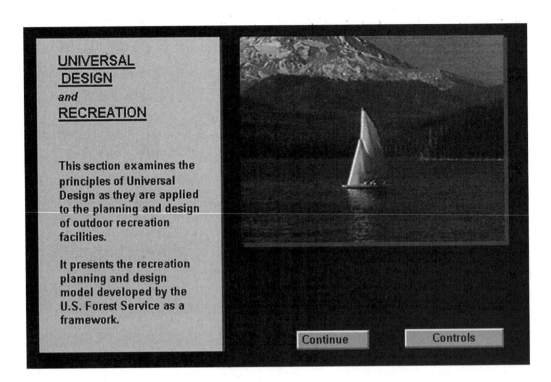

I have lined up one studio to experiment with universal design requirements and one technical course. I also plan to use one assignment early in the next semester studio as another test. This should give us some basis for evaluating the system. In fact, most of the students know we are working on the project, they know Dan, Rick, and I are working with the Forest Service. They know Dan has been offered a job because of his work with universal design and accessibility inventories. Already, two other graduate students have picked up universal design as the area of study for their theses. In studios, I hear many more references to accessibility questions in general, though I am not convinced that the idea of universal design has soaked in. Even the faculty are more aware of the issues involved in universal design than they have been in the past. I think Camp Build-a-Bunch did a lot to raise the level of awareness and to create talk among the students.

In other words, I don't know how we will isolate the effects of the multimedia work per se, but it is clear that universal design is a hot topic and students and faculty in a small program like ours pick up on these things fast. Just the fact that Dan, Rick, and I have several active projects and several more pending creates a certain level of interest and awareness. (Journal, 10/28/93, Principal Investigator)

Two assignments given during the fall semester explicitly required students to address questions of universal design in their work. One assignment was given in a

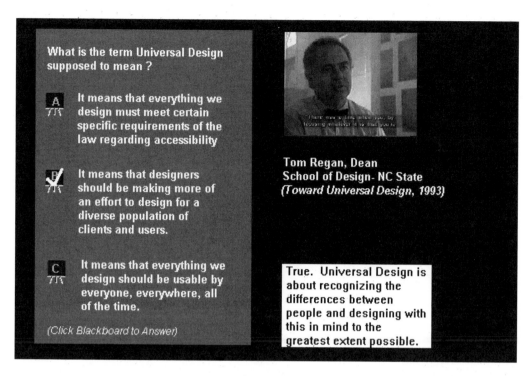

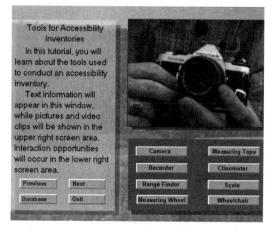

Multiple-choice questions help users understand the definition of universal design. Feedback occurs in the form of text and digital video.

graduate level Urban Design Studio. While much of the studio focused on urban design issues at the district or larger scale, a component of the studio involved design of a public open space, for which students were asked to address issues of design for a diverse user population.

Simultaneously, in a technical course called Materials and Details, both undergraduate and graduate students created and evaluated details incorporating a universal design perspective. Some graduate students were enrolled in both the studio and this technical course, affording them the opportunity to coordinate work between the two courses. These students had the opportunity to develop a design scheme in studio while developing related details in the technical course.

In the Accessibility Inventory module, tools used for fieldwork are described and demonstrated for students.

I did manage to copy the data files from the hard drive today and look at the results. So far, about 17 people have used the system. Three of these are Dan, Rick, and me. Among the remaining are a few that I know looked at it just to get an understanding of what we are doing with Authorware and a couple that are interested in doing research or thesis work on universal design. This too is a sign of the natural shift in student interest that comes about as faculty become involved in research in any topic area. As a result of faculty participation normally resources and easy contacts become available to students and this influences their choice of areas of study (along with other forces internal to the students to be sure). At any rate, it appears that about 12 people have somehow taken some time to look at the system, I have not checked to see how much time has been spent. (Journal, 10/29/93, Principal Investigator)

Evaluation

The tutorial application maintained an electronic record of student use. The table shows the raw data collected at the end of the fall semester 1993.

User	No. of Sessions	Avg. Time/Session *(in minutes)*	Total Time *(in minutes)*
1	1	16	16
2	1	7	7
3	1	33	33
4	2	7	14
5	1	7	7
6	9	7	63
7	1	3	3
8	1	3	3
9	1	15	15
10	1	3	3
11	1	2	2
12	4	22	88
13	1	4	4
14	1	43	43
15	1	18	18
16	1	2	2
	28	12	336

Approximately 150 graduate and undergraduate students had access to the system. Sixteen students took advantage of the tutorials. These students used the system for a total of 5.57 hours and spent, on average, 12 minutes each time they used the system. Only three students used the system more than once during the semester.

Little data on system use was recorded for the spring semester 1994. The computer on which the tutorials reside suffered some major operating-system problems during the course of this semester. For this reason, it is not clear whether the lack of data reflects actual use of the tutorials.

As the data indicate, it is doubtful that the tutorials had much direct influence on the attention students gave to universal design in their work. Students in each course were reminded that multimedia resources were available. Because the research objective was to test the use of multimedia tutorials in an open lab environment, the project team intentionally made no requirement to use them. Approximately one-third of the students enrolled in the studio used the tutorials. In the technical course, one-fifth of the students used them. Of the remaining one hundred (more or less) students in the program, only four individuals used the tutorials.

Design Studio (LAR 5704)

Use of the tutorials was substantially higher among students who had assignments with explicit universal design requirements. Still, not even half of the students who had explicit project requirements took time to view the tutorials.

Though the data is inconsistent, it appears likely that students attempted to use the tutorials more than the library (located one block away) to gather information about universal design. This may suggest that physical proximity is an important factor in getting students to use electronic learning resources.

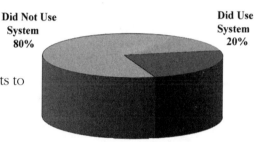

Technology Course (LAR 5984)

Our project team also evaluated the quality of student work from both courses. This evaluation identified few influences in the work attributable to use of the tutorials. A rigorous evaluation of the student work was planned. Unfortunately, the level of detail and communication in the work was not sufficient to warrant more than a cursory review. In the opinion of the reviewers, the products did not reflect the level of quality that is normal and expected from students in the program.

Reflection

Through UDEP, the project team has learned some things about teaching universal design and about computer-aided instruction. The team was surprised by how readily students embrace the notion of universal design. Once presented with the idea, students seem to accept at face value that design of the landscape should serve the needs of as many people as possible. Misjudging the student's willingness to incorporate universal design into their work caused our team to spend more effort than necessary on presenting basic foundations and justifications.

Based on professional experiences with universal design in recreational settings, the team believes that students must possess knowledge of universal design that goes substantially beyond proper values. Once a student espouses the value of universal design, the educational focus shifts rapidly toward acquiring technical knowledge about user needs and developing good judgment regarding its implementation. It is important to have access to technical facts, such as the required height of benches. These dimensions, however, take on new meaning when a wheelchair user explains how she transfers to the bench. The team members have worked with two consultants who use wheelchairs and each has very different needs and opinions about what is workable. Working with consultants helps in understanding the human dimensions of landscape architecture, but in the end, the responsibility of exercising judgment falls on the designer. This holds true even where issues of code conformance are concerned.

The reviewers feel that little of the work from either course shows much insight or inspiration with regard to universal design issues. One exception is a student who began to develop a system of universally designed streetscape elements. While the details had many errors and oversights, the concept of integrated arrangement and detailing of streetscape elements represents an intriguing universal design issue. The attention given to universal design issues, in both the design and technical courses, tended to take the form of standard curb cut, ramp, and drinking fountain details. In most cases, details were reproduced from published sources and were so poorly done that the student versions would not pass basic codes. Interviews with a professor, a graduate teaching assistant, and a graduate student indicate why the results may have been less than anticipated.

The project team felt that the universal design assignments were introduced too late in the semester to expect good results. One team member interviewed the studio professor and a graduate student who agreed with the team's assessment that "it's tough to introduce new material, substantial new material, after the Thanksgiving Break time of fall anyway."

Student: *I felt like the universal design was sort of a last minute thing that got pushed in there.... I felt more like it was there to acquaint us with it...but I was in a big rush that whole time.*

Professor: *Yeah, and that's something that Ben and I need to look at if we're going to do it again because according to his schedule it had to be the last part of the semester. But nonetheless, many of the [students] didn't get their feet into this project.... In a quick project you've got to get into it basically fast and they didn't—they were still wrapping up other things. It wasn't the presentation but it was other aspects of it. So, that was part of it too. You know, there were too many projects. And, I think you're right about trying to start something as a new piece.*

The studio professor expressed concern over misjudging the amount of work assigned to the students during the semester. She feels that one too many projects were required and that this adversely affected the students' performance in the studio.

Professor: *My conclusion about that project was that it was one too many projects for the semester. They didn't meet the objectives of the project which were to...take a space and work it through to the level of detail and materiality, and they didn't do that. As a matter of fact, most of them didn't even get to the point where they resolved the idea of the space and what they wanted to explore in terms of the community, let alone how they were going to express it. So, I didn't consider the project to be a success in terms of the objectives that were set up for it. There were too many projects. I mean, knowing that we had to have that project at the end of the semester I should have knocked out the first one...*

Among other things the lack of time resulted in students using few resources related to universal design in the completion of their studio work.

Interviewer: *You made reference to resources that they could pick up. Did you notice in the studio what kinds of things, if anything, were evident in terms of resources that were used to address accessibility questions?*

Professor: *No, I can't say that I did. When I said references, I meant that I...had a list of references and I included the module...and I spoke to them about the availability of the handbook and some of the other material that was available by way of guidelines. I did not, you know, follow it up to see whether they had gone to the library...and I can't say that I remember noticing much....*

The graduate student indicated that she was unable to find much resource information dealing explicitly with universal design.

Student: *And I just looked in all the books that I could find. But most things were dealing along the ADA guidelines. Universal design is fairly new. It wouldn't be in many of the books I was finding, would it?*

It appears that many of the students relied on a single lecture, given by a member of the project team to the technology course, for their understanding of universal design. In their interviews, both the graduate student and the teaching assistant mentioned that lecture as helpful.

In the studio, students spent much of the semester developing proposals at the urban district scale. The final component of the project was intended to be the design of an urban open space. As is common in studios, time ran out before all the students were able to complete all the work that the professor had planned. The studio professor expressed a need for about two more weeks of studio time to bring the work to the level she expected.

The exercise given in the technical course received relatively little weight in the final semester grade. Students appeared to "blow it off." Those who were in both the studio and the technical course struggled to create construction details because their schematic design proposals were not sufficiently developed. Unfortunately, the bulk of the work for both assignments took place at the end of the semester when the students are anxious and tired. As a result, there is limited value to evaluating the students' work.

Perhaps the prototype received little use because it provided only minimal technical and experience-related support to the students, a result of the team's decisions about content rather than limitations inherent in multimedia. While the computer will not replace the need for contact with end users, multimedia can be used to present case studies and technical information effectively. One reason the prototype did not move further in this direction was the difficulty encountered in locating resources for quality case studies.

The level of familiarity that students have with the computer influences their willingness to use it as an informational and instructional resource. The interviewed student who was quite familiar with computers tended to focus on the mechanics of the application and ignore the content.

> Graduate Assistant: *Actually, I was looking for more vocal material. I wanted it to talk more. It didn't talk enough. A couple things...actually the sound effects are what I was interested in the most. There were a couple of sounds that I can't remember...maybe there were some comic strips or something in a few of the images. I thought that was interesting*

His peer, less familiar with computers, expressed reluctance to use the tutorials without someone to assist.

> Student: *I think the fact that it is on a computer...I never would have done it if Howard (fellow student and computer literate) hadn't taken me in there, sat down and turned it on for me.*

The prototype tended to overlook these differences among end users. In choosing to use the tutorials to experiment with multimedia, the project team violated two well-documented principles of computer-assisted instruction. The tutorials did not present the user with a consistent interface and the level of user control was varied. As a result, the presence of the computer was emphasized rather than minimized.

By intention, use of the tutorials was not tied to any specific course in the curriculum. At the same time, the development of the database to attend the tutorials was delayed so that it was not in place during the evaluation. The interviews suggest that students are interested in access to raw information where the computer serves to facilitate searches. The tutorials with less user flexibility were seen as unduly linear and constraining (even for less experienced computer users).

Student: *Maybe because I didn't know how to use it, but sometimes there were parts I didn't want to deal with that you had to go through to get to the next part. I was looking for information rather than trying to answer all those questions to proceed to the next part at times.*

Considering the limited amount of use the tutorials received, it appears they should be used with some caution in open lab environments. The cost and effort involved in development of multimedia-based instruction that is not course specific may not be justified. On the other hand, the availability of user-friendly data-searching applications seems to hold much promise as a means of expanding resources available to design students.

At the outset the project team made a choice to emphasize values (through the development of tutorials) rather than information (through development of a database). Students readily espoused the values inherent in universal design when these were presented. Because this was occurring through a number of channels simultaneously, the importance of the tutorials was overestimated. In choosing to emphasize values rather than information, the project team misjudged the educational needs of its constituency.

The level of use and resulting influence of the tutorials appears to be less than anticipated. The data suggests that the presence of the project team had more influence than the tutorials. However, the range of activities and frequency of discussion related to universal design has substantially increased. If increased discourse about universal design will indeed change habits of practice, we can anticipate that a future generation of designers will place higher value on the needs of people with disabilities.

As noted in the principal investigator's journal, awareness and acceptance of universal design values and concepts increased substantially during the course of the UDEP work. The interviewed students indicated a desire to incorporate universal design concepts in their future work. Similarly, the interviewed professor expressed the intention to continue opening this issue to students in future studios and to adjust the schedule to better accommodate investigation. It is difficult to attribute this change to any single activity or intervention, but clearly the UDEP work has been a contributing factor.

References

Bruner, J. (1977). *The Process of Education.* Cambridge: Harvard University Press.

——— (1985). "Models of the Learner." *Educational Researcher,* June/July.

Dewey, J. (1963). *Experience and Education.* New York: Collier Books, Macmillan Publishing Co.

Dilnot, C. (1982). "Design as a Socially Significant Activity: An Introduction." *Design Studies* 3: 139–46.

McNally, D.W. (1977). *Piaget, Education and Teaching.* Sussex, England: The Harvester Press.

Schon, D. (1983). *The Reflective Practitioner: How Professionals Think in Action.* New York: Basic Books Inc.

Schon, D. and G. Wiggins (1992). "Kinds of Seeing and Their Functions in Designing." *Design Studies* 13, no. 2: 135–56.

Toward Universal Design (1993). Washington D.C.: The Universal Design Initiative.

With the successful completion of the first cycle of teaching universal design, many of the initial UDEP goals have been met. Ostroff's original vision of offering design educators an opportunity to enhance their teaching through a more inclusive approach to design has become a sustainable endeavor that will continue to provoke discussion about the fundamental values of good design. A second cycle of eight projects has begun; faculty from the first cycle are continuing to incorporate universal design principles in their teaching; and two projects are underway to produce materials critical to teaching universal design—exemplars and definitive principles.[1]

The first cycle of UDEP, a pilot, produced twenty-one case studies and opportunities for collective reflection on teaching universal design, in particular, and teaching design, in general. The case studies in this book document each school's intentions and outcomes and serve as a springboard for other faculty to develop their own universal design teaching strategies. The first four chapters of the book outline the context and structure of the project for design educators interested in undertaking curricular change. The book as a whole serves as a foundation for educators and practitioners to engage in broader critical inquiry about the nature of inclusive design.

The goal of UDEP was to stimulate innovation in design curricula that would lead to the development of products and environments that incorporate universal design concepts. In organizing the project to achieve this goal, Ostroff and Welch made several assumptions about the nature of successful curricular interventions informed, to some extent, by the outcomes of earlier curriculum development projects described in Chapter 3.

Integral to Ostroff's original vision, the first premise was the importance of every instructor developing teaching materials and techniques that fit within the culture of his or her respective department and school. This perspective was supported by the findings of one of the earlier projects: "no structural formula for intervention was found to be more viable than any other. The intervention must be tailored to the specific strengths and weaknesses of students, faculty and curriculum."[2] Since the objective of UDEP was to encourage faculty to incorporate a new value in design teaching, more emphasis was placed on understanding the dynamics of the experience in a given setting than on finding the most effective strategy for all settings. The organizers intended to support exploration of a range of teaching strategies, not to develop a single curriculum.

A wide range of strategies was proposed, illustrating the extent to which faculty thought broadly and creatively about how best to incorporate a new value into existing curricula. Six schools taught the material in the context of a studio. Eight schools introduced the material in both studios and lecture courses. Three schools taught universal design in a stand-alone class dedicated to the value. Four schools used events such as design charrettes and conferences to focus attention on universal design and to reach the largest possible group of students. In a few cases the strategy fit the existing culture of the department so well that the intervention was almost indistinguishable from the way barrier-free design had been taught prior to UDEP.

No one teaching strategy stands out as being most effective in raising students' awareness of the value of universal design. Design studios and classes with design assignments, however, offered more opportunities for students to incorporate their new awareness into their design thinking. In their effort to integrate universal design principles with the design process, students discovered issues that stimulated critical dialogue about design values, especially those espoused at their institution.

Finding the appropriate locations for introducing universal design into the design studio sequence had to be sensitive to the pedagogical structure of a department's curriculum. Even though the structure might not be ideal for teaching universal design, reshaping it was not within the scope of this project. Faculty did experiment with the level at which they introduced universal design. In the fourth-year studio at SUNY Buffalo, which used universal design as a vehicle for teaching good design, the faculty team decided that universal design principles needed to be introduced earlier, at the second year, with frequent, subsequent engagement building on the first early exposure. The awareness levels developed by Iowa State helped its faculty to plan, develop, and track the multiple exposures required for successful integration of the principles.

The second premise was that strategies infusing universal design principles throughout the curriculum had the greatest likelihood of changing students' attitudes and impacting their design decisions. An infusion approach would reinforce the notion that universal design is a way of thinking about user accommodation that permeates all design decision-making. If universal design were to be taught as a stand-alone course, it risked being identified as a skill area and being marginalized as non-essential material. The application package strongly encouraged proposals that offered multiple interventions and suggested that faculty collaborate across several design disciplines as well as with faculty in their own departments who might not otherwise incorporate universal design into their teaching.

A number of schools explored the idea of infusion by teaching beyond the boundaries of one department.[3] Eight schools took approaches that included students from multiple design disciplines. Four of those schools also formed faculty teams that represented at least three departments and used approaches that impacted all the departments. In addition to exposing the largest number of students and faculty to the value, these schools also exposed students to the breadth of applications for universal design across disciplines—products, buildings, outdoor spaces, and furnishings.

Another approach explored by several schools was infusion within a single department, targeting classes across all aspects of the curriculum and at every level of teaching that could incorporate the principles of universal design. Faculty collaboration for UDEP appear to be largely based on affinity between faculty members who already taught some aspect of universal design or user accommodation. At the schools where UDEP faculty tried to persuade others in their departments to address universal design, the outcome was not entirely successful. The problem remains that within departments, especially in architecture, universal design, like accessible design, is still viewed as the special interest of a few faculty. The ability to engage faculty with different design orientations in constructive dialogue remains a challenge, one that is not unique to this curriculum project. For true infusion, faculty across the spectrum of design perspectives must have an opportunity to consider how it fits their design pedagogy and to access resources that support its inclusion in the curriculum.

The premise that stand-alone courses do a disservice to universal design by treating it separately from the main body of the curriculum may be true, but the three schools that proposed stand-alone classes attempted to make linkages to other faculty and students' other coursework. Their courses were open to students from multiple disciplines and they developed compelling exercises to engage the students in questioning and rethinking assumptions about who is included and excluded by design. Two of these courses (Southwestern Louisiana and Cal Poly) broadened the focus to inclusive design—one by purposefully soliciting enrollment by students with disabilities, the other by addressing race and age as well as disabilities. Cal Poly also organized a universal design award that was open to every student in the school, establishing that the subject was important to design education beyond the impact of one course. Linkages to other faculty at these schools, however, did not occur, perhaps because the material was embodied in a single elective course.

The third premise was the importance of involving user consultants, in whatever form that best suited the intentions and style of the individual program. Drawing on the Lifchez project in which consultants played an essential role in challenging students' assumptions about the people who would use the building, UDEP hoped to demonstrate in a range of design disciplines that involving user consultants in teaching would increase students' awareness of the diversity of people who actually use products and establish the importance of user accommodation.

The faculty found that engaging user consultants in the classroom and studio was the single most valuable strategy for teaching universal design. The best teachers are the people who have a stake in universal design, whose needs are not well met by current products and environments. Design students and faculty are generally able-bodied users, so finding diversity of experience and expertise required going outside the design department into the university or community-at-large to find people who could represent varying degrees of ability and different points in the lifespan. Using experts who work with or are advocates for people with disabilities, older people, and other underrepresented users is not equivalent to bringing the real user into the classroom. Experts perpetuate the "we-they" dichotomy and the notion that the actual users need someone to speak on their behalf.

Every school with one exception used consultants at some point in teaching. The range of involvement ran the gamut from a discussion session between students and consultants to a design class at Southwestern Louisiana that enrolled nondesign students with disabilities and paired them up with design students to do assignments jointly. Faculty who had planned minor participation by consultants found the impact of consultants on students so powerful in communicating the essential principles of universal design that they would increase consultant participation in future teaching.

Consultants were most valuable in giving students an opportunity to see the world through another person's eyes and learning how a product or place looks from a different perspective. For many students it was like seeing for the first time a world they thought they knew. Several schools (University of Michigan, University of Tennessee) pointed out that having consultants of the same age and experience as the design students underscored the concept of being temporarily able-bodied and the relevance of universal design throughout the lifespan. Consultants were singularly effective at moving students (and faculty) beyond the technical focus of codes and at illustrating the variability in how people actually use the environment. Students met consultants whose needs might not be accommodated by following minimum code requirements. This reinforced that working directly with users is more informative than relying on abstract standards, especially when the designer makes judgments and sets priorities.

Many students were attracted to the novelty of having real people involved in the insular setting of the academy. The specificity with which some consultants spoke about their interactions with the environment gave students concrete information with which to make otherwise abstract design decisions. For some students, moving from studios based on hypothetical people to a studio with real people helped them engage more effectively in the design process.

The dramatic intervention of introducing users into the studio setting and review process elicited a range of responses. Some students experienced disbelief and outrage at the indignity of the misfit between people and the environment; some felt like inadvertent accomplices in their profession's careless attitudes; others remained skeptical that design could possibly respond to the range of issues that users present. In many of the courses and studios, students felt some degree of discomfort in their first encounter with consultants, especially if their physical appearance made them different from the students or their disabilities required students to adapt the "norms" of studio interaction. One school broke the ice by asking everyone assembled to describe how they got to the classroom that day and, predictably, a number of environmental barriers emerged in people's accounts—both consultants' and students'. In every situation, students expressed appreciation for the opportunity to get beyond the disability and to appreciate the consultants as real, complex people.

In selecting consultants it is very important to seek out a range of users, not just a token person who uses a wheelchair. One school included in its visit by user consultants a child, an older person, and a parent with an infant—all people who have a unique perspective on their surroundings. The wider the range of consultants the more likely students are to realize the essential principles of universal design. Lifchez emphasized the importance of presenting consultants to students as experts rather than as human beings who have unmet needs.[4] UDEP encouraged schools to compensate their user consultants to reflect the value of their expertise. Not every school had the funds to pay for consultants' time but provided free parking, meals, and acknowledgment of their contributions in the form of a framed certificate, letter from the dean, or public media coverage.

All schools discovered that involving user consultants in the classroom was most rewarding when well planned and consultants were clear about their roles. Not everyone is comfortable in the role of expert and some user consultants are intimidated by the unfamiliar culture of design studios, especially reading abstract drawings and understanding design jargon. Consultants who are comfortable talking about the details of their lives are most helpful to students. Two schools that used consultants to review a product designed and constructed by the students found that the presence of a real object facilitated meaningful discussion. Some schools found that consultant involvement did not have to be extensive to be effective. Even a single visit, when well planned, provided a powerful set of images in the students' minds to stimulate a semester's worth of discussion. Whatever the role of consultants, a formal agreement between the faculty and the consultant is very important for setting clear expectations.

Along with involving consultants in the classroom, the other most utilized technique was empathic exercises. At both UDEP conferences, this instructional stalwart came under heavy criticism from faculty and user consultants alike. Yet, all but one school employed some form of empathic experience. It deserves discussion because it is a teaching device that has been and continues to be used by many instructors throughout the design fields who know little about disability and employ it for its self-revelatory qualities. Its attraction for some faculty may be that it communicates to students the power of barriers without the faculty having to teach barrier-free design specifically. This technique has the potential for trivializing disability concerns, although it can illuminate environmental issues. The SUNY Buffalo team cites a study of disability simulations that shows that this technique does not "change attitudes" and "may reinforce negative perceptions about disability."

Chapter 26

Empathic techniques became popular in the seventies shortly after Leon Pastalan published his work on simulating the sensory losses associated with aging.[5] Pastalan and his colleagues had developed the simulation technique in an effort to "bridge the gap between the designer's need for personal experience which can be conceptualized in imageable terms—and the researcher's need to satisfy the rigors of science." Its imageability captured the attention of design instructors who were interested in getting their students to appreciate the needs of people different than themselves in a manner that informed design.[6] It is interesting that the University of Michigan team, which included Pastalan, used a gaming technique that it had developed as a more consistent and informative research tool for students to gain an understanding of the details of someone else's life. Their board game, *A Day's Journey Through Life,*© played with users, exposes students to a person's encounters with environmental barriers but emphasizes how an individual copes with the environment in daily activities.

Faculty who used empathic techniques as a part of their UDEP teaching generally reported that it had engaged students in the problem of environmental barriers quickly and memorably. "It's the environment that is disabling and we are responsible for this" was a common student insight after the exercise. However, just as often, students shared both a sense of pity and awe for anyone negotiating the environment using a wheelchair. It is this reaction that illustrates the shortcomings of the technique as a teaching device. Despite its intrinsic fascination for students, the empathic exercise risks misrepresenting the real issue and is a less direct approach to understanding users' issues than getting user consultants to participate in teaching.

There are several ways to use the empathic approach responsibly. Making environmental barriers visible is best done in collaboration with user consultants. Asking a student to take a walk with someone who is disabled by the environment and recording the experience and discussion—as happened at Pratt—is more likely to help the student understand how users adapt and cope. If students are asked to try empathic exercises, it is important that they understand that the purpose is to gather technical information about the environment and not about "what it's like to have a disability." It is also critical that students be aware that the wheelchairs that they use are probably old and have not been fitted to their bodies as they would for someone with a disability. Empathic exercises must avoid stereotypes and extend beyond using wheelchairs. Ideally, they simulate all the kinds of disabling experiences that the environment poses for a wide variety of users. Students in the class may be diverse enough that they can share experiences rather than simulating them. In the program at Texas Tech, the faculty member used every sprained ankle, bad back, and family history experienced by students as an opportunity to illustrate the value of universal design.

Drawing on the reflections by faculty and the commentary by students in the case study chapters and the free-ranging discussions that occurred at the two UDEP conferences, the following additional topics emerge as critical to the ongoing exploration of teaching strategies.

Evaluation. From UDEP's inception, evaluation was integral to its planning and implementation. Applicants were asked to include an evaluative approach in their proposals and evaluation techniques were discussed at the faculty colloquium. The most basic question—Was the teaching approach effective in teaching students the value and principles of universal design?—was the most complex to assess.

Generic "before" and "after" questionnaires were developed by the UDEP organizers and distributed to faculty with the understanding that they could use their own evaluative instruments if they chose to. Some developed their own evaluative instruments; others availed themselves of the "before" and "after" questionnaires; and some adapted them. The project questionnaire focused on awareness, attitude, and knowledge. The questionnaire results from most schools indicated that many students recognized the term *ADA* but were not able to accurately state what it was. Very few were familiar with the term *universal design*. After exposure to a class or studio that incorporated universal design principles, the proportion of students who could describe the significance of both terms rose dramatically. An open-ended question, "What were the three most important things that you learned over the course of the semester?" solicited many responses about the importance of involving users in the design process. It also evoked reflections on how the exposure to universal design had given them their first perspective on client accommodation. The University of Michigan and Eastern Michigan State collaborated with university statisticians to conduct a more rigorous assessment of changes in knowledge and attitude, comparing groups with different degrees of exposure to universal design values including a control group with no exposure. The results showed that classes taught by UDEP faculty caused a significant change in knowledge as well as in attitude.

Although the questionnaires indicated that the project was effecting change, they could not measure the most fundamental issue—whether students could incorporate their awareness and knowledge into their design projects. Some student work included in the case studies indicates awareness of universal design principles. The faculty suggested that a longer range and more reliable indicator of student learning would come from reviewing students' design work in subsequent semesters to see how well they are able to integrate what they learned about universal design into studio projects that do not place special emphasis on universal design. It raises the question of whether it will occur if there is not repeated exposure in other classes and studios.

Students may take several years to reach the level of integration described by Iowa. The awareness levels that Iowa established—from consciousness, engagement, and accountability to integration—form a useful model that establishes intermediate levels of achievement that can facilitate course planning, curriculum coordination, and standards for assessment. Some standard for design achievement would enhance evaluation efforts, but the design disciplines have rigorously avoided codifying indicators of effective design. The lack of shared criteria and techniques for evaluating design across disciplines and within disciplines limits the project's ability to conduct rigorous assessment of outcomes.

The other assessment measure for UDEP is its impact on the culture of the schools that participated. This can be measured partly by whether the universal design materials developed for studios and courses are used for teaching in subsequent years and, ultimately, by whether other faculty engage in finding ways to incorporate the value into their teaching. Many UDEP faculty report that they are continuing to teach the same courses with similar or enhanced materials or are integrating universal design into other courses that they are currently teaching. This suggests that, in addition to faculty commitment to the value, departments are either supporting the value or at least not resisting its incorporation into design teaching. Other measures of success at the institutional level would be the inclusion of universal design criteria in studio critiques and reviews at all levels, inclusion of universal design as a critical component of the curriculum, and discussion among all faculty at departmental meetings, but these would predictably take time to appear.

In the end, however, the universal design value resides in the individual, student or faculty, and not in the department. Even without departmental acceptance, the principles of universal design can be effectively communicated and taught. Other tests for students who have learned about universal design in coursework or studios are to study with an instructor who does not support or condone universal design and to work in an office that is unfamiliar with universal design principles. In those settings, they must be able to articulate the value, incorporate it into technical decisions, and be able to support and, possibly defend, their belief persuasively.

Communication. Directly related to the issue of evaluating student work is the question of how a student's drawings or models indicate that the solution supports the value of universal design. Most of the student work submitted for the book looked like student work coming out of any studio in any design school. Mace contends that "universally designed features tend to become invisible until pointed out."[7] In what way is universal design visible? It is difficult to evaluate whether students have understood the principles of universal design unless it is revealed or evident in the drawings and models that they produce. And yet, perhaps paradoxically, universal design is most successful when it is not apparent. Good universal design may not be visible like a ramp next to steps or a larger toilet stall. If universal design is most successful when it is invisible, some other form of presentation may be required to make apparent its attributes, especially for the purpose of teaching and evaluating the visual evidence of student accomplishments.

Most students' drawings were produced within the strong tradition of representation—site plan, plan, section, elevation, perspective. Few students ventured beyond the most common drawing and presentation techniques to communicate the new value that had changed their approach to design. An example might be the interiors student who designed a house for a person of small stature. Floor plans, her primary presentation drawing, reflected far less of her thinking about user accommodation and universal design than a section and elevation.

Drawings could be used more cogently as a form of exploration or a technique for communicating important ideas to others. At the simplest level a student might unravel a building in section to examine or illustrate the experience of moving through a space without barriers. For students with computer skills, there is the obvious opportunity to simulate three-dimensional experiences people of differing abilities might have moving about a building. Video was used extensively for recording events and activities but was not exploited as a tool for exploring how spaces could be experienced in a more universal way. A creative example of communication is the students at Texas Tech, who developed new entourage figures for their perspective drawings—a man jogging with a prosthesis or a traveler with three suitcases—to illustrate who might really use the landscape.

Some students started to investigate carrying the values of universal design into the design medium, making their design presentations accessible to a wide range of people. In many architecture programs today, drawings are largely inaccessible to all but the designer because students eschew conventions of labeling for artistic purity. Not only did UDEP faculty ask their students to make their design projects accessible to a variety of people but they also encouraged them to think about how they might make their presentation accessible to people who cannot read drawings. Students in several schools (Iowa State, Michigan State, Southwestern Louisiana) had to move beyond labeling and clear graphics to address these issues when confronted by user consultants who could not see the presentations. Students enthusiastically developed techniques for making drawings tactile and using compass points for verbal presentations.

Twenty years ago, when behavioral issues were gaining popularity in design schools and user participation required that drawings be read and understood by nondesigners, explanatory text on drawings was not only acceptable but resulted in a presentation aesthetic of sorts. The words were an essential component, since lines by themselves are open to multiple interpretations. Words were an effective, essential means of communicating how design decisions reflected particular values.

Extending beyond the ADA to universal design. Universal design is not a euphemism for teaching students how to use the ADA Standards for Accessible Design.[8] Although *universal design* is frequently used in the popular press interchangeably with *barrier-free design* or *accessible design,* it is not a new term for code compliance. The challenge of deciding how to teach universal design is that it is not only technical knowledge, it is also a value. Because building codes—and therefore accessibility—have been taught as technical information that students can append to the design process, it is sometimes difficult for faculty to visualize how else to incorporate universal design into their teaching. A premise of UDEP is that the goals of both the ADA Standards—for people with disabilities, and universal design—for all people throughout the lifespan, can be achieved by engaging designers' conscious imagination. A goal of UDEP is to demonstrate how the integration of the needs of diverse users at the beginning of the design process leads to good design.

Making objects, buildings, and places suitable for people of varying abilities does not mandate poor design. Many of the case studies demonstrate how to extend design thinking beyond the ADA Standards in a way that leads to good design. The Americans with Disabilities Act has great potential to stimulate discussion among designers because of its civil rights context, but it can quickly lose its intellectual potency when taught primarily as design standards and not as a basic consideration in the design process. Illuminating and reflecting on the design implications of universal design principles appears to be the most powerful form of inquiry for student learning. Teaching was most successful, as at SUNY Buffalo, when students were engaged in dialogues about the nature of architecture as a social construction—who is included and who is excluded. This critical dialogue was most likely to occur in the process of making design decisions in the problem-solving arena of studio.

Another goal of UDEP was to bring the level of discourse on inclusive design to a level where it could compete on an equal footing with the spatial ordering of formal elements for a designer's attention rather than being an intrusion into an otherwise perfectly ordered world. As the Kansas State team points out, the challenge is to create elegant architectural language that can give expression to the range of human needs. Critical thinking about universal design is the next important step to considering its place in design education.

Dynamics of change. The experience of faculty working on this project suggests that universal design principles pose more of a challenge for some disciplines than others. Architecture departments have had more difficulty engaging these issues than interior design departments, which had begun to embrace the value of universal design in teaching and practice before UDEP started. UDEP experience with industrial design and landscape architecture programs has been too limited to assess the academic response of those disciplines. As with architecture, a handful of individuals in landscape architecture and industrial design have made extraordinary contributions.

At the UDEP colloquium held before faculty started teaching universal design, faculty discussed the institutional obstacles they were likely to encounter when implementing the objectives of UDEP. Faculty enumerated the issues that might impede the project at their schools and then ranked their importance. The biggest problem was tenure. Universities have traditionally rewarded individual work over collaborative work and questioned curriculum development as a form of scholarship. Other major issues on the minds of faculty included the power of tradition and inertia in design educators' attitudes, inadequate time for course development, and the need for continuous reinforcement. UDEP was able to directly address the latter two issues. The UDEP stipend was used by some teams to employ graduate students to gather course materials and coordinate user consultants. The colloquium offered participants a degree of collegial reinforcement that faculty wanted to sustain. In addition to establishing an Internet connection so that faculty could communicate electronically, UDEP was able to fund advisor visits to schools, a reinforcement that faculty believed might help them promote and sustain their efforts, especially in departments that had exhibited little interest in the subject.

The advisors' role had been important in the original proposal, but as the project evolved, the value of their contribution was greater than anticipated. Among the most well-known and respected practitioners and educators in universal design, the advisors were lodestars for the overall direction of the project. They shared their expertise by giving presentations at the UDEP colloquium and agreeing to serve as mentors to faculty via monthly telephone calls. The phone contacts were difficult to sustain in the busy lives of multiple faculty although having an expert to consult was used by faculty on an occasional basis. The most valuable contribution of the advisors was the site visit, envisioned as a way to demonstrate the significance of universal design beyond the individual project. The visit from an outside expert, someone who is known to be an authority on the topic, was especially valuable for faculty who were in the minority within their department. The prestige of a nationally known person added to the credibility of the topic and provided additional avenues for discussion with colleagues, administrators, and students.

The visits varied from school to school. Most had a public component in which the advisor made a presentation on universal design to a broad audience, visited classes and participated in studio reviews, and met with departmental leadership to discuss the ramifications of universal design education, an audience that was sometimes not possible for faculty on their own. The interchange with deans and department heads was especially helpful in revealing how the project was perceived institutionally and academically. In future UDEP cycles, the advisor visit will be integral to developing a curricular plan, building on past experiences to guide schools in taking advantage of this useful resource.

Implications. This cycle of UDEP has been an opportunity to explore how educators, and by implication practitioners, could incorporate a more inclusive view of users into design thinking as well as to explore the implications of a shift in values for the design disciplines. It raised issues, not the first time for any of these disciplines, about who is served by design, who has a voice in design decisions, and how design reflects societal values.

The future direction for UDEP faculty and for other faculty teaching universal design will be to address two overarching issues. The first is the ongoing need for design educators to think broadly about making the structure and content of design curricula more inclusive. Based on the experience of this pilot project, single exposures, whether an element of a course or studio or an entire course or studio, are not enough for most students to fully engage the value of inclusivity and the principles of universal design. The long-range strategy for making design education more inclusive rests, in some part, on the extent to which the issues of universal design are infused across the curriculum, giving students repetitive exposure to and sustained emphasis on the value of an inclusive design approach. Multiple opportunities to explore and implement universal design will help students articulate a personal understanding of its value and principles, essential to their ability to integrate it into their design thinking.

The second critical issue is the recognition that teaching a value as opposed to information requires open discourse on the part of both faculty and students. As Dean Bork points out in his comments in the Virginia Tech case study, UDEP "has an inherent supposition that designers have an ethical obligation to serve the needs of all who may use the products and environments that they create." He adds that without further discussion of this assumption and lacking critical theory, educators are teaching "a nascent body of information that is largely political in its formulation and intent." Teaching universal design is not a matter of transmitting a body of knowledge; it is a process of exploring how a politically mandated and socially desirable value can be embodied by the design disciplines. Teaching universal design is one form of inquiry that can test these suppositions. Serious discourse about universal design both in teaching as well as critical practice, combined with ongoing projects to document exemplars and to refine and validate principles of universal design, will contribute to the development of critical theory.

Notes

1. With support from the National Institute on Rehabilitation and Research, the Center for Universal Design/Center for Accessible Housing is working with SUNY Buffalo and J.L. Mueller, Inc., to establish and validate principles for what constitutes universal design. Universal Designers and Consultants, Inc., and Adaptive Environments are collaborating with the Center, using the draft principles to evaluate slides that are being solicited nationally through a grant from the National Endowment for the Arts to develop a slide collection of fifty examples of universal design for practitioners and educators.

2. Shibley, R.G., L. Poltroneri, and R. Rosenburg (1984). *Architecture, Energy, and Education.* Washington, D.C.: Association of Collegiate Schools of Architecture, 10.

3. See the Matrix of Approaches on page 26 in Chapter 4.

4. Lifchez, Raymond (1987). *Rethinking Architecture: Design Students and Physically Disabled People.* Berkeley, Calif.: University of California Press, 84.

5. Pastalan, L., R.K. Mautz, and J. Merrill (1973). "The Simulation of Age-Related Sensory Losses: A New Approach to the Study of Environmental Barriers." In *Environmental Design Research,* edited by W.F.E. Preiser. Stroudsberg, Pa.: Dowden Hutchinson, and Ross.

6. Farbstein, Jay and Min Kantrowitz (1978). *People in Places.* New York: Prentice Hall.

7. Mace, R., G. Hardie, and J. Plaice (1991). "Accessible Environments: Toward Universal Design." In *Design Interventions: Toward A More Humane Architecture,* edited by Preiser, Vischer, and White, 174. New York: Van Nostrand Reinhold.

8. The ADA Standards for Accessible Design are the enforcable standards issued by the U.S. Department of Justice as part of the Final Rule for ADA Title III. When DOJ adopted the *ADA Accessibility Guidelines* (ADAAG) developed by the Access Board, as the appendix in Title III, they became the enforcable standards for new construction and alterations. When altering any building or space it is important to use the DOJ Final Rule where you will find not only the ADA Standards but all of the requirements for barrier removal and alterations.

Appendices

Faculty Contacts at Participating Schools

California Polytechnic State University at San Luis Obispo
Paul M. Wolff
California Polytechnic State University
Department of Architecture
One Grand Avenue
San Luis Obispo, CA 93407
(805) 756-1791
fax: (805) 756-1500
e-mail: pwolff@oboe.calpoly.edu

Iowa State University
Arvid Osterberg
Iowa State University
Department of Architecture
493 College of Design
Ames, IA 50011
(515) 294-8221
fax: (515) 294-1440
e-mail: arvido@iastate.edu

Kansas State University
Lyn Norris-Baker
Kansas State University
College of Architecture and Design
Seaton Hall
Manhattan, KS 66506
(913) 532-5953 / (913) 532-5945
fax (913) 532-6722
e-mail lyn@ksuvm.ksu.edu

Louisiana State University
Nikki Joan Spencer
Louisiana State University
Department of Interior Design
402 New Design Building
Baton Rouge, LA 70803-7030
(504) 388-8464
fax: (504) 388-8457

Massachusetts Institute of Technology
Leonard Morse-Fortier
Massachusetts Institute of Technology
Department of Architecture
77 Massachusetts Ave, Room 4-209
Cambridge, MA 01239
(617) 253-5569
fax: (617) 253-6152
e-mail: lfortier@mit.edu

Miami University
Barbara Flannery
Miami University
Housing and Interior Design
260 McGuffey Hall
Oxford, OH 45056
(513) 529-4900
fax: (513) 529-7270

Michigan State University
Roberta L. Kilty-Padgett
Michigan State University
Dept. of Human Environment and Design
Interior Design Program
College of Human Ecology
East Lansing, MI 48824-1030
(517) 355-3378
fax: (517) 432-1058
e-mail: kiltypad@pilot.msu.edu

North Dakota State University
Shauna J. Corry
North Dakota State University
Apparel, Textiles and Interior Design
178 Home Economics
Fargo, ND 58105
(701) 237-8604
fax: (701) 237-7174

Norwich University
Elizabeth Church
Norwich University
Department of Architecture
Vermont College
Northfield, VT 05663
(802) 485-2622
fax: (802) 485-2580
e-mail: echurch@norwich.edu

Pratt Institute
Brent Porter
Pratt Institute
School of Architecture
200 Willoughby Avenue
Brooklyn, NY 11205
(718) 636-3405
fax: (718) 636-3432

Purdue University
Bernie Dahl
Purdue University
Landscape Architecture Program
1165 Horticulture Building
West Lafayette, IN 47907-1165
(317) 494-1330
fax: (317) 494-0391
e-mail: mailhost@hort.purdue.edu

Ringling School of Art & Design
Ruth Beals
Ringling School of Art & Design
Department of Interior Design
2700 N. Tamiami Trail
Sarasota, FL 34234
(813) 351-5100
fax: (813) 359-7517

**State University of New York
  at Buffalo**
Edward Steinfeld
Department of Architecture
State University of New York at Buffalo
112 Hayes Hall
Buffalo, NY 14214
(716) 829-3483 ext. 327
fax: (716) 829-3861
e-mail: arced@arch.buffalo.edu

Texas Tech University
Jean Stephans Kavanagh
Texas Tech University
Landscape Architecture
Box 42121
Lubbock, TX 79409
(806) 742-2858
fax: (806) 742-0770
e-mail: b8kav@ttacs.ttu.edu

**University of Michigan
  and Eastern Michigan University**
Louise Jones
Eastern Michigan University
3808 Golfside Drive
Ypsilanti, MI 48197
(313) 487-0652
fax: (313) 484-0575
e-mail: hec_jones@emunix.emich.edu

University of Missouri
Ruth Brent
University of Missouri
Department of Environmental Design
137 Stanley Hall
Columbia, MO 65211
(314) 882-6035
fax: (314) 884-6679
e-mail: ruth_s._brent@muccmail.
  missouri.edu

University of South Florida

Alexander Ratensky
University of Southern Florida
Cooperative MArch Program
University Tech Center
3702 Spectrum Blvd., Suite 180
Tampa, FL 33612
(813) 974-4031
fax: (813) 974-2557
e-mail: ratensky@cfrvm.cfr.usf.edu

University of Southwestern Louisiana

Charlotte Roberts
University of Southwestern Louisiana
Department of Architecture
P.O. Box 43850
Lafayette, LA 70504-3850
(318) 482-5323
fax: (318) 482-5907
e-mail: cjr1173@usl.edu

University of Tennessee

Thomas L. Houser
Visual Arts Building
University of Georgia
Athens, GA 30602
(706) 542-1511
fax: (706) 542-0226
e-mail: thouser@uga.cc.uda.edu

Virginia Polytechnic Institute and State University – Interior Design

Julie Beamish
Virginia Polytechnic Institute and State University
Housing, Interior Design, and Resource Management
209 Wallace Hall, Virginia Tech
Blacksburg, VA 24061-0424
(703) 231-8881
fax: (703) 231-7157
e-mail: jbeamish@vt.edu

Virginia Polytechnic Institute and State University – Landscape Arch.

Dean R. Bork
Virginia Polytechnic Institute and State University
Landscape Architecture Department
202C Architecture Annex
Blacksburg, VA 24061-0113
(703) 231-5487
fax: (703) 231-3367
e-mail: dbork@vt.edu

University of Cincinnati

Frank Russell
College of Design, Architecture, Art and Planning
School of Planning
One Edwards Center, Room 548
University of Cincinnati
Cincinnati, OH 45221-0073
(513) 556-3283
fax: (513) 556-3288

Faculty Biographies

Ruth Beals received her B.F.A. from the University of Massachusetts. After ten years of commercial design, she began teaching upper-level courses in the Department of Interior Design at the Ringling School of Art and Design. During her eight years at Ringling, she has designed several projects that address accessibility and is considered an expert on the Americans with Disabilities Act. She is a principal at Adaptable Interiors, Inc.

Julia Beamish is an associate professor of housing in the Department of Housing, Interior Design, and Resource Management in the College of Human Resources, Virginia Polytechnic Institute and State University. She teaches a wide variety of courses including house planning, barrier-free design, and housing for special needs. Her research interests include the evaluation of housing design and the acceptance of affordable housing options by consumers and the local community, the acceptance of housing alternatives for the elderly, and the implementation of the Americans with Disabilities Act.

Susan Behar, principal at Susan Behar, ASID/Universal Design, Dunedin, Florida, is a licensed interior designer. She contributed to *Beautiful Barrier Free—A Visual Guide to Accessibility,* and was a consultant in the UDEP programs at the University of South Florida and the Ringling School of Art and Design.

Dean R. Bork, associate professor, has been a faculty member of the landscape architecture department at Virginia Polytechnic Institute and State University since 1980. His central focus is teaching, although he has been involved in numerous public service and funded research projects. Recently, his scholarly work has focused on improving education within the design studio.

Ruth Brent, professor and chair of the Department of Environmental Design in the College of Human Environmental Sciences, University of Missouri, currently teaches a graduate seminar and courses in professional business practices and resources and materials. Her research interests are in the areas of design education, aging and the environment, and design in the global context.

Nancy C. Canestaro, former associate professor of interior design at the University of Tennessee at Knoxville, has broad experience in facility planning and management, with emphasis on user-responsive space programming. She is recognized internationally for her gaming/simulation techniques.

Mark Chidister, an associate professor in landscape architecture at Iowa State University, has a people-oriented teaching career, with extensive writings on the use of public open space. He was recently appointed associate dean for academic programs in the School of Design.

Elizabeth Church is an assistant professor in the Department of Architecture at Vermont College of Norwich University. She teaches in the first-, second-, and third-year design studios and offers a required course for second-year students on human issues in design. Her research and design focus on housing needs of older people were realized in several multi-family housing projects in northern New England.

Steven Cooke earned a degree in architecture from the University of Florida and Virginia Polytechnic Institute and State University. He maintains his own practice in Lutz, Florida, while teaching first-year design, the introduction to technology, and materials and methods at the University of Florida, where he is an assistant professor.

Shauna J. Corry is an assistant professor and coordinator of the interior-design Program at North Dakota State University. She received a B.S. with a housing and interiors emphasis from Utah State University and completed an M.S. with an interior-design emphasis at Washington State University. She has research interests in Creativity and Partnering with Facility Managers and teaches creative problem solving. She is on leave through June 1996 completing her doctoral studies.

Bernie Dahl is an assistant professor of landscape architecture at Purdue University, where he teaches senior studio courses in planting design and regional design, as well as courses in universal design, computer visual simulation, and grant writing. He also has his own consulting firm that specializes in parks, greenways, and urban forestry.

Gary Day, associate professor of architecture at the State University of New York at Buffalo, has bachelor's degrees in architecture and social sciences and a master's degree in urban planning. He has taught in California, Virginia, New York, and Denmark. His primary interests are the impact of architecture on the site and the environmental factors that influence architecture.

Lily DeLeon has taught undergraduate and graduate courses in interior design at Michigan State University with research focuses on housing for the elderly and cross-cultural comparison. She is also a housing and health-care consultant in a project for the Saudi Arabian government.

Frank Dunbar was co-developer of the UDEP program at Purdue University. He has been a principal or staff landscape architect at several Southern California firms and has taught at the University of California at Los Angeles, University of California at Irvine, and Purdue University. His professional activities include the design of accessible trail and walkway systems. He is currently pursuing a graduate degree in environmental ethics.

Daniel Fechtner, a physician in rehabilitative medicine at Columbia University, collaborated with Robert Anders in developing a universal design curriculum at Pratt Institute and in writing the *Universal Design Primer.* Recently, he has researched universal design in Scandinavia and served as a team member on the Pratt project.

Barbara Flannery holds bachelor's and master's degrees from Iowa State University and a Ph.D. from the University of Minnesota. She currently teaches first-year design studio, design and human behavior, lighting design, and housing at Miami University. She previously taught at the University of Minnesota, Duluth. Her research interests focus on the behavioral aspects of design.

W. Lawrence Garvin holds undergraduate degrees from Washington and Lee University and Ohio State University and a graduate degree from Massachusetts Institute of Technology. He has held principal campus planning posts at MIT, Harvard University, the University of California system, and, most recently, Kansas State University. He joined the architecture department at Kansas State in 1990.

Brad Grant is an educator and practicing architect with a research focus on cultural and social factors in environmental design. He has taught courses, written articles, and designed several important projects related to the multicultural environment. He currently teaches in the architecture and ethnic studies departments at California Polytechnic State University, San Luis Obispo.

Theodore Trent Green holds a bachelor's degree from Hampton Institute and a master's degree from Harvard University. He worked for some time as an urban designer in Boston. He teaches architectural and urban design courses at the University of South Florida where he is an assistant professor.

Jason Hagin is a master's degree candidate in architecture at the State University of New York at Buffalo. He received a bachelor's degree in history with a minor in the fine arts from the College of William and Mary, and is currently a research assistant at the Adaptive Environments Laboratory at the School of Architecture and Planning.

Bruce Hannah, professor and former head of graduate industrial design at Pratt Institute, was founder of the Pratt Center for Advanced Design Research (CADRE). He is a multi-award winning designer whose work includes the Hannah desk system for Knoll International, which was named a "Design of the Decade" by the IDSA.

Robert Harvey has an international reputation in the restoration of historic sites and is studying the application of universal-design principles to historic sites and properties. He is a professor of landscape architecture at Iowa State University.

Gary Hennigh, associate professor of environmental design in the College of Human Environmental Sciences at the University of Missouri, has taught interior design studio, design communications, and history of design. His research and creative interests have been in the history of the designed environment and computer graphics.

Thomas L. Houser was an assistant professor of interior design at the University of Tennessee at Knoxville and is now teaching at the University of Georgia. He has extensive practical experience in interior design and education, with projects involving individuals from across the lifespan, many having physical and/or emotional disabilities.

Louise Jones, associate professor of interior design at Eastern Michigan University and research associate at the University of Michigan, has teaching and research interests that include design for special populations, universal design, and interior-design education. Her design practice includes work in showroom, hospitality, and residential design. Her current research activities focus on universal design and environment and behavior issues related to design for special populations, specifically those who are frail, aging, and/or disabled.

Jean Stephens Kavanagh, an assistant professor of landscape architecture at Texas Tech University, completed her undergraduate and graduate studies in landscape architecture at Cornell University. Her ongoing research in horticultural therapy and therapeutic landscapes reflects her investigations into environmental and human factors influencing design form in the landscape and has contributed greatly to her insights and expertise in universal-design education.

Roberta Kilty-Padgett, an interior-design educator since 1969, is an assistant professor of interior design at Michigan State University. Her teaching and research experience includes post-occupancy evaluations in relation to human needs, interior-design programming, ergonomics, and anthropometrics.

Margaret Leahy, an artist and interior designer, is an associate professor in interior design at Pratt Institute who has examined the aesthetic quality of design for people with disabilities. She is currently the leader of the Design Salon, an interdisciplinary group concerned with socially responsible design.

Theodore Lownie is a partner in the firm Hamilton, Houston and Lownie in Buffalo, New York, and a studio instructor at the Department of Architecture, State University of New York at Buffalo. He has extensive experience in the design of health-care facilities, public buildings, and historic preservation. He is currently the architect for the renovation of Frank Lloyd Wright's Darwin D. Martin house.

Dan Ashby Mahon is a landscape architect at Land Planning and Design Associates in Charlottesville, Virginia. He has a diverse background that includes experience as a medic in the U.S. Army, an art therapist, and a telecommunications designer. During the Universal Design Education Project, he was completing an MLA degree at Virginia Tech.

Fred Malven, an associate professor of interior design at Iowa State University, is a nationally recognized authority on healthy, safety, and welfare issues in design. He has given more than fifty national and international presentations on the subject to designers and public officials. His current interests focus on the differences in health and safety needs for populations of varying age, culture, gender, and physical/sensory ability profiles.

Todd Marsh is a studio instructor of design studies in the Department of Architecture at the State University of New York at Buffalo. He is a graduate of SUNY Buffalo where he completed his master's thesis on the differences between professional and non-professional values on architectural aesthetics.

Anna Marshall-Baker has an undergraduate degree in art and graduate degrees in interior design and developmental psychology. She has combined these interests in an investigation of features of the environment that affect development, particularly that of infants and young children. She is currently an assistant professor in interior design at Virginia Polytechnic Institute and State University, teaching foundation courses to beginning design students and advanced research courses to graduate students.

James Moore holds degrees from the University of Pennsylvania and Massachusetts Institute of Technology. He teaches design, thesis planning, and the introduction to technology at the University of South Florida, where he is an assistant professor.

Leonard Morse-Fortier, an engineer and assistant professor of building technology, teaches in the Department of Architecture at the Massachusetts Institute of Technology. He has a daughter with Down syndrome and is actively involved in several advocacy activities.

Ole Mouritsen is a professor of landscape architecture at the School of Architecture in Arhus, Denmark. During the Universal Design Education Project, he was a visiting professor in the Department of Architecture at the State University of New York at Buffalo, where he taught in the second-year studio program. He specializes in the relationship of architecture to landscape and the design of gardens.

Abir Mullick, industrial designer and urban planner, is an assistant professor in the Department of Planning and Design at the State University of New York at Buffalo. He teaches courses on product design and human factors. His research interests focus on product and environmental design for older people with disabilities, and the development of universal design criteria.

Lyn Norris-Baker is a professor of architecture and director of the Center for Aging at Kansas State University. She earned a Ph.D. in psychology, specializing in environment/behavior relations, from the University of Houston and a bachelor of architecture from Rice University. Her teaching experience includes courses in environment-behavior studies, architectural research methods, evaluation techniques, programming, and architectural design studio.

Roberta L. Null holds degrees from South Dakota State University, the University of Minnesota, and Ohio State University. She has taught housing and interior design courses at Purdue University, San Diego State University, and most recently at Miami University. Her research and teaching have focused on the design of supportive environments for special-needs groups, and now extend to universal design.

Arvid Osterberg has spent twenty years teaching, consulting, and conducting research in the areas of accessibility, universal design, building safety, and gerontology. He is a professor of architecture at Iowa State University, with a continuing interest in preservation and historic accessible design.

Richard E. Parrish, currently working as a freelance consultant and sales representative, specializes in design representation and multimedia hardware and software. He is completing an MLA degree at Virginia Tech.

Leon A. Pastalan, professor in the College of Architecture and Urban Planning, University of Michigan, is a recognized leader in the area of design for aging. He is director of the National Center on Housing and Living Arrangement for Older Americans, director of the Environmental Design for Aging Research Group, and editor of the *Journal of Housing for the Elderly.* His research, writing, and development of the emphatic model have been major contributions to the study of design for aging. His contributions to the field over a period of thirty years have directly influenced the development of the environment and behavior research discipline.

Brent Porter, project coordinator of the Pratt Institute Universal Design "Teach-In," heads his own architectural firm and is an associate professor of architecture at Pratt. His teaching concerns socio-psychological factors and energy consciousness in design.

Brian Powell, assistant professor of interior design at University of Southwestern Louisiana, teaches design studio, lighting, programming, and ergonomics. He has professional design experience and is a member of the ISID. He was recently selected to receive the AIA Research Council 1994, Design for the Aging Curriculum Package. He was also the recipient of a Graham Foundation Grant to create an interactive CD-ROM on universal design.

Daniel Powers hold bachelor's and master's degrees from the University of Florida. In recent years he has served increasingly as a forensic expert in court cases involving buildings. He teaches second-year design at the University of South Florida, where he is an associate professor.

Rachel Ramadhyani is currently a student in the landscape architecture program at Purdue University and has been an ethnomusicologist, semiotician, arts administrator, musician, author, and archivist.

Alex Ratensky is a graduate of the University of Pennsylvania and Princeton University. He is director of the architecture program at the University of South Florida and teaches the introductory course to the program.

Wellington Reiter, an associate professor of architecture at the Massachusetts Institute of Technology, is a designer and educator interested in cross-disciplinary activities including drawing, architecture, sculpture, and spatial experience.

Charlotte Roberts, an assistant professor in the interior design program at the University of Southwestern Louisiana, received a bachelor's and master's degree from that institution. She is a registered architect and has professional experience in architecture and interiors. She teaches design studio, interior systems, codes, and planning.

Joe Roberts, associate professor in communications design at Pratt Institute, played a chief role in bringing computer-aided design to everyday classroom instruction at Pratt. His firm, Klauber and Roberts Inc., is known for its innovative graphic design.

Virginia L. Russell, a registered landscape architect, has served on the board of trustees of the American Society of Landscape Architects. She has bachelor's and master's degrees in landscape architecture from the University of Kentucky and Ohio State University. She teaches site-systems courses that integrate the principles of universal design, formerly at Purdue University and currently as assistant professor in the School of Architecture and Interior Design at the University of Cincinnati. Her primary areas of study focus on the design of retreat centers and intentional communities.

Albert Rutledge, recently retired professor of landscape architecture at Iowa State University, has a thirty-year teaching career focused on people-oriented design including authorship of two books stressing the application of social factors in park planning.

Benyamin Schwarz, assistant professor of environmental design in the College of Human Environmental Sciences at the University of Missouri, teaches courses in studio design, housing, and design fundamentals. His research interests are in the areas of aging and the environment, design education, and cross-cultural design elements.

Ronald A. Sekulski, assistant professor at the School of Art, University of Michigan, is a recognized practitioner with twenty-four years of experience in product design. His research includes age-related human performance issues across the life span, working collaboratively with architecture, gerontology, and ergonomics. His consulting practice includes ergonomics and product design focused on the needs of special populations.

Michael Shannon has a varied background in interior design. His team-teaching involvement in the UDEP project was as a graduate student completing the requirements for an M.S. in architecture at California Polytechnic State University, San Luis Obispo. He has spoken at ASID national conferences and recently completed a five-week study of accessibility in Europe, as a designer and wheelchair user.

Madlen Simon received her bachelor of arts and master of architecture degrees from Princeton University. She has worked for Skidmore, Owings and Merrill, Edward Larrabee Barnes Associates, and in her own New York practice. She is currently an assistant professor of architecture at Kansas State University where she teaches design and professional practice. A recently completed commission, a life-cycle house, incorporated universal design thinking into her practice.

Ken Special holds degrees from the University of Connecticut and Virginia Polytechnic Institute and State University. He is currently teaching upper-division undergraduate interior design studios and computer-aided design at Miami University. Prior to entering academia he practiced as a senior interior design professional specializing in the field of health-care design with Healthcare Environment Design in Dallas. He has research interests in effective teaching and in the appropriate design of the near environment for user groups.

Nikki Joan Spencer, an associate professor at Louisiana State University for the past seventeen years, received her bachelor's degree in interior architecture and master of architecture degree from the University of Oregon. Her research interests include design education, design graphics, and design criteria, especially as they pertain to special populations.

Edward Steinfeld, professor of architecture at the State University of New York at Buffalo, is a registered architect and design researcher with special interests in design for older people and people with disabilities. He is director of the Adaptive Environments Laboratory, a center for research and technical assistance on design for accessibility, safety, and health. He is also the founding chairman of ASAP, the Association for Safe and Accessible Products. He has published extensively and is internationally known for his research. His current activities involve housing design for people with severe disabilities, research on home modification services for older people, universal design of bathrooms, and the development of criteria to evaluate universal design.

Eric Wiedegreen received his bachelor of design and master of architecture degrees from the University of Florida. He is a registered architect in Virginia and Florida with ten years of private practice in architecture and interior design. As an assistant professor at Virginia Polytechnic Institute and State University, he teaches courses across the spectrum from basic design to senior contract design.

Paul M. Wolff, an architect and professor emeritus at California Polytechnic State University, San Luis Obispo, has been teaching barrier-free and universal design for the past thirteen years. As director of the Barrier-Free Research Unit of the Design and Construction Institute at the College of Architecture and Environmental Design, he developed the *Access to Parks* guidelines for the program and facilities of the State of California Department of Parks and Recreation. He is now a consultant on issues of universal design.

Advisor and Staff Biographies

Robert Anders is currently serving a three-year term as president of the Academic Senate at Pratt Institute. He is also the head of the Design Management Program at Pratt. He has taught in the undergraduate and graduate programs of the industrial design department, with courses in ergonomics, computer-aided industrial design, professional practices, POP and exhibition design, and universal design. He has received research grants from IBM, Colgate-Palmolive, and Slik America. In addition to a long career as a design consultant to such companies as Mobil Oil, AT&T, and Ciba Pharmaceutical, he was director of staff design at Bristol Myers and director of visual merchandising at Revlon, Inc. As a consultant to federal government agencies, he directed the design of fifteen United States exhibitions at fairs in twelve countries. He currently serves as an expert witness in legal cases involving industrial design matters. His interdisciplinary executive graduate program in design management is the first in the United States. He co-authored, with Daniel Fechtner of Columbia University, both a curriculum and a primer on universal design. He was a UDEP advisor to the program at Miami University.

Dorothy Fowles, professor of interior design at Iowa State University, has integrated universal design concepts into interior design education for more than twenty years. She currently teaches lighting design and an interior design studio focused on institutional settings. Her students' studio projects have included care and living units for children, young adults, and elderly people with dementia, hearing impairments, learning disabilities, and mobility restrictions. These projects all have an emphasis on relevant social, psychological, and physical issues. She has lectured extensively on environmental and universal design, and has championed universal design concepts for the profession while serving on the ASID Barrier Free and Professional Development Committees. As former president of the Interior Design Educators Council, she integrated barrier-free addresses into IDEC programs over a decade ago. She has also served as editor of *The Interior Design Journal* (formerly *The Journal of Interior Design Education and Research*). Her interior design work has created opportunities in residential, hospitality, and office settings to apply theories of universal design to the real world. These projects have received international recognition through competitions and exhibitions. She was the UDEP advisor to the interiors programs at Michigan State and Virginia Tech.

Susan Goltsman, landscape architect, is a principal at Moore Iacofano Goltsman, Inc., and co-founder and director of PLAE, Inc. She has spent more than sixteen years creating policy, programs, and special environments that promote the development of children and youth. Her projects encompass a variety of environments, including parks, play areas, schools, daycare centers, courthouses, hospitals, and rehabilitation centers. Co-author of the *Play For All Guidelines* and *The Accessibility Checklist,* she has been recognized by the National Endowment of the Arts, the American Planning Association, and the California Parks and Recreation Society. She currently serves on a national committee that is developing standards for play area accessibility. She is also an adjunct faculty member in the Program on Urban Studies at Stanford University and is a past president of the California Council of the American Society of Landscape Architects. She was the UDEP advisor to the programs at Cal Poly at San Luis Obispo, Texas Tech, and the Virginia Tech landscape architecture department.

Paul John Grayson, president of Environments for Living, is an advisor on strategic planning, universal design, and accessible environments. As a consultant on ADA access issues, he has assisted entities such as Phillips Academy, the MIT Planning Office, the Marriott Corporation's MassPike Travel Plaza, DRI/McGraw-Hill, and the Ft. Lauderdale and Tampa international airports. He co-edited the book *Life Care: A Long Term Solution?* and contributed to the chapters "The Best of Design for the Elderly" in *Design Intervention: Toward a More Humane Architecture* and "Technology and Home Adaptations" in *Staying Put: Adapting the Places Instead of the People.* Holding a master's degree in architecture from Harvard University, he is a 1987 HGSD Wheelwright Fellow and a 1991 Fellow of the World Rehabilitation Fund's International Exchange of Experts and Information in Rehabilitation. He has lectured extensively on accessible housing, assistive technology devices that enhance independence for elderly and disabled persons, and health-care environments that reduce stress and strain on caregivers. He is a member of the American Institute of Architects, the Environmental Design Research Association, the Gerontological Society of America, and the Rehabilitation Society of North America. He was the UDEP advisor to the programs at Kansas State University, North Dakota State University, the Ringling School of Art and Design, and the University of Tennessee.

Daniel S. Iacofano, a principal at Moore Iacofano Goltsman, Inc., has over nineteen years of experience in urban and environmental planning, mediation, facilitation and meeting management, strategic planning, and participatory program design. He has consulted and lectured throughout the United States and Europe and has pioneered many innovative techniques for inter-agency collaboration and consensus building. He has contributed his management and facilitation skills to many projects, including the UC Riverside Long Range Development Plan, the Marin Municipal Water District/Marin County Open Space District Vegetation Management Plan, and the Downtown Phoenix Strategic Plan. In addition, he has combined his strategic and organizational planning expertise with meeting management techniques to assist countless communities, agencies, organizations, and companies in working together to articulate goals, strategies, and visions for the future, including Ventura County, the California State Department of Mental Health, the North Face Company, and the El Dorado Irrigation District. A visiting lecturer at Stanford University and UC Davis, he is author of *Public Involvement as an Organization Development Process* (New York: Garland Publishing, 1980). As co-facilitator of the UDEP Colloquium, he created the facilitation graphics documenting the event.

Ron Mace, principal investigator for the Center for Universal Design, is a nationally recognized architect and authority on design and program development for all people with disabilities. He has written extensively on accessible and universal design. He has been an author, researcher, participant, and consultant on milestone accessibility codes and standards development, including the Handicapped Section of the North Carolina State Building Code (1974), the American National Standards Institute ANSI A117.1 (1980), (1986), (1992), the Uniform Federal Accessibility Standard (UFAS 1984), and the Fair Housing Amendments Act (FHAA 1988). During his eighteen years as a full-time accessibility specialist, he has served as a design consultant, researcher, lecturer, mediator, and expert witness. His clients have included most federal agencies, many state and local governments, corporations, architects, attorneys, disability organizations, and trade associations. He has served as a technical specialist and consultant for physical and program accessibility whenever necessary and helping to mediate resolution of legislation policy and technical conflicts. While recognized as a strong advocate for accessibility, he has been able to obtain the trust and support of professionals in the building industry. In 1988, he was elected to the College of Fellows of the American Institute of Architects for his contribution to the profession in promoting access and universal design. He has received numerous awards including the Distinguished Service Award of the President of the United States for long-term contribution to furthering the rights and independence of people with disabilities.

Joe Meade, a recreational wilderness manager, is responsible for establishing a national access initiative including design standards, direction, and policy. Prior to moving to the Washington office of the Forest Service five years ago, he was the public affairs officers for the Ochoco National Forest Pacific Northwest region. He began his career with the Forest Service in 1977, working in interpretive services at a Forest Service visitor's center. Later, he branched into public affairs, serving as an assistant public affairs officer and forest public affairs officer. He is qualified as an incident information officer and has served on a national fire team for five years, serving on a number of campaign assignments. He has served the governor as chairperson, overseeing vocation rehabilitation on the state's Blind Commission and served as representative on the state's Independent Living Council. In 1986, he received the Presidential Award as the USDA's National Handicapped Employee of the Year; he had received a similar award from the state of Oregon in 1978. He now serves on the USDA Secretary's Advisory Committee on Disability Issues, and was recently appointed to represent the Secretary on the White House's Council on Domestic Policy. He was the UDEP advisor to the program at Pratt Institute.

Robin Moore, associate professor in landscape architecture at North Carolina State University, holds degrees in architecture from London University and in urban and regional planning from MIT. There he began to explore the design of urban neighborhoods to fully support human development, and continued through a series of action-research community projects involving a variety of age groups. His recent work included the Universal Garden and the Universal Neighborhood projects with the Department of Landscape Architecture and the Center for Universal Design at North Carolina State University. His desire to accommodate the needs of people of all abilities is also featured in his design and educational activities in Latin America. He is the author of *Plants for Play* and co-author of the *Play for All Guidelines*.

Jim Mueller, an industrial designer, has worked in the field of design for people with disabilities since 1974, when he joined the Rehabilitation Center at George Washington University. In 1982, he established his consulting firm, J.L. Mueller, Inc., whose clients include public agencies, private businesses, and individuals with disabilities. In 1992, he established the Universal Design Initiative. He is the author of *The Workplace Workbook 2.0* and other books and articles on job accommodation, universal design, and disability management. He is a member of the Industrial Designers Society of America and RESNA, the society for professionals involved in rehabilitation technology. He produced the video *Toward Universal Design* and is currently working with the Center for Universal Design to develop case studies of businesses that produce universally designed products and to develop criteria for evaluating universal design. He was the UDEP advisor to the programs at the University of Southwestern Louisiana and Louisiana State University.

Elaine Ostroff, co-founder and executive director of Adaptive Environments, is the director of the Universal Design Education Project. As an educator, she has been involved with accessible environments on a national and international level since 1971. In 1978, she began organizing national conferences on adaptive environmental design, bringing together many of the advisors who are now working with UDEP. In 1982, she convened the national seminar on Design for All People, which provided a framework for UDEP. In 1986, she developed the Best of Accessible Boston, an awards program honoring the architects and owners of buildings that exemplified good as well as accessible design, with Polly Welch as advisor to the jury. Much of her experience involves creating educational programs for non-designers, facilitating their advocacy as well as collaboration with design professionals. With the Center for Accessible Housing, she developed national conferences and seminars, including the Fair Housing Amendments Act Leadership Institute, Housing That People Can Control, and the Home Modifications Policy Task Force. She has been writing and producing ADA technical assistance materials for distribution through the nationwide ADA Technical Assistance Network and the Department of Justice. In 1995, she received the Achievement Award from the Environmental Design Research Association.

Chris Palames is director of Independent Living Resources, a disability rights collective and consultant to Adaptive Environments. He is a national expert on access policy who is a wheelchair user. Co-author of the *ADA Title II Action Guide*, he has provided training and public education programs nationwide on accessibility issues, consultation on barrier-free design, facility access surveying, and technical assistance to public and private agencies developing personal assistance services. Formerly he was assistant director for programs at the Massachusetts Office on Disability, a member of the Massachusetts Architectural Access Board, and chairperson of the Advisory Board of the Massachusetts Office on Disability. His experience in accessibility includes the following projects and clients: University of Indiana, Wesleyan University, Massachusetts Division of Capitol Planning, Tampa Airport, Florida Title II Transition Planning, Fair Housing Amendments Act National Training Program, Connecticut Access Monitoring Project, Massachusetts Executive Office of Communities and Development, Housing Accessibility Institute, Center for Accessible Housing, and the Boston Globe Foundation. He presented the history of disability rights at the UDEP Colloquium.

John P.S. Salmen, a licensed architect, has specialized in barrier-free and universal design for over nineteen years. He is the president of Universal Designers and Consultants, Inc., in Rockville, Maryland, where he is involved with code development, facility evaluation, design, construction, accessibility litigation, writing, research, and teaching. He is also publisher of the *Universal Design Newsletter*. A nationally prominent expert on the technical aspects of the Americans with Disabilities Act and the *ADA Accessibility Guidelines* (ADAAG), he was involved in the development of the ADA and has been on the ANSI A117.1 Committee for over ten years. He also represents the American Institute of Architects on the ADAAG Review Federal Advisory Committee. Since receiving his bachelor of architecture degree from the University of Minnesota, he has been involved in all aspects of design for the elderly and people with disabilities—while in private practice, as technical director for the National Center for a Barrier Free Environment in Washington, D.C., and as the director of technology and information for the American Hotel and Motel Association. He was the UDEP advisor to the programs at the University of Missouri and the State University of New York at Buffalo, and is currently directing a project funded by the National Endowment for the Arts to collect and disseminate images of universal design excellence.

Bob Shibley, architect, urban designer, and professor at the State University of New York at Buffalo, wrote some of the initial compliance regulations for the Department of Defense in the early 1970s when access was legislated by the old public law 90-480. Based on that and other experiences in federal construction, he worked with the review committees on ANSI standards research and development and has been a frequent reviewer for grant applications to the Architecture and Transportation Compliance Review Board and, more recently, the Department of Education. He directed a national curriculum and materials development project with eighteen schools of architecture on energy conscious design from 1979 to 1984. He has served as an advisor to the Adaptive Environments Center in several of its efforts to promote educational efforts in barrier-free and universal design. On a personal level, his son Loren was diagnosed with a mild ataxic cerebral palsy in 1972, resulting in his firsthand exploration into mainstreaming educational practices in three states as well as therapeutic endeavors related to the physical and mental challenges presented by that condition. He was the UDEP advisor to the program at Iowa State University.

Polly Welch, associate professor of architecture at the University of Oregon, has been involved in accessibility issues for over fifteen years as a practicing architect, as a consultant on user accommodation to public and private organizations, and as a public administrator. The programming and evaluation projects that she managed as a principal of Zeisel Research, Building Diagnostics, and Welch + Epp Associates have won design and research awards as have the numerous documents that she produced translating social research on housing needs into design guidance. She has designed accessible and adaptable housing for low-income families, older people, single parents and parenting teens, and people with disabilities. She was the principal author of *Design for Access,* an interpretive guidebook produced by Adaptive Environments for Massachusetts architects. In Massachusetts she served on the Architectural Access Board, the state's adjudicatory body; rewrote the state's access regulations to reflect its Fair Housing Law, the Fair Housing Amendments Act, and the Americans with Disabilities Act; and participated in developing questions on accessibility for the architectural licensing exam. In 1988, she was appointed deputy assistant secretary for public housing in Massachusetts and directed the siting and development of housing for families, people with mental and physical disabilities, and older people. While in practice, she taught at the Boston Architectural Center, the Professional Development Program at Harvard, and as a visiting professor at the University of Wisconsin–Milwaukee. In addition to helping implement this project and editing this book, she was the UDEP advisor to the programs at the University of Michigan, MIT, and Norwich University.

Selected Books and Articles

"Accessible Products: Aids to Universal Design." *Interior Design* 63, no. 11 (August 1992): 102–7.

Aging Design Research Program (in press 1996). *Design for Aging Resource Package.* Washington, D.C.: American Institute for Architectural Research.

Amundson, R. "Disability, Handicap, and the Environment." *Journal of Social Philosophy* 23, no. 1 (1992): 105–17.

Anders, Robert and Daniel Fechtner (1992). *Universal Design Primer.* Brooklyn, N.Y.: Pratt Institute Department of Industrial Design.

Barrier Free Environments (1991). *The Accessible Housing Design File.* New York: Van Nostrand Reinhold.

Bednar, Michael, ed. (1977). *Barrier Free Environments.* Stroudsburg, Pa.: Dowden, Hutchinson, and Ross.

——— (1987). *Adaptable, Marketable Housing for Everyone.* Washington, DC: Department of Housing and Urban Development. Available from HUD USER, Pub# HUD-1124-PDR, P.O. Box 6091, Rockville, MD 20849.

Behar, Susan (1991). "A Design Solution for 'Aging in Place.'" *The ASID Report,* January/February.

Bowe, Frank (1988). "Why Seniors Don't Use Technology." *Technology Review,* August/September, 32–40.

Brightman, Alan. *Ordinary Moments.* Syracuse, N.Y.: Human Policy Press, Center for Human Policy.

"Build Barrier Free Baths for Everyone." *House Beautiful Kitchens and Baths,* fall 1992.

Callahan, John (1989). *He Won't Get Very Far on Foot: The Autobiography of a Dangerous Man.* New York: Vintage.

——— (1990). *Do Not Disturb Any Further.* New York: William Morrow.

——— (1991). *Digesting the Child Within.* New York: William Morrow.

——— (1992). *Do What He Says! He's Crazy.* New York: William Morrow.

——— (1993). *The Night They Say Was Made for Love, Plus My Sexual Scrapbook.* New York: William Morrow.

———— (1994). *What Kind of God Would Allow a Thing Like This to Happen?* New York: William Morrow.

"A Celebration of Disability Culture." *The Disability Rag and Resource,* September/ October 1995. Louisville, Ky.: Advocado Press.

Cohen, Uriel (1981). *Mainstreaming the Handicapped, A Design Guide.* Milwaukee, Wis.: Center of Architecture and Urban Planning Research, School of Architecture and Urban Planning, University of Wisconsin–Milwaukee.

Cole, Thomas (1992). *The Journey of Life: A Cultural History of Aging in America.* Cambridge: Cambridge University Press.

Corbet, Barry (1993). "What's So Funny About Disability?" *New Mobility,* February/March.

Crosbie, Michael J. (1991). "Universal Hardware." *Architecture,* July, 88–89.

Davis, Jr., Thomas D. and Kim A. Beasley (1995). *Accessible Design for Hospitality: ADA Guidelines for Planning Accessible Hotels, Motels and Other Recreational Facilities.* 2nd ed. MacGraw Hill, Inc.

DeJong, G. and Lifchez, R. (1983). "Physical Disability and Public Policy." *Scientific American,* June.

Fisher, Thomas (1985). "Enabling the Disabled." *Progressive Architecture,* July, 119–26.

General Electric (1995). *Real Life Design.* Louisville, Ky.: GE Appliances.

Goffman, Erving (1963). *Stigma: Notes on the Management of Spoiled Identity.* Englewood Cliffs, N.J.: Prentice-Hall.

Greer, N.R. (1987). "The State of the Art of Design for Accessibility." *Architecture* 76, no. 1 (January): 58–61.

Hahn, Harlan (1988). "The Politics of Physical Differences: Disability and Discrimination." *Journal of Social Issues* 44, no. 1: 39–47.

Hevey, Dave (1992). *The Creatures Time Forgot: Photography and Disability Imagery.* London: Routledge.

Hockenberry, John (1995). *Moving Violations: War Zones, Wheelchairs, and Declarations of Independence.* New York: Hyperion.

Johnson, Mary, ed. (1992). *People with Disabilities Explain It All to You.* Louisville, Ky.: Advocado Press.

Kailes, June Isaacson (1984). *Language is More Than a Trivial Concern.* Available from June Kailes, 6201 Ocean Front Walk, Suite 2, Playa Del Ray, CA 90293-7556.

Kailes, June Isaacson and Darrell Jones (1993). *A Guide to Planning Accessible Meetings.* Houston, Tex.: ILRU Program.

King, Ynestra (1993). "The Other Body: Reflections on Difference, Disability, and Identity Politics." *Ms.,* March/April, 72–75.

Lebovich, William L. (1993). *Design for Dignity: Accessible Environments for People with Disabilities.* New York: John Wiley and Sons.

Liebrock, Cynthia, with Susan Behar (1992). *Beautiful Barrier-Free: A Visual Guide to Accessibility.* Florence, Ky.: Van Nostrand Reinhold.

Lifchez, Raymond (1986). *Rethinking Architecture: Design Students and Physically Disabled People.* Berkeley, Calif.: University of California Press.

Lifchez, Raymond and Barbara Winslow (1979). *Designs for Independent Living.* Berkeley, Calif.: University of California Press.

Longmore, Paul and Diane B. Piastro (1988). *Unhandicapping Our Language.* Available from Cryptography, P.O. Box 454, Long Beach, CA 90809-0454.

Lusher, Ruth Hall (1988). "Designing for the Life Span." *The Construction Specifier,* February, 31–32.

——— (1989). "Handicapped Access Laws and Codes." In *Encyclopedia of Architecture: Design Engineering and Construction,* vol. 3, edited by Wilkes and Packard, 646–59. New York: John Wiley and Sons.

Lusher, Ruth Hall and Ron Mace (1989). "Design for Physical and Mental Disabilities." In *Encyclopedia of Architecture: Design Engineering and Construction,* vol. 3, edited by Wilkes and Packard, 748–63. New York: John Wiley and Sons.

Mace, R., G. Hardie, and J. Place (1991). "Accessible Environments: Toward Universal Design." In *Design Intervention: Toward a More Humane Architecture,* edited by Preiser, Vischer, and White. New York: Van Nostrand Reinhold.

Mace, Ronald (1988). *Universal Design: Housing for the Lifespan of All People.* Available from HUD USER, Pub# HUD-1156-PA, P.O. Box 6091, Rockville MD 20849.

———— (1991). "Accessible for All: Universal Design." *Interiors and Sources* 8, no. 17 (September/October): 28–31.

———— (1992). *Definitions: Accessible, Adaptable, and Universal Design.* Raleigh, N.C.: Center for Accessible Housing, North Carolina State University.

Moore, Robin, Susan Goltsman, and Daniel Iacofano, eds. (1992). *Play for All Guidelines: Planning, Design, and Management of Outdoor Play Settings for All Children.* Berkeley, Calif.: MIG Communications.

Mueller, James (1992). *The Workplace Workbook 2.0: An Illustrated Guide to Workplace Accommodation and Technology.* Amherst, Mass.: Human Resource Development Press.

———— (1995). "The Case for Universal Design." *Ageing International*, March, 19–23. Washington, D.C.: International Federation on Ageing.

Mullick, Abir (1992). "What Did I Learn After All: Students' View of a Universal Design Project." In *Making Sense: Proceedings of the Industrial Designers Society of America.* San Francisco: Industrial Designers Society of America.

———— (1993). "Accessibility Issues in Park Design: Was Frederick Law Olmsted a Visionary?" *Journal of Landscape and Urban Planning.* Amsterdam: Elsevier.

Nolan, Christopher (1988). *Under the Eye of the Clock: The Life Story of Christopher Nolan.* New York: St. Martin's Press.

Nordhaus R., M. Kantrowitz, and W. Siembieda (1984). *Accessible Fishing: A Planning Handbook.* The Resources Management and Development Division of the New Mexico Natural Resources Department.

Null, Roberta L. (1989). "Universal Design for the Elderly." *Housing and Society* 16, no. 3.

"On the Eve of Universal Design: Homes and Products that Meet Everyone's Special Needs." *Home,* October 1988, 95–104.

Ostroff, Elaine and Daniel Iacofano (1982). *Teaching Design For All People: The State of the Art.* Boston: Adaptive Environments Center.

Peterson, Mary Joe (1995). *Universal Kitchen Planning: Design that Adapts to People.* Hackettstown, N.J.: National Kitchen and Bath Association.

Pirkl, James (1994). *Transgenerational Design: Products for an Aging Population.* Florence, Ky.: Van Nostrand Reinhold.

PLAE, Inc., USDA Forest Service, et al. (1993). *Universal Access to Outdoor Recreation: A Design Guide.* Berkeley, Calif.: MIG Communications.

Sachs, Oliver (1976). *Awakenings.* New York: Vintage Books.

———— (1985). *The Man Who Mistook His Wife for a Hat.*

———— (1990). *Seeing Voices: A Journey into the World of the Deaf.* New York: Harper Perennial.

Salmen, John P.S. (1994). *Accommodating All Guests.* Washington, D.C.: American Hotel and Motel Association.

Shapiro, Joseph (1993). *No Pity: People with Disabilities Forging a New Civil Rights Movement.* New York: Time Books.

Shibley, Robert G. and Laura Poltroneri, with Ronni Rosenberg (1984). *Case Studies in the Evaluation of the Teaching Passive Design in Architecture Workbook Series.* Washington, D.C.: Association of Collegiate Schools of Architecture.

Sinkewicz, Ruth Mercer (1989). *I Raise My Eyes to Say Yes.* Boston: Houghton-Mifflin.

Solomon, Andrew (1994). "Deaf is Beautiful." *The New York Times Magazine,* August 28.

"Special Universal Design Report." *Metropolis: The Urban Magazine of Architecture and Design,* November 1992.

Steinfeld, Edward (1987). "Adaptable Housing for Older People." In *Housing for the Aged: Satisfactions and Preferences,* edited by V. Regnier and J. Pynoos. New York: Elsevier.

———— (1990). "Designing for All People: Resources for Students and Educators." Outline for a college course.

———— (1990). *Methods for Teaching Barrier-Free Design: Less Restrictive Housing Environments Project.* Buffalo, N.Y.: Adaptive Environments Laboratory, State University of New York at Buffalo.

———— (1991). "Counter Culture: The Representation of Cultural Change." In *Reflections on Representation, Proceedings of ARCC Representation and Simulation Network Annual Conference.* Buffalo, N.Y.: School of Architecture and Planning, State University of New York at Buffalo.

————. "Design for the Life Span of All People? Spotlight on Adaptable Housing." *Rehab Brief* 10, no. 12: 1–4.

Steinfeld, Edward and Abir Mullick (1990). "Universal Design: the Case of the Hand." *Innovation,* fall.

Stewart, Jean (1989). *The Body's Memory.* New York: St. Martin's Press.

"Universal Design." *The Disability Rag and Resource,* March/April 1992. Louisville, Ky.: Advocado Press.

"Universal Design." Special Issue. *Interior Design* 63, no. 11 (August 1992).

Vanderheiden, Greg C. and Katherine R. Vanderheiden (1992). *Accessible Design of Consumer Products: Guidelines for the Design of Consumer Products to Increase Their Accessibility to People with Disabilities or Who Are Aging.* Madison, Wis.: Trace Research and Development Center.

Weisman, Leslie K. (1992). *Discrimination by Design: A Feminist Critique of the Man Made Environment.* Chicago: University of Illinois Press.

Wilkoff, William L. and Laura W. Abed (1994). *Practicing Universal Design: An Interpretation of the ADA.* Florence, Ky.: Van Nostrand Reinhold.

Wylde, Margaret, Adrian Baron-Robins, and Sam Clark (1994). *Building for a Lifetime: The Design and Construction of Fully Accessible Homes.* Newtown, Conn.: Taunton Press.

Wrightson, William and Cambell Pope (1989). *From Barrier Free to Safe Environments: The New Zealand Experience.* New York: World Rehabilitation Fund, Inc.

Zola, Irving Kenneth (1982). *Missing Pieces: A Chronicle of Living with a Disability.* Philadelphia: Temple University Press.

Selected Videos

Able to Laugh. Michael J. Dougan. 27 minutes. Available from Fanlight Productions, 47 Halifax Street, Boston, MA 02130, (800) 937-4113. Six professional comics—who happen to be disabled. This video is about the awkward ways disabled and able-bodied people relate to each other, and about how humor can remove some of the barriers of fear, guilt, vulnerability, and misunderstanding.

Accessibility and Historic Preservation (1994). National Park Service and Historic Windsor, Inc. Available from Historic Windsor, Inc., P.O. Box 1777, Windsor, VT 05089, (800) 376-6882. Resource guide and videotape.

Accessibility Regulations (1992). The U.S. Architectural and Transportation Compliance Board (Access Board). Approximately 13 minutes, open-captioned. Available for loan and copying, (800) USA-ABLE. One of two useful videos produced by the Access Board, it provides a brief but very clear overview of the federal accessibility regulations and whom they cover. It explains the origins of the Uniform Federal Accessibility Standards and introduces the Americans with Disabilities Act Accessibility Guidelines (ADAAG), along with a limited introduction to Title III of the ADA.

Accessible Design (1992). The U.S. Architectural and Transportation Compliance Board (Access Board). Approximately 19 minutes, open-captioned. Available for loan and copying, (800) USA-ABLE. This is the second of two useful videos produced by the Access Board. The technical specifications of the ADAAG are illuminated by showing them in use in several facilitiies by people with a range of disabilities. Both this video and *Accessibility Regulations* emphasize the universal-design aspects of these minimum standards, in creating buildings that can accommodate the eventualities of life.

Another First Step: From Institution to Independence, A Family Saga (1994). Michael Whalen. 51 minutes. Available from Filmakers Library, 124 E. 40th Street, Suite 901, New York, NY 10016, (212) 808-4980. This film introduces viewers to the concept of heritage. While it should be obvious to anyone that a person with a disability has both a family and a cultural heritage, this fact is too often missed.

Breaking Barriers (1989). The United Nations. 29 minutes. Available from The Altschul Group, 930 Pitner Avenue, Evanston, IL 60202, (800) 421-2363. Produced by the United Nations as part of the International Decade on Disabled Persons, this film focuses on the rights and abilities of disabled individuals cross-culturally.

Building and Remodeling for Accessibility (1993). Hometime. Approximately 30 minutes. Available from Hometime, 4275 Norex Drive, Chaska, MN 55378, (800) 535-7300. This do-it-yourself video from the public television series *Hometime* provides information and assistance for modifying entrances, bathrooms, and kitchens for accessibility. It also includes a segment on the construction of a new accessible home that shows construction details.

Building Better Neighborhoods (1984). Concrete Changes. 15 minutes, open-captioned. Available from Concrete Changes, 1371 Metropolitan Avenue, SE, Atlanta, GA 30316. This useful educational tool features a construction engineer for Habitat for Humanity discussing Habitat's practice of making every house it builds accessible; an architect describing how simple and cost-effective no-step entrances are to create; and several disabled individuals advocating universally designed and built housing.

For the Rest of Your Life: The Hartford House. Modern Talking Picture Service. 24 minutes. Available from Modern Talking Picture Service, 5000 Park Street North, St. Petersburg, FL 33709, (800) 243-6877. An overview of the Hartford House, a model accessible house designed and built by the ITT Hartford Insurance Group to raise public awareness of how environments through products and architecture accommodate an aging population.

Here. 13 minutes. Available from Advocado Press, P.O. Box 145, Louisville, KY 40201. Poetry performance by Cheryl Marie Wade, a poet who will forever alter any preconceived ideas about disability. Includes printed text of the nine poems performed.

The History of Disability Rights (1993). 22 minutes. Available from Adaptive Environments Center, 374 Congress Street, Suite 301, Boston, MA 02210, (617) 695-1225 (v/tdd) ext. 29. Chris Palames, a disability rights advocate, presents a personal and articulate description of the disability rights movement, which led to the passage of the ADA. He highlights the political background along with the legal and philosophical connections to other civil rights movements. Although this is a poor-quality video, shot at a bad angle during the UDEP Colloquium, it offers students a perspective and historical background not available elsewhere.

A House for Someone Unlike Me (1984). Written and produced by Bruce W. Bassett for the National Center for a Barrier Free Environment. 38 minutes. Available from Adaptive Environments Center, 374 Congress Street, Suite 301, Boston, MA 02210, (617) 695-1225 (v/tdd) ext. 29. This video vividly documents the architectural design studio led by Ray Lifchez at the University of California, Berkeley. Viewers get to witness the consultants with disabilities, the design students, Lifchez, and co-instructor Barbara Winslow in the midst of a creative and reflective design process, illuminated by personal stories of the consultants.

Interpretations. Black Boot Productions. 25 minutes, open-captioned. Available from Fanlight Productions, 47 Halifax Street, Boston, MA 02130, (800) 937-4113. Janice, a freelance photographer who is deaf, has taken on her first professional assignment. She has hired her long-time hearing friend Maureen to work for her as a make-up artist, as well as to serve as her interpreter for the project. The film is particularly successful at conveying the difficulties and frustrations of many deaf men and women who must work with interpreters in the hearing world.

Key Changes: A Portrait of Lisa Thorson. Cindy Marshall. 28 minutes. Available from Fanlight Productions, 47 Halifax Street, Boston, MA 02130, (800) 937-4113. This elegant video profiles a highly successful jazz singer who uses a wheelchair. Weaving performance footage with interviews, the video demonstrates how she challenges stereotypes and advocates for people with disabilities through her work.

Open for Business (1992). Ward and Associates, with Disability Rights Education and Defense Fund, Inc. (DREDF). Four versions of varying length, including closed-captioned and audio. Available from DREDF, 2212 Sixth Street, Berkeley, CA 94710, (510) 644-2555. Call for information and special discount rates. This fast-paced video shows two communities working together in one small town to learn what the Americans with Disabilities Act requires and how to achieve compliance with the requirements of Title III, Public Accommodations. The video explains the law and demonstrates attitudinal and architectural changes and the removal of communication barriers.

People in Motion (1995). WNET-TV. Available from People in Motion, P.O. Box 2284, Burlington, VT 05407, (800) 336-1917. Three-episode series. Episode 1, "Ways to Move," profiles dancers with disabilities; the 1995 Miss America, who is deaf; and a candidate for a California congressional seat. Episode 2, "Ready to Live," profiles Ed Roberts, a national disability rights activist and founder of the Center for Independent Living; Marilyn Hamilton, whose new wheelchair design gives people with disabilities more independence; and Luka Kristo, a Bosnian militiaman, who can write and draw pictures using prosthetic hands. Episode 3, "Redesigning the Human Machine," examines how space-age technologies assist people with disabilities.

Towards Universal Design. James Mueller. 15 minutes, open-captioned. Available from Universal Design Initiative, P.O. Box 222514, Chantilly, VA 22022-2514, (703) 378-5079. This video clarifies what the term "universal design" really means—design that considers people of all ages and abilities. It features candid viewpoints of design critics, educators, professionals, and students as they discuss the issues driving universal design: the growing power of older consumers in the marketplace, the implementation of the Americans with Disabilities Act, and the limitations that come to everyone who lives long enough.

When Billy Broke His Head (1994). Independent TV Service and Corporation for Public Broadcasting. 57 minutes. Available from Fanlight Productions, 47 Halifax Street, Boston, MA 02130, (800) 937-4113. An award-winning NPR producer and journalist who is partially paralyzed from a brain injury embarks on a road trip to chronicle the lifestyles and views of fellow Americans with disabilities and discovers the political dimension of disability.

The following commercial films are available on video and provide insightful perspectives on the lives of people with disabilities: *Awakenings, Children of a Lesser God, The Miracle Worker,* and *My Left Foot.*

Selected Periodicals and Other Resources

Access America. This is the official publication of the Architectural and Transportation Compliance Board (Access Board), 1331 F Street, NW, Suite 1000, Washington, DC 20004. Call (800) USA-ABLE for *Access America* and other technical assistance materials.

ADA Disability and Business Technical Assistance Centers. These ten regional centers, established by the National Institute on Disability and Rehabilitation Research, provide comprehensive information, referrals, and publications on all aspects of the Americans with Disabilities Act. The centers distribute many of the technical assistance and regulation documents produced by the federal government for free or at a minimal cost. Dialing (800) 949-4ADA reaches the center nearest your area.

ADA Information File at Local Libraries. To increase access to ADA information, the Department of Justice, through a grant to the Kansas State Library and the Chief Officers of State Libraries Agencies (COSLA), has sent an ADA Information File with 35 technical assistance documents to 15,000 libraries across the country. Most libraries have placed the file at the reference desk.

The Disability Rag and Resource. Produced six times a year by Advocado Press, this publication is available in print, disk, Braille, large print, and audio tape versions. For information, write to Advocado Press, P.O. Box 145, Louisville, KY 40201. Subscriptions are $17.50 for individuals and $35 for organizations.

Disability Studies Quarterly. This quarterly publication is available in print, disk, Braille, large print, and audio tape versions. For information, write *Disability Studies,* c/o David Pfeiffer, Office of Public Management, Suffolk University, Boston, MA 02114, or call (617) 523-3429. Subscriptions are $35 for individuals, $45 for institutions, $20 for students, and $50 for foreign institutions or individuals. Members of the Society of Disability Studies receive a $5 discount.

Internet Resources. The Adaptive Environments Universal Design Information Network on the Internet is available by Gopher and the World Wide Web. It includes information about universal design, related resources, and links to a number of other sites. The URL is http://www.aces.k12.ct.us/www/aec/aec.html. There is a universal design mailing list on the Internet that anyone can subscribe to at universaldesign-l@aces.k12.ct.us.

Mainstream: Magazine of the Able-Disabled. Published ten times a year by Exploding Myths, Inc., this magazine is available in print, disk, Braille, large print, and audio tape versions. For information, write *Mainstream,* P.O. Box 370598, San Diego, CA 92137-0598. Annual subcriptions are $24.

Universal Design Newsletter. This illustrated newsletter is published four times a year by Universal Designers and Consultants. An index is available for the first eight issues. For information, write Universal Designers and Consultants, 1700 Rockville Pike, Suite 110, Rockville, MD 20852, or call (301) 770-7890. Annual subscriptions are $75.